Praise for
JOHN S

MW00462101

"Morbidly fascinating and wickedly entertaining . . . John Stark Bellamy II is the historian your mother warned you about . . . he offers bad guys and wanton women, unspeakable tragedy and murder most foul." —*The Plain Dealer*

"Bellamy . . . [is a] Homer of our homicides, wandering through dark places and remembering." —*Free Times*

"[Bellamy's books] relate, in detail, the reasons, methods, and repercussions of a couple of centuries' worth of grisly acts. You'd have a tough time finding somebody in town more learned—or enthusiastic—about the city's history of death and disaster." —*Scene Magazine*

"Blood and tears drip from the pages." —*Akron Beacon Journal*

"Bellamy writes with razor-edged wit and his own particular brand of charm." —*Medina County Gazette*

"Bellamy writes his stories with the sensibility of a late 18th century reporter . . . Certainly, he chooses to write about crimes, but what emerges between the lines are stories of human suffering, stories of class struggle, stories that speak as much to the criminal mind as to the crime itself. And Bellamy clearly relishes his criminals. Sometimes he pokes fun. Sometimes he wonders at the humanity of it all. But always he tells his tales with sympathy, compassion and a good old-fashioned, if not antiquated, flair for storytelling." —*Sun Newspapers*

"Bellamy's way with words turns history into a current event."
—*Ohio Magazine*

"Bellamy blends details culled from old newspaper clippings, trial transcripts and other sources into an exploration of the city's seamier side." —*West Life*

"Colorful and richly detailed writing." —*Chronicle Telegram*

"Bellamy's morbid subject matter, vividly drawn characters and flowery prose are reminiscent of Victorian murder mysteries, although the subjects hit closer to home." —*Maple Heights Press*

THE LAST DAYS OF CLEVELAND

And More True Tales of Crime and
Disaster from Cleveland's Past

John Stark Bellamy II

GRAY & COMPANY, PUBLISHERS
CLEVELAND

Some of the contents of this volume were previously published, generally in considerably truncated, attenuated, or mutilated form:

"I Die an Innocent Man!" and "They Say I've Been Killing Someone" appeared in e-book format as Chapter 2 of *By the Neck Until Dead: A History of Hangings in Cuyahoga County* on the Cleveland Memory Project website of the Special Collections Library of the Cleveland State University Library: www.clevelandmemory.org/speccoll/bellamy.

"Fireman's Fireman: The Legend of George Wallace," was originally appeared in extremely embryonic form in the January/February 1995 issue of *The Watch Desk,* published by the Western Reserve Fire Buffs Association.

"Ohio City Shootout: The 1975 Murder of Michael Kick," was originally published in the Fall and Winter 2002 issues of *The Hot Sheet,* a publication of the Cleveland Police Historical Society.

"My First Disaster" was originally written for my memoir in progress, *Wasted on the Young,* several other chapters of which may be found at the *Cool Cleveland* website (coolcleveland.com).

Library of Congress Cataloging-in-Publication Data
Bellamy, John Stark.
The last days of Cleveland : and more true tales of crime and disaster from Cleveland's past / John Stark Bellamy II.
p. cm.
ISBN 978-1-59851-067-6
1. Crime—Ohio—Cleveland—History—Case studies. 2. Disasters—Ohio—Cleveland—History—Case studies. 3. Cleveland (Ohio)—History. I. Title.
HV6795.C5B448 2010
364.109771'32—dc22   2010034621

Gray & Company, Publishers
www.grayco.com

Printed in the United States of America

10 9 8 7 6 5 4 3 2 1

*To Egidijus Marcinkevicius and Julia Burgess,
with affection, admiration, and thanks for their friend-
ship and support—and who will be the first persons I call
if I ever get into the kind of trouble I write about.*

CONTENTS

PREFACE

As my Cleveland woe books now amount to an octet (six compilations and two anthologies) and this my eighth preface, there is little left to be said about why I devote myself to such material, what larger value I assign to it or What It All Means. As one of my favorite philosophers, Frank Zappa, once remarked, "I don't want to spend my life explaining myself. You either get it or you don't." It is what it is, and I have long since been too immersed in and entranced by Cleveland woe to estimate the quality or endurance of the tales I have tried to tell in over 150 tales of Cleveland's past. I simply and sincerely hope you enjoy reading them as much as I enjoyed researching and writing them.

A couple of explanatory notes about the contents of this book are necessary. When I was younger and far more naive about the labor involved, I once nourished the hope of chronicling the death of every Cleveland policeman killed in the line of duty, a gallery of heroes that amounts to more than 100 officers. As "Time's winged chariot" grows ever noisier in my ear, I now realize that I shall never accomplish that noble goal. But I did manage to compose and publish seven such accounts before I left Cleveland and I now add two (Chapters 5 and 12) more to this labor of love. Both of them are dedicated to retired Cleveland police officer Joan Patrici, who also happens to be my sister-in-law.

Another of my uncompleted ambitions was to memorialize all the Cleveland firemen who have been killed in the line of duty. I never got around to that either, although I did chronicle some of these heroes and the fires that killed them. So it is a special pleasure to include here a chapter on George Wallace, Cleveland's greatest fire chief and just the caliber of public servant the City of Cleveland so sorely lacks now.

It is my frequently articulated and possibly cranky opinion that

Cleveland has not been blessed with many superior or even readable historians. One chapter of this book is devoted to an unabashed championing of the work of a forgotten titan of Cleveland chroniclers: S. J. Kelly, whose 800,000-word memories of bygone Cleveland may have set the record for prolixity for Cleveland historians. Some of the chapters in my Cleveland woe books, including this one, were stimulated by Kelly's original narratives on these subjects—which ones I leave to readers to discover for themselves.

On a more personal note, this anthology also includes an account of my first disaster. It was a story that, as the expression goes, "could not be told" until after the death of my sainted mother, who cunningly delayed its publication by living to the age of almost 92. My only additional observation on this particular story is that I never expected to be able to exploit my dumbest acts in print.

Once again, I thank George Condon and Peter Jedick. Their books of Cleveland history and their kind encouragement and aid offered me rare models of excellence in my struggle to become a Cleveland historian. I owe an additional obligation to George for encouraging my exploration of S. J. Kelly's pioneering work. I will forever be grateful to Doris O'Donnell and Faith Corrigan, crack reporters whose sandals I am not worthy to touch, who inexplicably believed in my Cleveland woe enterprise and were present at the creation. At the research level, I was much aided in the compilation of all my Cleveland stories by William Barrow, librarian at the Special Collections Library of Cleveland State University and knowledgeable custodian of the *Cleveland Press* Collection of clippings and photographs. I will always be in debt to the erstwhile magazine clerks at the Fairview Park Regional library—Rebecca Groves, Jennifer Gerrity, and the late Marty Essen—who unfailingly aided me in my eternal microfilm researches and silently endured my odious habit of pencil chewing. I also wish to thank Cuyahoga County Public Library librarians Avril McInally and Vicki Richards. Avril has assisted me on every book since the ancient days of *They Died Crawling,* and Vicki has served as a highly appreciative first audience for my most shocking and macabre stories. The opening story, "Suffer the Children," is dedicated to her. A special debt is owed to Denis Wood, geographer *par excellence*, who, more than four decades ago, helped open my eyes to the wondrous detail and storied past of my Cleveland environment.

Special thanks are owed to my brother Stephen and his wife, Gail Ghetia Bellamy, yet another Bellamy writer in the endless extended family. They provided decisive support and expertise in my initial search for a publisher and have remained steadfast in their aid and enthusiasm for my unusual craft. I also wish to thank Evelyn Theiss of the *Plain Dealer* and that same paper's former book editor, Janice Harayda, for their enthusiastic encouragement throughout my long, strange trip into the annals of Cleveland woe. And a *huge* thank-you to John Lanigan and Jimmy Malone, who, from the day I first stuttered through my baptism of fire on *Lanigan & Malone* in December 1995, have done more than everyone else put together to spread the gospel of Cleveland woe.

It is again with great pleasure that I thank my wife, Laura Serafin. I managed to finish one book without her—*They Died Crawling*—but I couldn't have managed the others, and it wouldn't have been worth the trouble. After all, it takes a very special kind of woman to live in enduring felicity with the man *Plain Dealer* journalist Joe Dirck once described as "The Cleveland Historian Your Mother Warned You About."

I wish to thank my readers. Sixteen years ago I sat shivering many a winter's night in an ill-heated garret as I composed my first tales of Cleveland woe and wondered how and whether they would find a like-minded audience of Cleveland readers. I never did find that audience—they found me—and it is in great part due to them that I have enjoyed a second act in the ongoing melodrama of my life.

John Stark Bellamy II
Somewhere in Vermont

THE LAST DAYS OF CLEVELAND

Chapter 1

SUFFER THE CHILDREN

The 1907 Curtis Horror

Dedicated with great relish to Miss Vicki Richards,
a real connoisseur of Cleveland woe

Never give a German a rope on a rainy day.
—Proverb passed down in the
Jean Dessel Bellamy family

It's a hard world for little things.
—Lillian Gish line in the 1955 film
The Night of the Hunter

Seventeen years. That's how long I've been mining the inexhaustible vein of Forest City dismalia. Seventeen years, nearly 150 tales of crime and calamity—and I have yet to discover a more heartbreaking story than the awful fate of the Curtis girls. Take it from me: there is simply no more poignant tale in the annals of Cleveland woe.

It's difficult to have any sane perspective on the Curtis suicides—if suicides they were. The Cleveland of 1907 was a different place and a different time. Now-alien notions and values prevailed, and no chapter of human life was viewed more differently than childhood. What today would be considered child abuse was more often than not adjudged "good discipline," and what was even then viewed as intolerable cruelty most often went unpunished. Diligent readers of these melancholy chronicles may remember the childhood of Tremont's Otto Lueth, the teenaged killer of little Maggie

Thompson in 1889. A grim feature of his murder trial was abundant and unchallenged testimony that his mother had habitually, indeed enthusiastically, abused him throughout the duration of his young life, kicking and beating him, tearing his hair, and even repeatedly slamming his head in a door to underscore her admonitions. Perhaps the most startling aspect of such testimony—at least to modern ears—was the fact that none of its auditors seemed to think her cruelty remarkably unusual, many of them simply discounting it as "good German discipline." And on a personal note, let me relate a family story told by my maternal grandfather, who grew up in a similarly rigorous German home in 1890s Iowa. One Christmas morn in the early years of that gay decade, he and his brother Leo crept downstairs to peek at the family Christmas tree in the parlor, a transgression expressly forbidden by Frank Dessel, their stern Prussian father. Indeed, he was secretly waiting for them—and he hit Leo so hard with an iron poker that he broke his leg. And perhaps the most interesting aspect of the incident was that Leo's brother, recalling the incident 70 years later, still considered their father's brutal act a perfectly just act of paternal discipline. Frank was well matched with my mother's other Prussian grandfather, Frederick Radkey. Fred was so enraged when his daughter Margaret (the author's grandmother) sneaked off to a high school dance that he shaved her head when she returned home in the wee hours. So, bearing Otto, Leo, and Margaret in mind, let us journey back to the harsh world of 1907, more specifically, the Helen Curtis household in the Village of West Park. (West Park, now a neighborhood of Cleveland's far West Side, existed as a separate village of Rockport Township until it was annexed by Cleveland in 1922.)

It is the month of June and things are not going well in the Curtis family. Other residents of Greater Cleveland may be concerned with recent public events, such as the Memorial Day interurban train crash in Elyria (six dead and many frightfully injured) or Cleveland mayor Tom Johnson's controversial plan to eliminate the Erie Street Cemetery on East Ninth Street. But in the modest Curtis house at 40 Lakota Street in the newest "Lennox Park" allotment, a mile west of Cleveland proper, all concerns are domestic and chiefly focused on two of the four children there. They are

Helen, 11 years old, and Marguerite (usually called Margaret), 10. Surviving photographs of the two girls subtly suggest their impending grim fate. Nicely dressed with beribboned hair, they stare at the camera, frowning forlornly, as if seeing something invisible to the viewer—something inescapable, something inhuman, something terrible. They probably do—for both Helen and Marguerite have been trying to kill themselves for some time. And despite family efforts to stop them, they will both get their death wish granted on June 7, 1907.

The real truth of the Curtis family tragedy will never be discovered. Aside from a limited amount of the testimony at the inquest into their deaths, most of what is known about Helen and Marguerite's life consists of mere neighborhood gossip, mostly malicious, and the stark medical details of their self-destruction. A century later, we know only that they were unhappy, but we will never know just how much they were pushed—or pulled—into committing the final act that took their young lives.

CHILDREN TAKE POISON AND DIE

Inheriting Mania for Suicide From Mother, Two Girls Eat Rat Mixture.

OFTEN TRIED TO TAKE OWN LIVES

Once Attempted to Burn Sister in Stove, but Screams Brought Assistance.

Cleveland Leader, June 8, 1907.

For us, the Curtis family story begins in Liverpool Village, Medina County, not long after the Civil War. There, William Curtis, sometime sawmill proprietor and tavern keeper, lived and reared his family, including his wife, Helen, and sons Leland, Frank, and Freeman. Sometime in the early 1900s, William succumbed to stomach cancer, but his death only accelerated the ongoing exodus of his family from Liverpool. His son Leland had long since settled in Kansas with his wife, Louise, and four children, and by 1906 Leland's two brothers were living with their widowed mother Helen in the newish, two-story frame house on Lakota Street. The

CHILDREN WHOM SUICIDE IMPULSE AFFLICTS AND THEIR FATHER.

Clarabel, aged four.   Helen, aged eleven; Marguerite, aged ten.   Leland Curtis, the father.

Plain Dealer, June 8, 1907.

dynamics of their household changed dramatically on March 12 of that year, when Leland's four children—Helen, 10, Marguerite, 9, Frank, 7, and Claribel ("Clara"), 3—came to live with their grandmother Helen.

The simple explanation for the children's arrival was that their mother was dead. Beyond that fact, her story gets morbid and murky. After the tragedy of Helen and Marguerite's suicides, Leland's mother, Helen, would insist that a mania for self-slaughter ran like a red streak in Louise's family. Louise's German-born mother, Helen claimed to reporters, was obsessed with suicide and had often tried to kill herself. And the unfortunate Louise had inherited her mother's suicidal bent, continually threatening to kill herself. And Louise didn't stop at threats, according to her mother-in-law:

> She was accustomed [to] awaken [her husband] at midnight and tell him that she was going to take her life . . . Upon awakening, he often found his wife gone. He said searching parties then were formed to hunt through the woods and river banks, where it was her custom to go when resigned to melancholia.

Ultimately and inevitably, Louise made good on her repeated threats. One winter night in 1905 while Leland was sleeping, she fled from their farmhouse in her nightgown. He tracked her down the next morning, but she contracted pneumonia from her exposure and died a few days later. Living on a rough rural farm with four young children age 10 and under, Leland naturally did what was usual in such family situations in that age. He sent the four children to his mother, Helen, in Cleveland, believing that they needed a woman's care. Such arrangements were common, virtually automatic in that age of extended families; my own mother and her brother were duly shipped to their aunt's home when their mother died suddenly in 1924.

If Leland's mother was telling the truth in the aftermath of her granddaughters' suicides, she must have understood the risks of her new family commitment. Leland, she later stated, had tried to keep his children with him after their mother died but soon found himself unable cope with their own suicidal tendencies. The two eldest, Helen and Marguerite, often talked of doing away with themselves, and Helen made at least one attempt, drinking most of a bottle of whiskey. Doctors saved her life by using a stomach pump, but it proved the decisive incident in their transfer to Cleveland.

Life in their new Cleveland home would have been difficult for the children under any circumstances. The arrangement was for the children to live there and attend West Park schools while Leland continued his work at a Waukee, Kansas, grain elevator and sent his mother remittances for their support. But Mrs. Curtis was now 59 and, although not quite an invalid, suffered from both a heart condition and a painful lameness, which limited her agility and movement. But there may have been other circumstances specifically inimical to the mental health of the Curtis grandchildren. Although Freeman Curtis, when questioned at his nieces' inquest, painted a portrait of his mother as a loving, tender parent, other voices were heard during that public investigation. Mrs. Angeline Worth, the proprietor of the Miller Hotel in Liverpool, had known Helen Curtis for many years, and she remembered some things Freeman may have forgotten:

Well, I know that she tied Freeman to his chair when he was a little fellow and left him. He fell off the chair and against a hot stove. He would have been roasted to death if neighbors had not heard his screams and saved him. He carries the scar to this day. I know that Leland was driven away from home by his mother and went to Kansas to shift for himself when he was a real young boy.

Mrs. Worth also recalled Helen Curtis, who was given to jealousy, chasing her husband, William, with a butcher knife after deciding he had been too accommodating to flirtatious females. And another inquest commentary on Helen Curtis's parenting style came from John Wolf Sr., likewise a longtime Curtis neighbor in their Liverpool years. He recalled that she had so starved her own children that they used to come begging to his house for even a crust of bread.

Not long after the arrival of the Curtis children, disquieting stories about life at 40 Lakota Street began circulating in the Lennox Park neighborhood. Mrs. Curtis's son Freeman would later state that it was the worst community he had ever known for vicious tale-bearing—and the Curtis neighbors certainly had many tales to bear. Marie Bodenlos, who kept a grocery and school supplies store a block away from the Curtis home, often saw Helen and Marguerite as they stopped by on the way to and from school. When they first started begging her for something to eat, she assumed they were simply eating between meals. But one day she teasingly asked them if they didn't get anything to eat at home—and was shocked when they told her that Mrs. Curtis only gave them stale bread to eat. When she probed further, they told her that Mrs. Curtis bought 10 loaves every Tuesday and Thursday from a man who came by with his bread wagon. The bread would then be left in the basement to soften before being doled out to the hungry children. Helen told much the same story of nutritional abuse to Miss Jennie Albers, her teacher at the West Park school, adding that it was sometimes topped with jelly. Alice McClennan, who spent two weeks at the Curtis house while the children were there, would later testify that she saw no meat served to them during her sojourn. Mrs. Curtis would unequivocally deny such stories at the inquest, angrily insisting that her usual daily menu included potatoes, bread and butter, and gravy for breakfast, with the same at lunch, plus "bread and jell." She added that they sometimes had chicken but maintained a coy indefiniteness as to how often. And whatever the deficiencies of her cuisine, she excused them with the plea that Leland Curtis did not send enough money to subsidize a more generous diet for his children. Considering that Leland regularly sent his mother $25 a month, not to mention the presence of two able-bodied Curtis sons in residence, Mrs. Curtis's defense of her table was a remarkable statement. It was also noted by Lakota Street neighbors that while at home the Curtis children were habitually dressed in burlap bags, although their school garb was relatively normal, if drab and unchanging. Jennie Albers would later remember that Helen was so ashamed of her clothing that she ran away from school the day the class photograph was taken. Another neighbor commenting on the girls' clothing, Mrs. George Heine, expressed the opinion that Helen and Marguerite's grooming and garb made them resemble "gypsies more than white children."

Far worse tales than those of Mrs. Curtis's alleged short rations and clothing allowance circulated amongst her West Park neighbors. Mrs. Marie Prior, janitress of the West Park school and wife of school board member Frank Prior, would later recall that she saw the children tied to their chairs with their hands behind their back. She also remembered that they were often locked in the cellar for hours after they returned from school and then sent to bed without supper. During her fortnight's stay in the Curtis home, Alice Mc-Clennan likewise witnessed the rituals of chair binding and cellar imprisonment. Truly, "good German discipline" was well in force at 40 Lakota Street.

Was Mrs. Curtis's abuse even worse than that? During the last months of Helen and Marguerite's lives the chief confidant of their childish sorrows was their teacher, Jennie Albers. Helen told her frequently of the unstinting beatings and whippings administered by Mrs. Curtis to her grandchildren. She eventually admitted, though, that there was no "whip" involved: Helen Curtis's favorite instrument of chastisement was a piece of fence rail, which she laid on without restraint. Sometime in the spring of 1907, Helen came to school janitress Marie Prior and teacher Jennie Albers with bruised and bleeding wrists and hands. She allowed Mrs. Prior to bandage her up, but she refused to admit how she had been injured, saying only that her grandmother would not allow her to tell.

After the girls' spectacular death, Mrs. Curtis, of course, had her own contrasting version of events. It was equally, if not more gothic than the child abuse narrative generated by the girls and the Curtis neighbors. According to Mrs. Curtis, the presence of Marguerite and Helen in her home had been a disaster from the beginning. Although she agreed with Jennie Albers's assessment that the two girls were "bright," she also insisted that they were "light-headed" and, worse, hell-bent on suicide from the moment they crossed her threshold in March 1906. Shortly after she arrived in Cleveland, Helen disappeared, after telling Mrs. Curtis that she was going to lie down on some railroad tracks until a train put her out of her misery. She was subsequently found on the tracks and rescued, but she continued her threats to thus end her life. Soon after that, Mrs. Curtis returned home to find Marguerite hanging out of a second-story window, a clumsy but frightening attempt at suicide. Soon, the girls were sharing their suicide wishes with the Curtis neighbors and, eventually, with Jennie Albers. Helen's final threat in Albers's presence occurred on May 29, a little more than a week before her death. She told Albers she could no longer endure the agonies of life with her grandmother and that she and Marguerite would kill themselves to escape her cruelty. To her regret, Albers never took the suicide threats very seriously. But even before Helen's final threat she was concerned enough about such morbid words and about the apparent neglect reflected in the girls' clothing and chronic hunger to report the situation to West Park school superintendent S. H.

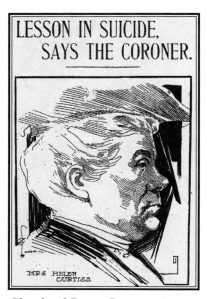

LESSON IN SUICIDE, SAYS THE CORONER.

MRS HELEN CURTISS

Cleveland Press, June 11, 1907.

Pincombe. He first sent a truant officer around to the Curtis home—Helen had been absent for about six weeks at Christmastime—but the officer could not find anyone at home to answer the door. The officer than scoured the neighborhood to find someone to swear out a warrant for child abuse against Mrs. Curtis. Notwithstanding the many armchair critics of Mrs. Curtis's childrearing methods, he found none, so a puzzled Superintendent Pincombe wrote to Leland Curtis in Kansas. The denouement of Pincombe's investigation would be predictable to anyone conversant with abuse allegations. A baffled Leland turned the letter over to his brother Freeman, who later told a Cleveland *Plain Dealer* reporter:

> It was a shock to me, that letter. I had never seen the children abused. I asked my mother about it, and she said, "Ask the children." They denied that my mother had been cruel. Then I went to Mrs. Prior and to Miss Albers. They told me what they had heard from the children themselves—stories of beatings and neglect. But I was unable to get the girls to confirm it. "Grandma is good to us," they told me. I am inclined to believe that the charges are trumped up by the people in the park. They were not on good terms with my mother; they have always seemed to me to be maliciously persecuting her.

Freeman did not disclose to the reporter that he had taken it upon himself to reply to Albers's original letter, a response which she simply termed "impertinent." And so the matter was dropped. Subsequently, Leland was further lulled into complacency by a letter from Helen and Marguerite in late May 1907, in which they assured him that they were "happy" and growing "fat as pigs" on their grandmother's cooking.

Lacking much evidence, and with the lapse of a century, it is difficult to defend Mrs. Helen Curtis from charges of flagrant child abuse. Freeman Curtis, her son and most vociferous defender, ascribed all the accusations to lying, malicious neighbors—but his feigned ignorance of what was going on in his mother's house is tellingly belied by his residence there at the time. On the other hand, it was clear, notwithstanding his mother's behavior, that at least three of the Curtis children were, by any criteria out of control. Frank Curtis seems to have led a fairly normal life, but Helen and Marguerite continued to make suicide threats and attempts. One day they approached Mrs. Bodenlos and asked her for money to buy some carbolic acid. (A common household antiseptic, carbolic acid was often used to commit suicide, especially by turn-of-the-century females.) When asked why they wanted carbolic acid, they replied, "We want to commit suicide." Failing to secure a supply from Bodenlos, they approached a saloonkeeper, who likewise refused to sell it to them. No matter—four-year-old Clara Curtis eventually found some in a trunk and, doubtless aping her older siblings, drank enough of it to burn her mouth and be sick for weeks. During that same eventful year, Helen and Marguerite also made at least three or four attempts to set the house on fire, one with a candle, one with a gasoline stove. The closest they came to a fatality was when they stoked a fire in a wood stove and tried to thrust Clara's head into the blazing interior. Either the aperture was too small or Clara's screams too loud, as alerted neighbors soon put an end to this appalling episode. But it burned all of Clara's hair off and did not deter Helen and Marguerite from further morbid adventures. At some point Helen, too, tried the carbolic acid route to death, noticeably scarring her mouth but without securing her desired end.

Given this background of suicidal mania, something ghastly was bound to happen—and it took place on Friday, the seventh day of June 1907. No one knows what happened that morning, although an imaginative *Cleveland Leader* reporter later gussied up the emotional background of the tragedy with suitable foreshadowing:

> Yesterday morning both girls seemed to be more cast down than usual and complained of the canker that was consuming their happiness. After a time they were seen crying as if their hearts were breaking. A little later the girls disappeared.

The actual sequence of the fatal event was a bit more prosaic. Shortly before noon, Mrs. Curtis, preparing for lunch, asked Helen and Marguerite to go down to the cellar, bring up some potatoes, and pare them. They dutifully descended the stairs, followed by little Clara and, a little later, their brother Frank. Owing to recent rains and poor sewerage, the cellar held two feet of water, so retrieving the potatoes would have been a risky business in any case. But they weren't interested in the potatoes—and headed directly for some shelves built against a cellar wall. Climbing up to the top shelf, Helen picked up a container of "Rough-on-Rats" and brought it back down. Removing it to a dry patch of the cellar, she opened it and offered it to Marguerite . . .

An irresistible digression here. In turn-of-the-century America, Rough-on-Rats was likely the most popular anti-rodent preparation of the day. Developed by pharmacist E. S. Wells of Jersey City, its *very* active ingredient was arsenic, and Wells single-handedly created its vigorous advertising copy and such complementary proprietary compounds as Rough-on-Bile, Rough-on-Catarrh, and Rough-on-Corns, Itch, Pain, Piles, Toothache and Worms. Most of his advertising graphics pictured an impressively dead rat, whose side sported the reassuring mottos "Don't Die in the House" or "Gone Where the Woodbine Twineth." There was even a Rough-on-Rats song by composer Jules Juniper, which included this catchy chorus:

R-r-rats! Rats! Rough on Rats!
Hang your dogs and drown your cats;
We give a plan for every man
To clear his house with ROUGH ON RATS.

It is only fair to state that such Rough-on-Rats propaganda was not taken quite as seriously as inventor E. S. Wells might have desired. A brief sample of the kind of heartless parodies it inspired will suffice:

Willie and three other brats,
Ate up all the Rough-on-Rats.
Papa said, when Mama cried,
"Don't worry, dear, they'll die outside."
—Anonymous

Meanwhile, back at the foot of the cellar stairs, the moment of truth had arrived. Looking at Helen's proffered palm of rat poison, Marguerite stared back and said, "I will, if you will." A moment later, Marguerite tipped the can to her mouth and then handed it to Helen, who did likewise.

Clara, who was sitting on the cellar stairs, probably had no clear notion of what her sisters were doing. But brother Frank, coming down the stairs, realized what they had done when he saw the poison can in Helen's hand. Leaving him in no doubt, one of them said to Frank, "We are going to die." Running up to the kitchen, Frank found Mrs. Curtis and screamed, "Marguerite and Helen said they are going to kill themselves!"

What occurred during the next few minutes is a bit hazy and supported mainly by the contradictory evidence offered later to newspaper reporters and to Cuyahoga County coroner Thomas Burke at the inquest. Mrs. Curtis, who was lame, took some time to get to the top of the cellar stairs. As she got there, she saw Marguerite, already in convulsions as she attempted to totter up the stairs. There was a telltale green stain on her lips from the rat poison and she managed to croak out the words, "Gran'ma, I'm dying!" before falling at the feet of Mrs. Curtis. Seconds later, Helen staggered up the stairs. She could no longer even talk, her face was deadly pale, and she fell almost on top of her sister.

Mrs. Curtis may have fainted at this point, or perhaps a bit later. At some juncture, however, she tried to administer home remedies to the unconscious girls, dosing with them with milk and a solution of baking soda and water. She later claimed that she thought they had poisoned themselves by drinking paint—hence the stains on their lips—but whatever her initial surmise, it was soon obvious that they needed real medical help. Alerted by her ensuing screams, neighbors started flooding into the house, one of them snagging Dr. Henry C. Kelker, who just happened to be walking past 40 Lakota Street. Examining the unconscious girls, he found a faint pulse in both of them but after summoning A. R. Nun's ambulance service admitted to Mrs. Curtis, "There is little hope." Mrs. Curtis would later claim—without any corroboration—that before the girls were taken away, they both completed exonerated her and acknowledged full responsibility for their suicidal act.

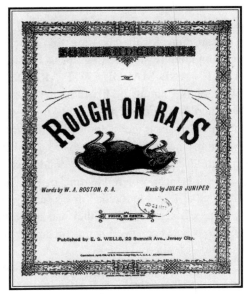

Sheet music cover to "Rough on Rats."

Rushed to St. John's Hospital, the girls were attended by Drs. Joseph O'Malley and Frank Kuta and put into adjoining beds, and the deathwatch begun. The poison did its work on Marguerite faster, and she only regained consciousness once, about 4 p.m. that day. Opening her eyes, she gazed feebly around her and began mumbling the words of the Our Father prayer. She got about halfway through before lapsing back into unconsciousness and then drifted quietly off to her death at 7 p.m.

Helen fought longer and harder for life, but her end was never in doubt. She managed to regain consciousness late in the afternoon, long enough to talk to her uncle Freeman. According to Freeman—a perhaps unreliable witness—she told him the reason for the double suicide: "We took the poison because Grandma wanted us to go to school." Asked if she had any message for her father, she said, "Tell him I've been a bad girl. Tell him I hope he will forgive me." Unaware that her sister was already dead, she begged an attending nun, "I want to speak to Marguerite." No one wanted to tell her of her sister's fate, so the nun asked, "What do you want to say to her?" "Bring her over and I'll tell her," replied Helen. "Ah, after a while," said the nun. Asked a few more questions about how she and Marguerite had obtained the poison, she simply replied, "I won't tell," before falling unconscious for the last time. She died at 9:55 a.m.

Mrs. Curtis immediately sent a telegram to Leland Curtis that simply said, HELEN AND MARGUERITE ARE DEAD; COME HOME. Ignorant of the nature of his daughters' deaths, Leland arrived in Cleveland late Sunday night, only to be overwhelmed by the details of his family tragedy and the pestering attention of Cleveland's four daily newspapers. Whatever he really thought or knew about his children's history in Cleveland was consistently concealed by a public façade of unyielding denial. Insisting that there was no history of "suicide mania" in his family, he was likewise adamant in his claims that his mother was a loving custodian and that his children had been well cared for and happy. Talking to reporters, Leland defended his family and placed the blame for his daughters' deaths on culture shock, his mother's uncharitable neighbors, and the cruelty of the West Park children:

> I believe that they were urged on to do this thing by being tantalized by the other children about the neighborhood who told them all manner of things and made them discontented with life. The girls were raised on a farm, and until eighteen months ago were used to living in the open. They often wrote me that they wanted to come back west, but always said that they were getting along with their studies fine, so I took it that they were contented.

Pending an official investigation and awaiting input from Leland Curtis, Coroner Burke ordered Frank and Claribel Curtis removed to the children's detention home.

By the time Coroner Thomas Burke's inquest opened on Monday, June 10, it is likely that the public mind had been thoroughly poisoned against Mrs. Helen Curtis. The story of Helen and Marguerite's double suicide had dominated the four Cleveland papers since Saturday morning, and every available scrap of incriminating gossip and rumor had been thoroughly exposed and almost endlessly recycled by the time Burke's proceedings began at 10 a.m.

Nor did Burke himself disguise his own preconceptions about the case, discounting, only a day after the deaths, the theory of a familial suicide compulsion. Indeed, he went much further in a *Cleveland News* interview, presenting a harsh, albeit purple-prosed indictment of the childcare dished out by Mrs. Helen Curtis:

> I can readily see the impelling cause that drove those two little girls to their death. The lives of children need love and laughter, as plants need sunlight and the rains, that they may flourish. I do not believe that heredity had anything to do with their deed. Heredity would scarcely manifest itself in that way before the fourteenth year, and they were only ten and eleven. But consider the situation of children whose longings and pleasures are looked upon by their guardians from the severe standpoint of old age; to whose protectors dolls are silly and tag is idiotic. Think of children who go mournfully from home in the morning, and return with fear at night; whose innocent plays are condemned with a cuff on the head; whose whole lives are compassed about with puritanical severity. Children ponder these things and feel them deeply. If you have ever been whipped as a child, you will remember the heartbreak and the wishes that you were dead. Extend this feeling over years and you have a cause that would drive any child to suicide.

In the actual event, Burke's inquest was, on the whole, a fair one, although its tone seemed fatally prejudiced against Mrs. Curtis at the outset. After hearing Marie Bodenlos relate her memories of the girls' unhappiness and hunger, Alice McClennan took the stand to talk of their starvation bread diet, the rags that served for their clothing, the chair-tying and cellar-locking discipline, and their general air of depressive misery. "They were not happy children—morose and never smiled—never had a chance to smile." More ominously, she remembered Mrs. Curtis saying to her, "I wish those children were out of my sight!"

Finally, after eliciting from McClennan every incriminating circumstance of her two-week sojourn at the Curtis house, Burke got to the $64,000 question—and he wasn't subtle about it. Nor was McClennan's reply, a model of incriminatory evasion:

> Burke: Do you think that Mrs. Curtis put the rat poison where the children could procure it, or were they induced to eat it when put on bread?
> McClennan: I cannot say. If those two little girls took it of their own volition they were pretty game. I know I would not have taken poison myself at ten years of age.
> Burke: Do you think that Mrs. Curtis put the rat poison where the children could procure it, or were they induced to eat it when put on bread?
> McClennan: I cannot say.
> Burke: Was a physician hurried in?
> McClennan: I think that Mrs. Curtis did not do so on account of the expense.

Jennie Albers followed McClennan, and offered copious and heartbreaking testimony of the girls' unhappiness and preoccupation with suicide. In her emotional testimony she told the inquest jury:

> They were bright children, and many times I bought them paper and pencils. Morning after morning they would come to school crying. I would ask them what was the matter, then both little girls would reply, "Grandmother is mean to us."

Albers, who had already talked much to Cleveland newspaper reporters, was given ample opportunity to recall Helen and Marguerite's numerous allegations of abuse before Coroner Burke led her to his ultimate question:

> Burke: Under oath I want you to answer this question: Was that poison put where Helen and Marguerite Curtis could get it?

Hesitating for a moment, Albers looked up at the ceiling. Then,

Cleveland News, June 10, 1907.

with quivering chin and a shaking voice, she answered Burke's question with her own: "Why did Mrs. Helen Curtis lock up food and not lock up poison?"

Albers's rhetorically charged question set the stage for Mrs. Helen Curtis. Not surprisingly, she denied that she had been cruel to the dead girls and even that they had ever talked of suicide, much less repeatedly rehearsed it. (This was much at odds with her earlier disclosure to reporters that she knew the girls were suicide prone and that she had attempted to hide all household poisons and had even buried a tempting can of green paint in the ground.) She wisely refrained from criticizing the dead girls, saying that they were "happy and obedient" children. And she insisted that they had been well cared for, amply fed, and adequately dressed, even after Coroner Burke confronted her with one of the burlap sack dresses. Failing to make a dent in her impassive equanimity, Burke concluded the morning inquest session with a scathing and unequivocal indictment of Mrs. Curtis's veracity and moral responsibility:

> My dear woman, the testimony of your neighbors does not bear you out in the statements you have made here. You are not telling the truth, and also that you, before God, are the murderer, perhaps morally, of those two children, Helen and Margaret Curtis.

There was less to Burke's thundering accusation than met the ear.

Although his last words to Mrs. Curtis were hailed with applause by the crowd of 25 neighborhood women in the inquest room (led by Jennie Albers), Burke's peroration was undoubtedly spoken for mere grandstand effect. The canny Burke, no stranger to politically sensitive inquests, knew exactly how much legal wiggle room was involved in the words *perhaps* and *morally*. So, even before hearing the rest of the inquest witnesses—most of them likely prejudicial to Mrs. Curtis—he issued the following statement at noon on Tuesday, June 11, a kind of apotheosis of irrefutable legal reasoning and bathetic, if crowd-pleasing, slobber:

> Justices Kennedy and Babcock have held that to prove a case of criminal negligence a violation of some law must be shown. In this case that seems impossible. For, even if Mrs. Helen Curtis placed the poison before the eyes of the children and then left the room, she would have violated no law; hence a charge of criminal negligence would not be feasible. We would have to show that she actually gave the children poison or placed it in food, which she knew they were to eat, and there is absolutely nothing to indicate that. But I do think that the inquest will be of broad benefit. An exposure of conditions which have been related here will tend to bring babes nearer to their mothers.
>
> There is no offspring as helpless as a human child. The animals almost from birth are able to care for themselves. So are the birds. The human babe is helpless. Also, the thorough inquest conducted will make mothers more careful where they leave deadly poisons when there is a possibility of a child being near.

Mrs. Helen Curtis's critics got in a few last licks before the formal end of Burke's inquest on June 12. A delegation of former neighbors from Liverpool appeared Wednesday, most of them eager to relate delicious gossip and hearsay to her detriment. Angeline Worth, who apparently still nourished jealous suspicions about her husband William's bygone attentions to Helen, led off the parade with her characterization of Curtis as a "hard, grasping, avaricious woman." Moving on to how Helen had mistreated her sons Leland and Freeman, she eventually got around to the demise of her husband:

There were suspicious circumstances surrounding his death. He was a big, strong, healthy man. For a few months he was a little sick and then he died quite suddenly. The rumors that all was not right were so persistent, that I think an autopsy was held by a doctor who is now dead. I do not think he ever gave the result of the autopsy to the public.

Prodded by Burke, Mrs. Worth couldn't remember whether Mrs. Curtis had purchased any arsenic before William's death, but she helpfully volunteered that she'd seen Helen chasing him with a butcher knife. Two final witnesses appeared on Wednesday morning, one testifying to Mrs. Curtis's fine character, the other swearing that William Curtis had died of stomach cancer instead of spousal poisoning. Burke's formal conclusion to the inquest was more masterful treacle for the sentimental public he served:

This investigation has accomplished this much, I hope. It has impressed on the public the need of individual love and care in the bringing up of children. There is nothing in the testimony upon which I can hold any one legally responsible for the death of these little girls. But the inquest has accomplished something. During the first year of a baby's life there does not exist a living thing more helpless. Older children hunger for love and caresses and personal attention, which these little girls, it appears to me, did not always get.

And that was the end of the Curtis tragedy, save for the funeral and burial of the dead girls. On Tuesday afternoon, June 11, the Reverend Amos F. Upp of the Simpson Methodist Church conducted a short and simple service for Helen and Marguerite at the Curtis home. Before and during the service the Curtis yard was crowded with neighbors and the simply curious, many of whom audibly speculated about Mrs. Curtis's responsibility for their tragic end. In his brief remarks, the Rev. Upp alluded only gently to the circumstances of the deaths, saying, "God is our judge, not man. He knows our motives and our thoughts." Then the funeral party headed for the West Park Cemetery, with Mrs. Curtis and her sons leading the way. At the graveside there, Simpson spoke briefly, again delicately alluding to the suspicions swirling around Mrs. Curtis, praying, "God give us strength. Give us everything we need in this hour of trial. Dispel the clouds that hang over us." Then, as Helen and Marguerite's maternal aunt Maggie sobbed helplessly and little Clara looked uncomprehendingly over the open grave, a sweet-voiced female sang "There's a Land That Is Fairer Than Day" (a hymn also known by the title "In the Sweet By and By"). Ten of the dead girls' West Park school classmates served as pallbearers, while two others carried wreaths and bouquets sent by fellow students and teachers, displays which, as a Cleveland *Plain Dealer* reporter wrote, "almost seemed to mock in their futile prettiness the barrenness of the dead girls' lives." Then the dirt was shoveled over the coffins and everyone present resumed their lives.

As stated at the outset of this unspeakable story, no one will ever know the truth about the Curtis horror. But even if one allows that Helen and Marguerite Curtis were pathological liars—an instance not unknown in my experience of apparent child "victims"—it was clear that Mrs. Curtis was not telling the whole truth in her account of her life with the doomed children. And surely Freeman Curtis was correct when he opined—too late—"Mother is too old to have the care of children."

The final word about this malignant Cleveland Cinderella story belongs to Mrs. Helen Curtis, last recorded wearily sinking into a chair at her Lakota Street home after the funeral. "What I have said is the truth," she sobbed. "I don't care who hears it. Some other time I may have more to say."

Chapter 2

SOME PEOPLE NEVER LEARN

The Specs Russell Saga

Make no mistake about it: Joseph ("Specs") Russell was a two-bit thug. He was a simple-minded, trigger-happy punk: cowardly (except when he had a gun), always driven by only the most shallow and short-term goals, and altogether no damn good. True, he lacked the flashy style or more durable success of a Shondor Birns, a Danny Greene, or even a "Big Jim" Morton—despite the fact that he was far younger than they when he started his criminal path. But give Specs his due: during his short but sensational career as Public Enemy #1 the diminutive bandit ran the Cleveland Police Department ragged and managed, more often than not, to make its officers look like idiots.

Joseph Russell's origins were obscure but reputedly respectable. His father's name was Anthony, and Specs was born about 1908 near DuBois, a small town located in one of the more remote regions of north-central Pennsylvania, much of it nearly a howling wilderness of forest and degraded mining terrain. What drew his parents and older brother Angelo to Cleveland, and when, is unknown. What is known, however, is that young Joe turned to the bad at a very tender age. His first arrest came when he was eight. Mocked by a neighbor who jeered at his bell-bottomed trousers, Joe went looking for a gun and, when he found it, menaced his sartorial critic with extreme consequences. Appearing in Cuyahoga County Juvenile Court four times before his ninth birthday, Joe was eventually remanded to the Hudson Boys' Farm for moral improvement. It took him two months to contrive his first escape, an interval he would labor strenuously to reduce. During his early teenage years several more juvenile court appearances and more stints in Hudson failed to improve his character or prospects. A measure of his criminal precocity was his increasing taste for assuming aliases, such as "Joseph Russo" and "Giuseppe Russell," to mask his illicit activities.

Joe's mature career as a recidivist thug officially began on August 4, 1921. Arrested for motoring without leave in an automobile belonging to S. C. Boland of 1329 East 84th Street, Joe was subsequently sentenced to the Boys' Industrial School in Lancaster, Ohio. Out of compassion for his extreme youth, the sentence was suspended, only to be enforced when, on May 10, 1922, he and his raffish companions were surprised while breaking and entering several homes. Placed in the Cuyahoga County Detention Home on Franklin Avenue (now the Cuyahoga County Archives) pending trial, Joe soon escaped, taking some jewelry and clothing with him. (Faithful readers of these humble chronicles may recall that Sam Pupera, one of the boyish killers of industrialists Wilfred C. Sly and George K. Fanner in 1921, was also an escaped alumnus of the impressively porous County Detention Home.) Quickly recaptured, Joe was duly sent to mend his ways at the Ohio Reformatory in Lancaster.

He did not. Paroled in October 1923, Specs was arrested on March 31, 1924, for burglarizing the home of Joseph David, 5808 Whittier Avenue, a theft which netted Joe some jewelry, a revolver, and, on April 2, another scholarship to the Ohio Reformatory, this time at the Mansfield facility. (Cleveland justice was apparently a bit speedier back in the Roaring Twenties than now.) Paroled the following July, Specs was ordered back to Mansfield on October 24, 1925, for violating the conditions of his parole. The next day, however, he detoured to Cleveland to stand trial for the robbery of Morris Gimplin of 12304 Kinsman Road. For reasons unknown, Cuyahoga County prosecutor Edward Stanton, never a softy on crime, nolled the case, and Specs returned to Mansfield to complete his sentence. When he was paroled from the Mansfield Reformatory in 1927, Specs swore he would never return.

The young hoodlum who emerged from Mansfield was not, at

first glance, a very prepossessing figure, much less a physically imposing one. Perhaps 18 or 19 years old, Joe was no more than 5 feet, 4 inches in height (probably less) and weighed only 120 pounds. His dark-complexioned face sported several largish pimples, and his voice, a harsh-voiced twang, was apparently his incompetent attempt at a "hard-boiled" tone. Usually appareled in a light suit, he was shod in polished black shoes and wore a soft straw hat in summer. Most memorably, he generally sported a pair of smoked glasses when doing business—and his business was armed robbery.

In light of his later notoriety, it is remarkable that Specs's initial robberies attracted such meager police or public attention. But 1920s Cleveland, with a population pushing 900,000, had a lot of crime, so perhaps a baby-faced and bespectacled thug repeatedly holding up small groceries, gas stations, and retail shops initially seemed hardly worth the notice of a police blotter or a couple of lines on page 12. Specs's career as a stickup artist began on June 2, 1927, but it was June 28 and several dozen robberies later before police officials and journalists began to take notice of his malign doings, most noticeably by dubbing him "Specs" and the "smoked glasses kid." That evening Specs, wearing his trademark shades, walked into the Spayne & Reich clothing store at 7002 Superior Avenue. Pulling out a .45-caliber automatic, Specs aimed it at clerks Adolph Klein and Elmer Koenig and rasped, "Stick 'em up!" Relieving them of their personal cash, Specs then herded the two men into a back room and locked the door. Removing $150 from the store's cash register, he ambled back to the street, slid into the front seat of his stolen car, and drove away.

The average robber might have called this a good day's work and clocked out. But not Specs Russell, who was just warming up. An hour later he sauntered into Louis Wieder's clothing store at 2943 Woodhill Road. Drawing his .45, he again snarled out his "Stick 'em up!" patter and calmly departed with $147.

In his brief career Specs Russell had already developed a number of professional habits, aside from his smoked eyewear, clichéd dialogue, and the flourishing of his .45-caliber revolver. One of them was pushing his luck, which he now demonstrated in dramatic fashion. After an hour of aimlessly riding around in his stolen car, he decided to rob Joseph Polk's drugstore at 12803 Kinsman Road. Forcing Polk and clerk Louis Rudin to lie on the floor, Specs covered them with some automobile tires and told them to keep still. Polk did not. While Specs rummaged in the cash register, the druggist managed to wriggle his way to his own gun and start shooting at Specs. The stunned bandit returned fire, and he and Polk ultimately exchanged a total of 15 shots, with Polk getting off the lion's share of nine. But neither man was a very good shot, and their noisy battle ended with a panicked Specs fleeing the drugstore on foot, leaving both loot and automobile behind him.

Another characteristic of Specs Russell was that he liked to keep his opponents on the Cleveland police force guessing. Most any other armed robber, especially one as recognizable as the bespectacled Specs, might have cooled it after his latest crime spree. But not the counterintuitive Specs, who showed up the very next evening at Nelson Vixier's pharmacy at 1511 Hayden Avenue. Forcing Vixier and clerk Fred Snowberger into a back room, he ordered them to lie on the floor. Perhaps mindful of his previous tire mishap, he covered the two men with bottles and warned them that he would shoot them dead if he heard so much as a bottle fall. A minute later Specs fled the store with $40 in cash and a wristwatch.

Two days later, Specs shifted his operations to the West Side. He was accompanied this time by an accomplice, probably Joseph Rutsynski, a 17-year-old runaway from the Boys' Industrial School at Lancaster. Pulling up to the Bosworth Drug Store at 11501 Lorain Avenue in a stolen Essex Coach automobile, Specs and his henchman walked inside, flourished their guns, and commanded owner Ben Gladstone and clerk Arnold Goldberg to "stick 'em up!" But a man passing by the drugstore had seen Specs go in. Realizing that he was the "smoked glasses kid" described in the Cleveland newspapers, the man fomented a crowd while Specs and his accomplice were inside. Emerging with $250 from Gladstone and $5 from Goldberg, Specs was confronted with a crowd of about 100 persons when he came through the door. But Specs could be quite nonchalant when he was the only one with a gun, so he calmly leaned against the door and stared the crowd down while Rutsynski ran and started the Essex. As the engine roared to life, Specs

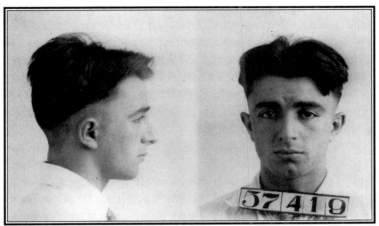

Joseph "Specs" Russell.

sprinted for it, jumped in, and rode away.

By now Specs was the talk of Cleveland and embarrassed police officials were devoting more and more time to their dragnet for the smoked-glasses bandit. By early July, squads of heavily armed police officers and detectives were even staking out some of Specs's most likely targets: neighborhood grocery stores, gasoline stations, and small retail outlets, such as shoe stores. During the previous month he had committed as many as three dozen armed robberies, and repeated declarations by Cleveland safety director Edwin Barry and Cleveland police chief Jacob Graul that the mysterious Specs would be apprehended "soon" were wearing thin. It was clear that Specs, while in no peril of being mistaken for a Forest City Robin Hood, had built up a certain personal mystique with the public, and his ability to elude Cleveland cops was hurting both their morale and reputation. But not everyone was taken with Specs, especially Cleveland *Plain Dealer* business columnist John Love. In a July 1 column, after noting the pitifully small amounts of money bandits like Specs usually garnered at the risk of their lives, he cast a skeptical glance at both the mentality and modus operandi of the "smoked glasses kid":

The "smoked glasses" robber who has been annoying Cleveland is just another curious example of specialization. The glasses may have no real importance, but by this time he has succeeded often enough with smoked glasses that he musn't leave them off. He is superstitious about them. Criminals have little imagination, and one scheme that works is better than a lot of experimenting. Because they lack imagination we are saved from pitying the poor criminal whom the police won't allow to vary his repertoire, like the actor whom the public won't allow to play tragedy because he does farces so well.

In the end, Love would prove correct about Specs's lack of imagination. He was also right about the economic lunacy of Specs Russell's criminal enterprise: during his two-month heyday, Specs pulled approximately 52 robberies, for a total cash take of about $4,000. That comes out to an average of only $76.92 per robbery, any one of which could have gotten him killed.

Specs's 1927 crime spree makes even less sense when you consider that his high-risk robberies didn't even bring him the glamour and affluence he so desperately sought. After he was finally caught, Specs laid bare his primal motivation to his archnemesis, Cleveland Police detective inspector Cornelius W. Cody. It was simply sheer seething envy that drove Specs Russell to a life of crime, and a very unsophisticated strain of envy at that. As he confessed to Cody:

Why, I see these guys wearing flashy clothes, sporting snappy cars and dragging out enough bills to choke a cow. They got diamonds, rings, everything. They make me sore. So I thought I'd get those things for myself.

In fact, during the period of his crime spree, Specs and his various confederates were hardly living off the fat of the land. When not sleeping in various stolen cars, they were living in their hideout, an abandoned Bailey Company warehouse and stable at 733 Hill Avenue. There, surrounded by filthy walls, sagging floors, and numerous rats, they slept on piles of excelsior piled on a ratty old mattress, one eye ever cocked for the cops. When they were awake, many of their leisure hours were spent avidly reading newspaper accounts of their exploits. Not surprisingly, no one in the area paid attention to them or to the succession of stolen cars parked behind the warehouse. The Haymarket district had always been one of Cleveland's scruffiest neighborhoods (discerning readers of these chroniclers may recall that the nefarious bandit and cop killer "Blinky" Morgan had his hideout there back in the 1880s), and the derelict warehouse was soon slated for demolition as part of the clearance for the Van Sweringen brothers' huge Terminal project.

Never content to rest upon his laurels, Specs picked up the pace again on Wednesday, July 6. There was a crap game going on in the old Newcomb Block on Ontario Street in the Haymarket district, and Specs was playing with Rutsynski and a 16-year-old boy named Mike Matyas. While rolling the dice, Matyas overheard Russell telling Rutsynski that they could make some "easy money" holding up some more stores. Realizing that he was privy to their plans, they turned to menace him. Realizing that he was trapped, Matyas blurted out, "I'm on the rocks myself and would like to join you fellows."

The three men walked to Broadway and Orange Avenues, where they piled into Specs's latest car, a stolen blue Overland roadster, and motored up to Kinsman Road and East 83rd Street. Russell then disappeared for a few minutes, returning with three guns: a .32-caliber pistol for Matyas, a .38-caliber revolver for Rutsynski, and his own trademark .45-caliber revolver.

Minutes later, about 3:50 p.m., they parked the Overland on the south side of Superior Avenue at East 80th Street. Entering the Home Provision Company at 8045 Superior—just three doors east of the Thirteenth Precinct Police Station—the trio ordered some ham and cheese, and Matyas ducked back out the front door to act as lookout. Then Russell and Rutsynski pulled their guns and told store manager Howard Pollock to "stick 'em up!" Locking Pollock in a refrigerator, they took $55 in cash and fled to their car. Turning north, they sped up East 81st Street and threaded their way north before turning west on St. Clair Avenue.

Their next stop was the Meyer Miller shoe store at 6304 St. Clair. Rutsynski at first pretended he had come to be measured for a suit of clothes, but before long the guns came out and the robber trio locked Miller and clerks Louis Kurnick and Morris Kreiger in a back room. They took $32 from the register and were probably just walking out the door when the alarm for the Home Provision Company came in to the Thirteenth Precinct station. As Specs had not worn his smoked glasses on that heist, the police didn't follow up the robbery report with much urgency until they realized, after hearing of the trio's work at the Miller store, that Specs was involved. The usual squads, bristling with sawed-off shotguns, rifles, and pistols, were dispatched, and with the usual results.

Once again, Specs was a step ahead of his baffled pursuers. About the time the alarm for the Miller robbery came in, Specs and his two gunsels parked their car in front of William Charein's shoe store at 12512 Kinsman Road. With Russell standing at the door as lookout, Matyas asked Charein to measure him for a pair of shoes. Then, as Charein leaned down, Rutsynski hit him over the head with his gun. But just as Charein crumpled to the floor, a young woman walked into the store. Specs hadn't planned for such a contingency, and he panicked. Shouting "Beat it!" to his comrades, he led by example toward the street. As Matyas and Rutsynski fled, they hastily grabbed boxes of shoes and socks as they headed after Specs. After driving around aimlessly for a few hours, they stopped at Joseph Pantrell's restaurant at 1947 West 25th Street. Robbing Pantrell and a night-owl customer of $69—it was already 11:45 p.m.—the robbers called it a day. To the humiliation of the Cleveland Police, the following morning's Cleveland *Plain Dealer* featured a page 1 story headed:"SMOKED SPECTACLES KID" ROBS THREE STORES; ONE PLACE WITHIN THREE DOORS OF THIRTEENTH PRECINCT STATION.

In their defense, the chief difficulty for Cleveland police in finding Specs was simply that they didn't know just who he was. Based on descriptions by his ever-swelling crowd of victims, they knew he was young, they knew he was cocky, and they knew he habitually wore smoked glasses and was a bit on the trigger-happy side. They also knew he was not very tall, and Cleveland's journalists no doubt gratified the ranks of Cleveland's Finest with their frequent and insulting references to the "midget" bandit terrorizing Cleveland. But they didn't know his name, his family, or that his nominal residence was at 2416 East 89th Street. Not that he would have gone back there now, for no lair was likely more secure than his Hill Avenue ruin.

Specs's modest reign of terror continued at its feverish pace. The next night, July 7, Specs, Rutsynski, and Matyas cornered grocery owner John Bulford alone in his store at 2527 East 46th Street. Leveling his .45, Specs demanded that Bulford "stick 'em up." When Bulford refused, Specs fired at him once. But even as he pulled the trigger, Bulford dropped to one knee, grabbed *his* gun from underneath the counter, and fired back. Both men missed, but the trio ran out without getting Bulford's cash. Fifteen minutes later, Specs and Rutsynski—apparently Matyas had lost his nerve at Bulford's store—showed up at the confectionary of Peter Paris at 6503 Fullerton Avenue. A minute later they departed with a modest $45 in cash, plus some cigarettes and candy.

Perhaps all three robbers were chastened by Bulford's armed resistance, as they took the next day off. Well, more or less, if we can exclude the two-tone Willys-Knight roadster that Specs stole that Friday afternoon from a parking lot at East 61st and Waterman Avenue. He and his boys spent the rest of the day joyriding the car around Lorain County. It would be much the worse for wear by the time its real owner, Raymond A. Parker of 4141 East 120th Street, saw it again.

The police finally got a break early on the morning of Saturday, July 9. Responding to an anonymous tip that four young men in a Willys-Knight roadster at East 138th St. and St. Clair Avenue were acting "suspiciously," a flying squad of six policemen descended on the scene. They found no one there when they arrived—but their visit triggered yet another anonymous tip, which led them to the home of Mike Matyas. Rousting him out of bed, police interrogators questioned him vigorously—he would later, of course, claim that his confession was tortured out of him—until he told them the whereabouts of Rutsynski. A police flying squad soon collected him, and he, no doubt after rigorous interrogation, confessed not only the real identity of the "smoked glasses kid" but also the vital fact that Specs had arranged for the trio to meet at noon that very day at the Hill Avenue hideout.

Led by Cleveland police captain Joseph Sweeney, six massively armed squads of police were waiting when Specs showed up at about noon in his Willys-Knight roadster. Two of them were Detectives Frank Brown and Joseph Munley, who spotted Specs as he drove past them. But Specs spotted them, too, and led them a spirited chase until they forced his automobile to the curb at Broadway Avenue and Ontario Street. Hauling Specs out of his car, Munley and Brown patted him down for weapons and found two revolvers, one a .32 caliber, the other a .38. They then brought Specs back to Hill Avenue, where Detectives Patrick McNeeley and Carl Zicarelli joined them in questioning Specs. They were still unsure if he was the bandit ringleader they sought, and the wily Specs told them only that he had been instructed to show up with a fourth gang member at a house at West 5th Street and Literary Road. So the police took him there, and then they decided that three of the detectives would search the house there while Carl Zicarelli guarded the handcuffed Specs in the squad car outside.

That was not a good idea. Shortly after the three detectives entered the house, Specs, complaining of pain in his arm, asked Zicarelli if he could unlock the handcuff on his left wrist. Zicarelli, no doubt to his lasting regret, agreed to do so and unlocked the left handcuff, which he retained in his hand. The instant the cuff came off, Specs crouched down, reached into his pants, and pulled out his trusty .45 automatic, which Brown and Munley had somehow missed when they patted him down. Pressing it against Zicarelli's side, Specs pulled the trigger twice. Nothing happened—miraculously, the hammer of the gun had jammed. But even as the stunned Zicarelli groped for his own gun, Specs lurched out of the squad car door, dragging Zicarelli down and after him. A second later, the hapless detective hit his forehead on the pavement and was knocked unconscious

Such was the story that Detective Zicarelli told his fellow policemen after his regained consciousness. Almost a month later, following his ultimate capture, a boastful Specs claimed that he had never pulled the trigger on Zicarelli and that the frightened detective had either fainted or become so paralyzed with fear that he was incapable of resistance. While Specs's version of the events seems unlikely, neither explanation reflects credit on the professional habits of Detectives Zicarelli, Munley, and Brown.

Specs didn't stick around to see if Zicarelli was dead, unconscious, or just plain scared. Sprinting away from the police car, he ran into the house of Mrs. Anna Ulicky at 716 Literary Road. Mrs. Ulicky, in the rear of her home, was unaware of Specs's presence as he fled upstairs and hid underneath a bed. But a few minutes later her son went upstairs and screamed when he saw Specs peeping at him from under the bed. Leaping up, Specs ran to the rear of the house, threw up a window sash, and leaped out. Landing unhurt on the ground 20 feet below, he ran down an alley, where Dr. F. N. Richardson of 2149 West 14th Street saw him climb a fence, run through a yard, and then jump on the back of a moving van coming down the street. When last seen that afternoon, Specs was still on the van as it sped eastward toward downtown Cleveland on the Central Viaduct. Later that evening, Cleveland police detective George Zicarelli, Carl's brother, briefly sighted Specs as he drove westward on the Central Viaduct in an old touring automobile.

It was soon evident that Specs Russell's sensational escape and his humiliation of the Cleveland Police meant the gloves were coming off in the search for the daredevil bandit. Citing Specs's alleged attempt to kill Zicarelli, Safety Director Barry issued a rare "shoot to kill" order to his men, permitting them to fire on sight at the elusive bandit. By Sunday morning, the greatest concentrated Cleveland manhunt since the 1923 pursuit of cop killer John Leonard Whitfield was in full force, with dozens of policemen and detectives following up clues and staking out Specs's reputed haunts and likely targets. (For a narrative of the Whitfield episode see "God, the Devil, Man or Beast" in the author's 1995 volume *They Died Crawling*.) The most practical and useful tool for the police was the creation of a wanted poster with Specs's picture, his Bertillon measurements, and facts about his mannerisms and habits. (Invented by Frenchman Alphonse Bertillon in 1882, the Bertillon system was a biometric system for identifying criminals by measuring their bodily dimensions and peculiarities—length of limbs, size of head, tattoos, etc. It was used widely until supplanted by fingerprint evidence. Bertillon also invented the mug shot.) Within a couple of days 500 copies were sent out to Ohio communities and neighboring states. But, unfortunately, most of the tips and clues provided by Clevelanders only added to the confusion, uncertainty, and general Keystone Kops ambiance of the Specs manhunt. During the first 24 hours after his escape a report came in that Specs was speeding toward Akron in a Wills St. Claire roadster; another sighting found him driving down Professor Avenue, while yet a third reported him in a gray Chrysler on the Central Viaduct. Over the next week there were at least 40 false sightings—and they all consumed police time and resources and even provoked a flurry of false arrests, as young-looking, runty men in automobiles were rousted by nervous policemen. The climax of such confused efforts came on Wednesday, July 13, when police raided a home in Euclid with sawed-off shotguns and arrested some hapless fellow there on suspicion of being Specs Russell. As the week after his escape elapsed it became clear that the search for Joe was not going well, despite the repeated assurances of Cleveland officials that he would soon be caught. An unidentified police spokesman perfectly captured the fatuous tone of official certainty with the comment, "His methods are identical in every case and his days are numbered because he is so easily identified." More surprisingly, just 48 hours after Specs's spectacular escape from Zicarelli, Safety Director Barry publicly exonerated all of the detectives involved in the Saturday afternoon fiasco, simply stating, "They did a fine piece of work in apprehending Russell and his two pals. Russell would be in jail now, had the detectives not been over-anxious."

Whatever their public bravado, police anger and anxiety rose higher and higher as the days after Joe's escape went by. It would be some time before authorities discovered his movements after he jumped on the moving van, but Specs, as usual, didn't let the grass grow under his feet. Although he still had a police handcuff hanging from his right wrist, Specs managed to conceal himself from scrutiny until he somehow hammered it off, probably with a large railroad bolt or "fish scale" he found by some switch tracks of the Big Four Railroad near Lorain Avenue and not far from the New York Central Railroad tracks. Sometime later that Saturday evening he stole the car that George Zicarelli saw him in on the Central Viaduct, and eventually Specs made his way to the apart-

Writer at his craft: Specs Russell in the
Ohio State Penitentiary.

ment of Eleanor Flanigan at 1947 West 77th Street. Eleanor was the
fiancée of his brother Angelo, who was there with Eleanor when his
younger brother showed up, his wrist still bleeding from his efforts
to remove the handcuff. Angelo had always looked out for his errant
younger brother, and he and Eleanor quickly agreed to help him
escape from Cleveland. As Eleanor later explained to Cleveland
police, "Brothers will be brothers, you know." Angelo and Eleanor
had been planning a trip to Niagara Falls anyway, so Specs suggested that they drop him off there, where he might be able to slip
across the Canadian border. But after some discussion it was agreed
that they would wait until the heat subsided, perhaps a couple of
days. Meanwhile, an unchastened Specs bragged to Eleanor and
Angelo for several hours about his various exploits and successful
defiance of the police. Sometime early Sunday morning, Eleanor
decided to go to Angelo's house, lest the police trace back her con-
nection to Specs's brother.

If you think that Specs Russell spent those days in quiet hiding at Miss Flanigan's flat, you haven't been paying close attention to his story. A little more than 12 hours after his escape, at 3:45 a.m. Sunday, July 10, Specs brought his latest stolen vehicle, a Ford coupe, to a halt at the all-night Brooks Oil Company gas station at East 107th Street and Carnegie Avenue. Attendant James Foster was on duty when Specs pulled in, but walked inside after watching Specs sit in his car for a few minutes. He was standing behind a roll-top desk when Specs finally ambled in and, without prelude, pulled his gun and snarled "Stick 'em up!" To his shock, Foster merely laughed at him and retorted, "Be yourself!" Startled, Specs came at Foster with his .45, slowly backing him toward some oil drums. As Foster halted at the drums, Specs jammed the gun into his side and ordered him to open the cash register. Instead of complying, Foster grabbed Specs, pressed the robber's left arm against his side, and pinned Specs's gun between his arms and ribs. A second later, Specs pulled the trigger.

This time the .45 went off, but the bullet bounced off an oil drum and ricocheted around the room without hurting anyone. Specs, for once, did not push his luck. Dashing to the Ford, he jumped in, started the car, turned onto East 107th Street—and nearly hit a man and woman crossing the street. Bellowing "Stand aside and let a man pass!" Specs gunned the engine and roared north on East 107th. Edward Rosenbloom of 9507 Euclid Avenue was across the street in his Chevrolet when Specs left the gas station. He had heard the sound of the gun and immediately surmised what was happening. He decided to pursue Specs, hoping he might encounter some helpful police along the way. Finding none—or perhaps yielding to some sober second thoughts—he abandoned the chase when the two cars reached Superior Avenue. Later shown a Bertillon photograph of Specs, James Foster identified him as the man who'd shot at him.

Eleanor Flanigan would later insist that she, Angelo, and Specs left Cleveland that Sunday night. But it seems likely they killed another day there, because Specs was spotted by a friend on Monday morning. Driving a stolen Chrysler, he halted the car in front of the Barrett Company factory at 1730 Walworth Run to say hello. "What are you going to do?" his friend asked. "The police are on your trail!" "I don't care; they won't get me!" said Specs, laughing, as he drove away.

Specs's friend reported his encounter that very day to Cleveland police captain Emmet J. Potts, but that was the last solid hint to police about Specs's trail for almost a week. All of his favorite haunts in the Haymarket, the Roaring Third precinct, and the area around Hough Avenue and East 79th Street were kept under constant scrutiny. And the usual false sightings continued to pour in, each one investigated and disproven. Grocer Sam Weizman reported that a suspicious trio had come to his 6517 Quincy Avenue store at 5:45 p.m. on Wednesday, July 13. His colorful story was that one of them, a man in women's clothing and a red wig, entered the store and drank a bottle of near beer and purchased a pack of cigarettes before departing. Weizman was sure the near-beer drinker was Specs Russell. The same day, two girls told police they had seen three men wearing women's clothing entering one of Russell's suspected hideouts on Commercial Road. And Mrs. Bert Greenbaum remained positive that Specs, visibly nervous and wearing a turban on his head as a disguise, had stopped by her husband's furniture repair shop at 1712 Crawford Road the same day. Reports of additional Specs sightings poured in from Warren, Youngstown, and Columbus. The only real progress in the Specs case came on Friday, July 15, when Specs's juvenile henchmen, Mike Matyas and Joseph Rutsynski, had their day in court. Appearing before Judge Harry L. Eastman, the two youths were charged with the robberies at William Charein's Kinsman Road shoe store and the Home Provision Company heist. Claiming that they didn't even know Specs Russell and that their previous and prolix confessions to multiple robberies had been beaten out of them by Cleveland policemen, Matyas and Rutsynski called several of their adolescent chums to swear that they had been playing baseball in a vacant lot on all of the alleged robbery dates. Judge Eastman, alas, found the testimony of the boys' victims far more persuasive, especially after Charein pointed out that Matyas was wearing a pair of shoes he had grabbed as the robber trio fled from the shoe store. Despite the emotional plea of their attorney that Matyas be sent to the Hudson Boys' Farm, Eastman sentenced both of them to the Mansfield Reformatory for terms of at least 14 months. Scoffing at the idea that their tender years excused their crimes, Eastman concluded:

These boys have mapped out a career of crime for themselves. They are set in one path. They won't turn back. I must send them to a place where they can't do any more harm.

Meanwhile, Specs was in none of his reported locations. Specs's plan was still to go east, but he told Angelo to first drive west, as a way of throwing the Cleveland Police off his track. The threesome got as far as Fort Wayne the first day, stopping there for gas. But while Specs was in the gas station buying cigarettes he discovered one of his wanted posters on the wall and thought the gas attendant was eying him suspiciously. So they turned around and headed for northeast Pennsylvania, where Tom Russell, cousin to Angelo and Specs and a man of reputed wealth, had a home in the small town of Byrndale. Driving east through Ohio, they carefully skirted Mansfield, Joe fearing that he might be too much of a familiar face to some of the reformatory guards. Touching West Virginia briefly, they turned north again into Ohio before heading toward Niagara Falls. There, Specs telephoned his cousin Tom, who brusquely told him he did not want to have *anything* to do with him.

Uncertain of his next move, Specs parted from Eleanor and Angelo at Niagara Falls. While they continued on to Canada, he decided to head for the Byrndale-DuBois area, where he had friends and a solid grasp of local geography, most of it a forested wilderness. By the latter part of the week, he had found a rough but adequate lodging in a cabin at the top of Bootjack Mountain, a heavily wooded area with but a single road leading to the top. The terrain for miles around was also honeycombed with abandoned mines, mining shacks, and ravines. Better yet, Specs's summit shelter afforded him a glimpse of anything that might be coming for him from miles away. With a view to the longer term, Specs also visited the nearby Weedsville State Bank, where he talked to its president, Joseph Mitchell. Specs's intention was to transfer $300 from an account at the Cleveland's Union Trust Company to the Weedsville bank, but it was not to be. By Saturday, July 16, he had learned that

Cleveland lawmen knew of his presence in the area and were ready to arrest him if he showed up at the bank. Specs's rising fears must have been stoked by a visit to the Weedsville post office, where he spied his own picture on the wall.

It is not clear how Cleveland police learned of Specs's hideout on Bootjack Mountain. But they were much aided in their search for the fugitive by officials of the Cleveland Automobile Club, who put their considerable resources and the services of attorney J. Frank Merrick at their disposal. The Automobile Club's interest was provoked by Specs's penchant for stealing cars, and their sleuthing soon paid off. By the weekend of July 16–17, the area around Bootjack was crawling with Cleveland policemen and Pennsylvania state troopers, heavily armed and all preparing for the capture of Specs Russell. It was assumed that Specs would not surrender without a gun battle, but Angelo Russell, who had been jailed as an accessory upon his return to Cleveland, was brought along in hopes he could persuade his brother to surrender peacefully.

The Cleveland contingent was led by Detective Inspector Cody and included Detectives Charles Cavolo, Patrick McNeeley, James Ruff, Ernest Clerment and Harry Weis. Armed with tear gas, rifles, and shotguns, they planned a joint assault with a squad of Pennsylvania state troopers on Specs's cabin at 3 a.m. on Monday, July 18. On Sunday night at sundown they closed down the sole road to the mountaintop.

Cody's carefully planned capture did not go off as scheduled. Specs, who had many friends in the area willing to help him escape, was fully aware of police plans for his capture and enjoyed a bird's-eye view on their bustling preparations from his mountain eyrie. Now armed with a .38-caliber pistol, Specs issued an unveiled warning to his pursuers, having boyhood friend Steven Rebo tell them, "I wouldn't even harm a bird around here, but I'll shoot the first cop who tries to get me."

No cop got a chance at Specs this time. Sometime after midnight on Monday, July 18, Steve Rebo and another man met Specs at his cabin. Concealing Specs under some canvas in an old Ford, they drove him down Bootjack Mountain via some unmarked but hair-raising route, with the Ford's headlights off all the way down.

Twelve miles later, shortly after 3 a.m., they arrived in Ridgeway, just in time for Specs to catch the 3:25 Buffalo, Rochester & Pittsburgh Railroad train to Buffalo. By the time Cody's men, led by Cleveland police corporal Edward Smith, entered the cabin, Specs was already en route to Buffalo. At the cabin Smith and his men found Steve Rebo, who calmly and without remorse told them how Specs had escaped their dragnet.

Amazingly, Specs's incredible luck continued to hold. His train was due in Buffalo shortly after 7 a.m., which theoretically gave his pursuers plenty of time to alert authorities there. But, owing to the remoteness of the Bootjack area, local telephone service there did not begin daily operations until 7. Alerted to this fact, Cody and his men sped through the darkness over risky mountain roads to Ridgeway, where they called Buffalo just after 7 a.m. They were too late—Specs's train had arrived at 6:45, and Specs had already vanished from the train station.

The following week was not a happy one for Cleveland police officials. As details of Specs's latest escape emerged, criticism showered down on them, especially Safety Director Barry and Detective Inspector Cody. It seemed they could do nothing right, although they made frantic exertions to pick up Specs's trail again. Charles Cavolo and other Cleveland detectives spent many frustrating hours during the next week following up frequent but futile "sightings" of Specs Russell in the Buffalo area, including Niagara Falls, Tonawanda, and La Salle, plus Conneaut, Ohio, and various Canadian locales. All these searches were in vain, although Cleveland police spokesmen continued to insist that Specs's capture was "imminent."

The irony of such frenzied searching was not that Specs was absent from any of these locations, but that he was actually in . . . Cleveland. As he later proudly explained to police, he decided to return to Cleveland as soon as he realized that Buffalo was too hot for him. But he had no money left, so he hied himself down to the Buffalo docks, where he soon found employment as a casual laborer on the *Seeandbee,* the elegant passenger steamer that plied the Great Lakes between 1913 and 1941. Two days later, he got off the boat in Cleveland and decided, with his characteristic lack of imagination, to pick up exactly where he had left off. On Sunday, July 24, he entered the home of Mrs. Edward E. Schwartz at 1577 East 117th Street and departed with $2,500 worth of her property.

Specs announced his return more dramatically with a robbery on the evening of Tuesday, August 2. He once again donned his smoked glasses, and with two new companions in crime, one a hunchback, he walked into Albert Hauzar's grocery store at 14646 Saranac Road. Sporting two revolvers, Specs made Hauzar lie on the floor while his two accomplices rifled the register for $25. An hour later, Specs's two confederates entered Henry Hecht's grocery store at 1590 Hayden Avenue. While Specs stood lookout at the door, they took $175 and left the store.

It was at precisely this juncture that Specs's luck finally and decisively turned. Piling into a two-door Ford, the trio sped south on Hayden toward its intersection with Sixth Avenue, where they crashed into another automobile. Shaken but unhurt, they abandoned the car and began fleeing on foot. Their crime spree almost ended right there, as they were pursued by an impromptu and angry citizens' posse, who had witnessed the hit-and-run accident. The robbers managed to escape without injury from their pursuers, although they lost two straw hats, a fedora, and a .22-caliber pistol in their undignified fight.

The abandoned and smashed-up Ford was the clue Cleveland police had been hoping for. Detectives Fred Bartlett and John Lynch were assigned to the case, and they soon learned that the Ford was a rental car. Better yet, it had been rented by the hunchback goon, who had provided his genuine naturalization papers when he rented the car. Those papers included his actual address, an apartment flat at 2409 Cedar Avenue. Hurrying there at 6:30 the next morning, the police did not find Specs but they did surprise the hunchback asleep in a bed. He told them Specs had been living there since July 22 and was expected back soon. Jailing the hunchback in a cell at the Central Police Station, lawmen staked out the Cedar Avenue address and awaited events. And in case you seek more proof that the world was a different place in 1927, consider this: although Cleveland newspaper reporters were told the location of Specs's Cedar Avenue lair *before* police laid their trap for him there, all the journalists observed the secrecy requested of them.

The moment long and eagerly awaited by Cleveland policemen

finally came on Thursday, August 4. This time they left nothing to chance. Anticipating Specs's return to the Cedar Avenue flat that afternoon, everyone was in readiness for his arrival. Sitting in an unmarked car six doors west of the apartment were Detectives Fred Bartlett and John Lynch. Waiting in another car five or six doors east were Detectives Joseph Doran and Fred Kosicki. Across the street, diagonally, on a porch hidden by trees were Detectives George Zicarelli and William Hussman. Upstairs on the second floor of the apartment house was Detective Gustav Reese, concealed behind a banister that looked over the stairs to leading to Specs's room. Behind the door to Specs's flat lurked Detective Charles Cavolo, like Reese, armed with a sawed-off shotgun. It was a hot, sticky, uncomfortable summer day, and virtually all of the officers and detectives had been working on the case for nearly 24 hours.

The trap worked perfectly. Suddenly, about 5 p.m., Specs came sauntering down Cedar Avenue. He was just returning from the Stillman Theater at Playhouse Square, where he had taken in an afternoon showing of *The Big Parade,* one of the silent film hits of the year. As he came up the street he passed the car containing Lynch and Bartlett. Lynch was slouched down in his seat, but Specs eyed him warily and made a motion toward his waist, as if about to pull a gun. Lynch had once arrested Specs for burglary and was fearful that he'd been recognized. But the moment passed, and Specs headed for the door to 2409. As he reached the front stoop, he stopped and looked around for a moment. From there he could see the car containing Doran and Kosicki, but the late-afternoon sun on its windshield screened their faces from him. Satisfied, he opened the door and began climbing the stairs.

He never got into his room. As he reached the second-floor landing, he was startled by a commotion downstairs. It was Zicarelli, Hussman, Kosicki, Doran, Lynch, and Bartlett coming through the door with guns drawn, but before Specs had time to react, Reese had a shotgun in his back and was saying—how could he *resist?*— "Stick-'em up!" Prodding Specs toward the apartment door with his gun, he added, "You're caught" and, as Cavolo opened up the door, "Here he is, Charlie." Cavolo also had a shotgun directly pointed at Specs, and as Joe meekly put his hands up, Lynch reached around him and pulled a .22-caliber pistol out of his pocket. It was all over, and as the next morning's Cleveland *Plain Dealer* put it, "an animal was never caught in such a flawless trap." Recovering his usual insouciance as they marched him out to a squad car, Specs whined, "What's this for? I haven't done anything since I got back to Cleveland!"

Considering the past animosity between Specs and his police foes, the scene several hours later that evening at Detective Inspector Cody's office in the Central Police Station on Payne Avenue was more in the nature of an affectionate "roast" than a police interrogation with reporters present. Newly shaven, sporting a neat black mustache, his hair parted perfectly in the middle, and attired in a light brown suit, soft white shirt, blue-gray tie, and admirably polished black shoes, Specs fielded questions from his audience in a relaxed, bantering, and, more often than not, boastful manner. It was like a scene out of *The Front Page* or *Roxie Hart,* a public spectacle during which Specs was treated more like a glamorous celebrity than the cheap hoodlum he was. Winking broadly at Safety Director Barry, he kicked things off by noting he was wearing stolen clothes. He then ostentatiously fished in the watch pocket of his trousers, drew out a bulky roll of bills, and handed them to Cavolo. Specs's roll amounted to $140, and Cody told Cavolo to give $5 to Specs for pocket money and hold the rest for evidence. Then it was on to the questions, many of which Specs answered flippantly, improvising new lies in almost every sentence. He chortled as he described his escape from Carl Zicarelli and laughed again as he explained how he had outwitted his pursuers at Bootjack Mountain. Contrary to repeated police claims that his third gun had been concealed in a special pocket near his crotch, he insisted that he had simply stuck the gun behind his belt and shirt. He denied pulling any robberies since his return to Cleveland, with or without a hunchback accomplice. He bragged that during the week before his capture he had frequently been in the presence of Cleveland policemen at public places like Euclid Beach Park and the Woodland Hills swimming pool. But when Barry offered him a cigarette, he primly declined, saying "I don't smoke." "You don't smoke, you don't drink," retorted Barry sardonically. "I presume you do nothing but hold up? I wish we had some of your habits and you some of ours."

Specs was especially insistent on the delicate subject of his age,

Specs Russell in his middle age.

which he claimed was not more than 20. This was a crucial matter for Specs, as he knew that if it could be proved he was over 21 and he was convicted of felony robbery, he could well face life imprisonment in the Ohio Penitentiary in Columbus, rather than a shorter and less harsh term in the Mansfield Reformatory. Interestingly, Specs's father, Tony, had already volunteered to the police that his son was at least 21 years old.

The wheels of justice moved with uncharacteristic swiftness for the "smoked glasses kid." Less than 24 hours after his capture, Cody, Cavolo, and Police Prosecutor Burt W. Griffin appeared before a Cuyahoga County grand jury to present evidence against Specs. Minutes later, that grand jury indicted him on two counts of robbery and one of housebreaking and larceny. The first robbery count was for the June 28 robbery of Louis Wieder's grocery store on Woodhill Road, and the second was for his role in the July 6 heist at the Home Provision Company. The housebreaking/larceny charge was for the July 24 robbery at the Schwartz home on East

117th Street. While the grand jury did its work, more than a score of Specs's robbery victims dropped by the Central Police Station to confirm that it was Specs who'd robbed them.

The next afternoon, in a special Saturday session, Specs was arraigned at 2 p.m before common pleas court judge Frederick P. Walther. Specs's attorney, Joseph Zinner of the law firm of Ackerman, Krewson & Selzer, had previously intimated that Specs might plead not guilty by reason of insanity. But as soon as he was arraigned, Specs pleaded guilty to the first robbery count and the housebreaking/larceny charge. However, Cuyahoga County prosecutor Edward Stanton was unable to prove that Specs was over 21, so Judge Walther ruled he had no choice but to send him to the Mansfield Reformatory. He then turned to Specs and said:

> Well, Russell, I have no option but to send you to the reformatory because you are not yet 21. When you do reach the age of 21, however, you will be brought back for trial on other indictments, and then I think you will go to the penitentiary. You have forfeited all claims for consideration. You have challenged the police department, and you have challenged society. There is no one to blame but yourself, and I hope your case will prove an example for others. Why, you are lucky you never killed anybody!

The irrepressible Specs couldn't keep silent, muttering "I've got better sense than that!" When asked by Walther if he had anything else to say, Specs simply said, "I'm sorry I did it." I suppose you are," responded Walter, then added rather sententiously, "It doesn't pay, old boy; it doesn't pay. I am glad you are sorry but it's too late now."

Specs was unsure whether to gloat or not as he returned to his jail cell that evening. There he spent several uncomfortable hours with pencil and paper, trying to "dope out" his likely term of imprisonment. His anxiety increased when he learned, the following day, that Ohio attorney general Edward C. Turner had issued an opinion that, contrary to Judge Walther's ruling, Specs did not have to be over 21 to be sent to the Ohio Penitentiary. For the nonce, how-

ever, Specs took the optimistic view and began plotting his strategy
to win early parole from Mansfield. Only three days after Judge
Walther pronounced sentence, Specs sent nearly a dozen letters to
persons who might be helpful to this end, including Cornelius Cody,
Edwin Barry, and Mansfield Reformatory superintendent T. C. Jen-
kins. The text of the letter to Barry was nearly identical to the rest,
and in it Specs expressed a tone of abject contrition:

> I have done my heartiest to cooperate with you . . . and I am
> ashamed of myself, I am. Please do this for me as I know
> you are square and I want to show you and Inspector Cody
> that I can and will behave myself and show society I can be
> placed back and live a clean, honorable life. Thanking you
> in advance for what you have already done, I am "yours" in
> earnest, Joseph Russell

Alas, Specs's humble epistolary efforts proved futile. Ohio legal
authorities eventually decided that Specs's age was no bar to sending him to Columbus, and Specs, hoping to appear cooperative
and thereby get a lesser sentence, pleaded guilty on August 22 to
the second robbery count. Imagine Specs's stunned surprise, then,
when Walther sentenced him to 55 years in the Ohio penitentiary,
a virtual life sentence. But as Cornelius Cody presciently remarked
at the time, "Not much use sending a robber to the penitentiary for
life. A crook can commit all kinds of murder nowadays and be out
on the bricks again in six or seven years."

Specs's early days in Columbus did not go well. Still in a state
of denial, he thought he'd been treated unjustly and was surly and
uncooperative. Taken to Chardon in November to testify at another
trial, Specs snarled at his guards, "I'll never go back to that place
alive!" But he did, and soon his hopes were rekindled by the appeal
of his sentence filed by attorney Walter Krewson. But on October 5,
1928, the Court of Appeals of the Eighth Ohio District upheld Judge
Walther's sentence. The opinion was written by Judge Roy Williams, with Judges Manuel Levine and John J. Sullivan concurring.

Surprisingly, the end of his legal hopes seems to have had an
improving effect on Specs Russell. For all of his imprudent behav-

ior, he had always been considered a bright fellow by his childhood teachers, and he had fitfully demonstrated both verbal and musical abilities. Specs now decided to exploit those talents. He had learned to play the trombone during one of his youthful reformatory stints, and he returned to the instrument, soon rising to the first trombone chair of the Ohio Penitentiary Band. Then, in 1928, he began writing and selling freelance articles, first to such musical magazines as *Etude* and eventually to more general, mainstream periodicals like *Good Housekeeping* and *Reader's Digest.* Most of his articles were about music or prison life, but even poetry held no terrors for the ambitious Specs, whose poem "Twilight," published in the January issue of *Good Housekeeping,* included this choice quatrain:

Across the earth bursts forth a hushed note:
A million feathered creatures thrill
Their vigil hymn to God, from fluttering throat—
Then night falls down, and all again is still.

Specs's startling strides in personal growth in prison were accompanied by an equally astonishing moral reformation. On January 19, 1930, Specs wrote this letter to Cuyahoga County prosecutor Ray T. Miller, a missive that might have melted the heart of even the most cynical lawman:

Dear Mr. Miller. I am writing to ask you a favor. As I have learned to see life in a different light, I now desire to make full restitution to all from whom, in my reckless days, I took anything. You have the names and addresses of those in your files, and I am wondering, if you will not, please, be good enough to let me have the list. You see, Mr. Miller, I now realize the seriousness of my mistakes. . . . I am glad my mistakes came when I was a kid. They have helped me to see life right and to determine to be the sort of man I ought.

Three months later, as heroic evidence of his moral redemption, Specs repeatedly risked his life to save prisoners who would otherwise have remained trapped in their cells during the terrible

Ohio Penitentiary fire on April 21, a legendary blaze that killed 322 inmates the day after Easter.

If there was anyone who believed in Joe's newfound goodness it was his sister-in-law, Eleanor, now the wife of Angelo. During the early 1930s she initiated a petition drive to persuade the Ohio Board of Pardon and Parole to commute Specs's 55-year sentence. Eventually attracting over 4,000 signers, Eleanor's submission to the Board included the names of 25 magazine editors, 25 prominent Cleveland lawyers, 18 ministers, 18 physicians, and such luminaries as writer H. L. Mencken, former Cleveland mayor and U.S. Secretary of War Newton D. Baker, Western Reserve University's Charles Thwing, and *Saturday Review* editor Henry S. Canby. Specs Russell, Eleanor gushed to anyone who would listen, was a changed man. He was steadily repaying his former robbery victims with income from his freelance writing, had written a 400-page instructional text for trombone players, and had profoundly realized the error of his former life. Attributing his change of heart to the death of his father, which occurred shortly after Specs entered the penitentiary, she proudly underscored the sentiments Specs had expressed in a recent letter to Ohio governor George White. Samplerworthy, they included his insight that "true happiness comes only to those who rightfully deserve it" and an admission that he had once been a "showoff" but now realized he was "the biggest fool." More edifying yet was the inspirational advice he offered to aspiring trombone players in the pages of *Etude* magazine: "The germ of success lies in the persistent and diligent efforts of the individual to bring his purposes to reality."

Not *everyone* was persuaded by Specs's apparent reformation. The voice of the Cleveland *Plain Dealer* editorial page (most likely this author's grandfather, then editor-in-chief Paul Bellamy) remained adamantly opposed to any kind of break for the "smoked glasses kid." After noting the copious petitions and letters to newly elected Ohio governor Martin L. Davey beseeching Specs's release, the editorialist acidly scorned public gullibility about his alleged reformation and demanded he serve out his whole term:

> Citizens who sign Russell's petitions become, we like to think unwittingly, instruments for turning loose on society

one whose record of crime is unbroken from the time he was arrested for thieving in grade school. They become partners in the underworld's fight against society and the law. They aid in seeking freedom for a criminal whose grandstand play and love of the spotlight has made a life of robbery and hold-ups irresistible. Outside of his own self-refuted testimony, there is no evidence that Russell has now reformed.

Another skeptic about the "new" Specs was Adolph Klein, who hadn't forgotten the $8 taken from him during the Spayne & Reich robbery on June 28, 1927. As his parole campaign revved up, Specs took every available opportunity to mention how much stolen money he'd already restored to his victims. He claimed, in fact, that several of his victims had spurned restitution out of sheer goodwill toward him. Decidedly not Adolph Klein, who wrote to Specs in June 1932, asking him for the $8. But even Klein was politely apologetic about asking for the money, explaining:

Under ordinary circumstances, and in conformity with my theory as to the distribution of wealth, I would not trouble you with this request. Unfortunately, though, besides having suffered from ill health I have been unemployed for the last year, and now find that the return of $8 would be of in estimable benefit. Consequently, waiving the accrued interest, I hereby make application for the preferred place among the beneficiaries of your "conscience funds." With kindest personal regards and best wishes for the success of your musical and literary endeavors, I am, Adolph Klein.

It appears that Specs was unable or unwilling to grant Klein's wish, for several weeks later the jobless clerk complained that Specs had still not sent him the $8. "I guess his secretary is too busy to reply," Klein commented sarcastically to a reporter. Two months later, Specs ruefully commented to an interviewer that he still owed $1,800 to his victims, admitting "Believe me, it's easier to stick 'em up than to pay 'em back."

Specs's drive to win parole was surely not aided by a violent episode in 1933 that recalled his bandit glory days. At 10:25 on the morning of February 2, two men entered the Marshall Drug store at Huron Road and East Ninth Street. Manager Thomas Rees guessed they were robbers as soon as they walked in and attempted to stall them with conversation. But at that point a third man entered the store and pulled a gun on Rees. It was Specs's old pal Joseph Rutsynski, and he said, "This is no joke—it's a stickup!" Forcing clerk Eric Benz and a customer to the floor, Rutsynski made Rees give him the $250 in cash in the register, and then the three robbers fled out a door onto East Ninth Street, headed south

It was another unlucky day for Joe Rutsynski, who, following his apprenticeship with Specs, had further honed his criminal chops under Joe Filkowski, the "Phantom of the South Side." By blind chance, a squad of Cleveland police detectives, including Detective Sergeant Audley Bramer and Detectives John Cull, Clarence Smith, and Francis McVery, happened to be on the street, where they had been conducting a routine crime prevention tour. As they ran down East Ninth Street the three robbers almost collided with the four detectives, and Bramer ordered them to halt. Declining the invitation, Rutsynski turned around and shot at the detectives. The chase was on.

As they ran into Erie Street Cemetery, a bizarre gun battle erupted amid the ancient gravestones between the four policemen and the three robbers. At least 50 shots were exchanged to no ill effect, but one of the robbers, with the curiously apt name of Chester Morbidelli, managed to knock himself unconscious when he hit his head on a grave marker. Eventually, Rutsynski and his accomplice, Adam Ellis, escaped from the cemetery and ran south toward Woodland Avenue. But Cleveland police detectives George Clark and Robert Wehagen just happened to be cruising in the area, and they commanded the running duo to stop as they ducked into an alley. There, Wehagen handcuffed Ellis, and Clark removed a .45-caliber automatic from Rutsynski's belt. When Rutsynski refused to turn around and made a sudden motion toward his pocket, Clark knocked him cold with a blackjack.

The years went by. Every few months some sympathetic journalist would write a column about the reformed Specs, his musical triumphs, his writing career, and his persisting hopes of release.

But his sister-in-law's campaign for his freedom suffered a major setback in June 1936, when Ohio attorney general John W. Bricker ruled that under Ohio law Specs would not be eligible for parole until 1941. Once again, a Cleveland *Plain Dealer* editorialist poured salt on Specs's emotional wounds. Noting that his prior career as a chronic parole violator made Specs a poor risk, it scoffed at the notion that he was a reformed character deserving special treatment:

> That Russell is paying back the money he obtained from holdup victims is a commendable gesture, but it in no way excuses him from paying the penalty for his crimes. In view of his record there is justifiable ground for doubting his reform now. The attorney general's ruling that prisoners are not entitled to parole "as a matter of right" should go a long way toward strengthening the present laxities. Easy parole has been an incentive to crime on the part of those who lack a sense of responsibility to society. Russell is no worse and no better in the eyes of the law than hundreds of others in prisons. He is not entitled to special privileges from the law. Justice will be served by the law taking its course and not by a campaign of misdirected sympathy.

Specs's parole crusade hit another obstacle the following year. By that time he had been transferred from the Ohio Penitentiary to the more pleasant venue of the London prison farm. But in August 1937, Ohio Penitentiary Warden James C. Woodward abruptly ordered Specs back to the Columbus prison. He did not state his reasons, but word soon leaked out that Specs had been using the farm prison's printing plant to run off copies of his parole petitions.

The hopes of Russell and his supporters rose again in 1939, when a new parole law went into effect on May 3. Under its provisions any prisoner sentenced to a term of 15 years or more (excepting those sentenced for treason or murder) became eligible for parole consideration. And, sure enough, on June 13 of that year, the Ohio State Pardon and Parole Commission decided that Specs would go free on October 1.

He almost made it this time. But on September 28, just three days before his scheduled release, the Commission revoked his parole, citing his "unsatisfactory prison activities." Those activities included smuggling liquor and narcotics to fellow inmates and, worse yet, Specs's promises to them that he would, by virtue of his employment in the prison records office at London, alter their records. There was no evidence that any records were altered, but it was clear that Specs would have to stay for at least another year.

And then—suddenly—it was over. On January 2, 1941, Joseph "Specs" Russell walked out the gates of the Ohio Penitentiary a free man. Brimming with confidence, he told everyone he would employ the literary talent which had so unexpectedly flowered during his 13 years in prison. And why not? For as he asserted in a *Plain Dealer Sunday Magazine* article later that year, America's penal institutions abounded with unknown and unexploited talents like his, just waiting for society to give them a break. And wasn't he Exhibit A to prove his claim that "once the human mind has been directed into the right channel, rich man or poor, free or a prisoner, who can estimate its possibilities?"

It would be nice and uplifting if the Specs Russell story ended right here. But it didn't, and in the end his anonymous adversary at the *Plain Dealer* proved correct about Joseph Specs Russell. His initial post-prison months seemed a dream come true, as writing commissions poured in from such prestigious periodicals as *Reader's Digest, Coronet, True Detective, Scribner's Commentator,* and *Master Detective Stories.* It seemed that Specs was living up to all his promises, and he soon got permission to travel outside Ohio. For, as he told M. J. Hanchin of the Ohio Parole Board, he needed the enhanced travel permission because it appeared he was about to be sought by Hollywood and New York producers. They were particularly interested, Joe told his parole officer, in developing one of his prison memoirs, a tale he'd published in *Reader's Digest,* entitled "The Most Unforgettable Character I've Ever Met." This was truly the high water mark of Russell's unlikely "literary career"—the "Most Unforgettable Character" series was one of the most popular *Digest* features, running for years and years and often featuring profiles by celebrities and well-known authors.

Specs's dreams of legitimate success ended abruptly on the afternoon of Thursday, October 23, 1941, less than 10 months after his parole. At 4 p.m. he entered the main Buffalo, New York, post office to check his mailbox. Waiting for him were Buffalo police detective Sergeant Louis Kirschmeyer, and U.S. Post Office Inspectors L. J. Brennan and Clarence F. Ford. They trailed him from the post office and when Specs realized they were pursuing him, he jumped into an automobile and sped away. But he was cornered only four blocks away and surrendered meekly after Kirschmeyer fired four shots at him. Taken before U.S. Commissioner Boyce H. Butterfield the next day, Specs was arraigned on charges of plagiarism and using the U.S. mails for fraudulent purposes.

Specs's literary career, it seems, had been largely bogus. Sometimes using his own name but more often employing as many as 50 aliases (his favorite being "Giuseppe Rosselli"), Specs had repeatedly stolen material from magazine writers and submitted it to other magazines. A surprising amount of such purloined material had been published, and Specs had been well compensated for it. And when not simply stealing material, Specs had just made it up, He had been particularly inventive with his true-crime tales, claiming that his gritty tales had been told to him by such imaginary officials as the "Honorable Theresa T. Livingston, Judge of Domestic Court, Buffalo"; "Steve J. Krull, deputy in charge of Jamestown County office"; "James W. Atone, Rochester Commissioner of Police"; "Bryan McClure, Erie Chief of Police"; "Lieutenant Steve Ryan, head of Pittsburgh auto theft bureau"; and "Steve Benson, head of detectives, Erie, PA."

Naturally, Specs's eternal editorial foe at the *Plain Dealer* could not resist comment on the latest plot turn in his checkered life. Under the title of "Slippery Slip Horn Player," the editorialist flirted with a tone of "more in sorrow than in anger," but his vindictive glee at Specs's downfall remained unconcealed. A scathing review of his bandit career was followed by withering words on his failed rehabilitation:

So far it was Hollywood stuff, and it continued as such. The motley posse had captured a rather high type of boy. He not only had gone to high school, but was a good student. He had a flair for writing. He had an ear for music and played the slide trombone. It is a human tragedy when any boy turns to crime, a deeper one when a youth of civilized talents goes astray. His name was Russell, and the name of "Specs Russell" immediately became known far and wide. Specs was so repentant and so determined to succeed that he endeared himself to many hearts. Fourteen years constitute a prison stretch few could survive, but his soul did not wither. He played his horn. He wrote. Money he thus obtained he used to reimburse his robbery victims.

As the prison years trudged by many persons became interested in his parole. When it finally came and the young man got a job and toiled long and hard on horn and typewriter, these people were happy. Such being the story, we believe that all who have followed it are more sad than revengeful now that Specs is jailed as a forger and plagiarist. None will indict the whole parole system because of Specs. They are merely sad in disappointment, for they believed Specs was made of better stuff.

On February 4, 1942, Specs pleaded guilty to seven counts of mail fraud before federal judge Harold P. Burke in Buffalo and was sentenced to three years in a federal prison. He must have behaved himself there, as he was released sometime before the beginning of 1945. We know this because by July of that year, the Federal Bureau of Investigation was looking for Specs Russell in Cleveland. It seems that in January the Idle House Night Club in Savannah, Georgia, had been burglarized for a haul of $200 in cash and liquor. They couldn't pin that rap on Specs, but he could not shake the forgery habit he'd prosecuted so well in his literary days. On October 1, 1947, he was sentenced to a term of between 15 and 30 years in the Western Pennsylvania Penitentiary in Pittsburgh, his comeuppance for forging checks under fictitious names.

Specs was probably still in the Keystone State slammer when his long-suffering but supportive sister-in-law, Eleanor Russell, died suddenly around Christmas in 1952. His destiny after that remains obscure until 1959, when the Federal Bureau of Investigation began tracking the activities of one "Abe Friedman," a suspected check forger. Pretending to be an "associate" in an imaginary financial services firm, Friedman prosecuted his forging activities in New Orleans until the Big Easy became too hot for him. Heading west, accompanied by a peroxide blonde, aka, "Azile Mona Kelly," he touched down at such fleshpots as Las Vegas and Reno before vanishing in California. Ms. Kelly was not so fortunate, as she was arrested and sent to prison on federal charges stemming from her work with "Friedman."

Sometime in early 1960, a middle-aged man identifying himself as "Charles Richard Peters" showed up in Cleveland. The FBI soon became aware of him, and on Monday afternoon, April 11, he was quietly arrested at a downtown Cleveland intersection while waiting for the traffic light to change. The following day a fingerprint check revealed that Charles Richard Peters, alias Abe Friedman, was none other than the Cleveland "smoked glasses kid" of Roaring Twenties legend. When last seen in the available historical record, Specs, now 52 and looking every second of it, was facing a five-year prison term. Some people never learn.

Chapter 3

"A LITTLE EXCITEMENT"

The Star-Crossed Corrigan Family

O Lord, methought what pain it was to drown:
What dreadful noise of water in mine ears!
What sights of ugly death within my eyes!
Methought I saw a thousand fearful wracks;
A thousand men that fishes gnaw'd upon;
Wedges of gold, great anchors, heaps of pearl,
Inestimable stones, unvalu'd jewels,
All scatter'd in the bottom of the sea.
Some lay in dead men's skulls; and in those holes
Where eyes did once inhabit, there were crept,
As 'twere in scorn of eyes, reflecting gems,
That woo'd the slimy bottom of the deep,
That mock'd the dead bones that lay scattered'd by.
—Shakespeare, *Richard III*, Act I, Scene 4

It isn't really immoral to feel sorry for the misfortunes of the rich. But for most of us it isn't—for obvious reasons—an instinctive reaction. It is true that, a few deviant socialists and other cranks notwithstanding, Americans have always worshipped holders of great wealth. But, more often than not simultaneously, they have also savagely applauded the reverses and disgraces of the rich. Envy is, after all, but an inverted form of praise, and it seems an almost universal impulse, as Kenneth Grahame noted, for a "playful populace" to rejoice at "the sight of a gentleman in difficulties." That

said, only a heart of stone could remain unmoved by the enduring woes of Cleveland's illustrious Corrigan family. Every family
has its tragedies, but the shattering catastrophes of this seemingly
cursed clan over threescore years conquer indifference and challenge probability.

The Corrigan family saga began like much like that of another
celebrated 19th-century Cleveland family, the Rockefellers. Both
clans of relatively obscure background produced sets of ambitious
brothers who would bring their families wealth and renown in the
Forest City. Born in Ontario, Canada, during the latter half of the
1840s to Johnston and Jane Corrigan, James and John Corrigan
began striving even as teenagers for the riches and eminence they
would secure as adults. At the age of only 17, James went out as
a seaman on the Great Lakes. By the late 1860s he was in Cleveland, where, along with John D. Rockefeller and other farseeing
entrepreneurs, he began refining oil. A decade later, like most of
his fellow oilmen, he found it prudent to lease his oil interests to
the Standard Oil colossus and exploit new opportunities. He found
them in Galicia, a province of Austrian Poland, where he produced
oil and sold it in Austria, Hungary, and Germany. It was in Galicia
that his only son, James William Jr., was born in 1880. Returning to
America in 1883, James sold his oil properties to John D., receiving 3,000 shares of Standard Oil stock in return. Soon after that, in
league with John D.'s brother, Frank Rockefeller, Corrigan made
huge investments in the Lake Superior iron ore fields. As America
moved toward the climax of its Steel Age these proved very profit-
able, as did a fleet of Great Lakes steamers and kindred investments
in industrial and transportation properties. But then came the bad
economic times of the early 1890s. Hard pressed for cash, Corrigan
borrowed large sums from John D. to protect his iron ore purchases,
using his Standard shares as collateral. Eventually, as the effects of
the Panic of 1893 worsened, Corrigan was forced to sell some of
that collateral back to John D. When, some months later, the price
of the shares spiked, Corrigan and Frank Rockefeller cried foul,
accusing the wily John D. of profiting from insider information
about the securities. Corrigan eventually took his case to court but
ultimately lost. By 1900 the disputed shares and their accrued divi-

dends were said to be worth $1 million, an outcome that finalized Corrigan and Frank Rockefeller's estrangement from John D.

Even before his lawsuit ended, however, James Corrigan had taken the plunge into steelmaking that would make him truly rich. In 1890, building on his ownership of iron ore deposits and the lake vessels to carry them, he, his older brother John, and prominent Cleveland industrialist and jurist Stevenson Burke formed Corrigan, Ives & Company to manufacture steel. The firm went under during the 1893 panic but was reconstituted two years later as Corrigan, McKinney, and Company. The name change reflected the ascent of Price McKinney, the firm's bookkeeper and future nemesis of Corrigan's son, James W. Jr. Under the later name of Corrigan-McKinney Steel it would become one of the dozen largest steel empires in the United States.

By the turn of the century, James Corrigan had come far from his years of humble struggle. From their offices in the Perry-Payne Building, he and his brother John controlled a lucrative empire of steel mills, mineral ore deposits, fleets of Great Lakes ships to transport and service them—and even gold mines in Mexico. And the lifestyle of the brothers, especially James, fully advertised the material success that had come their way since their modest beginnings in Ontario. Blessed with a large family, including his wife Ida Belle, son James Jr., and daughters Nettie Belle (Mrs. Charles Rieley), Jane Anderson, and Ida May (oft called "Toots" or "Tootie"), James Corrigan enjoyed the kind of lifestyle appropriate to his class and means. Like many a Gilded Age millionaire he was often too busy to enjoy his wealth, but his wife and children were well fed, well garbed, and heavily bejeweled, and lived a life never lacking in leisure, luxuries, or servants to answer their every whim. When not ensconced in their handsome home at 1340 Willson Avenue (now East 55th Street), the James Corrigan family was likely to be found either at their lovely Wickliffe summer home (now the Pine Ridge Country Club) or aboard the pride of James C. Corrigan's recreational life: the sailing yacht *Idler*. And that is where the Corrigan family tragedy truly begins.

Captain James—as he liked to be called—was no bathtub sailor. Starting as a deckhand in the 1860s, he had spent much of the next three decades contending with the perils and surprises of Great Lakes sailing. Both he and his brother John were experienced and enthusiastic sailors, and it was inevitable that at least one of them would eventually aspire to the ownership and display of that 19th-century totem of true mogul status: the luxury yacht. And so it came to pass, during some evil hour in the fall of 1899, that John C. Corrigan purchased the sailing schooner *Idler*.

Constructed as a luxury yacht at New Haven, Connecticut, in 1864 by the shipbuilding firm of F. Colgates, the *Idler* was built to compete at the highest level of international boat racing. During the late 1860s and early 1870s she sailed with minor success in the America's Cup races before passing into the ownership of Commodore Archie Fisher of the Chicago Yacht Club. But as the years passed, the *Idler* proved chronically unsuccessful as a racing vessel, and in 1890 Fisher sold her to John Cudahay, the millionaire owner of the Cudahay Packing Company, then a pork-processing firm that rivaled the Armour empire. But after Cudahay lost his fortune in the 1893 panic, the *Idler* was left to rot, unused and neglected, in a Lake Michigan harbor slip of the Illinois Central Railroad. Then, in 1896, W. D. Boyce bought the yacht, refurbished her, and raced her unsuccessfully for a season before consigning her to renewed oblivion. By 1899, the once-proud yacht was reduced to serving as a training ship for naval militias and was in dilapidated condition. But her fortunes turned for the better in the fall of 1899 when Albert Rumsey, chief shipping master of the Lake Carriers' Association, acting for James Corrigan, bought the *Idler* as a pleasure craft. Taken to Fairport on Lake Erie, she was almost completely rebuilt and freshly repainted in gleaming white in time for the 1900 sailing season. No expense was spared to ensure that the boat was a safe and comfortable craft for Corrigan's family and guests, and it was said that the *Idler*'s refurbishment consumed the better part of $8,000.

Virtually every sailor with any experience of the *Idler* considered her a splendid and eminently seaworthy craft—if properly handled. Ninety-seven feet long and 23 feet in the beam (width), the *Idler* had a gross tonnage of 84, carried six tons of ballast, and drew about 10 feet of water. Possessing several commodious and

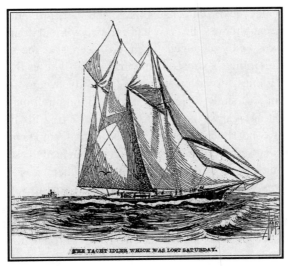

THE YACHT IDLER WHICH WAS LOST SATURDAY.

Sketch of the yacht *Idler*, *Plain Dealer*, July 10, 1900.

well-appointed cabins for its guests, it was also a comfortable home for its captain, Charles Joseph Holmes, and its crew of six. The latter included mate Samuel Biggam and sailors Olaf Neilson, Severn Neilson, Charles Kelly, Charles Johnson, and Jacob Antonson. During its final voyage, the *Idler* crew was supplemented by carpenter William Summers and cooks Charles Hackett and George Welch. Biggam had sailed the Great Lakes for 19 years, and the crew, mostly Norwegians, had considerable experience on both fresh and salt waters.

Captain Holmes must have seemed a good choice for master of the *Idler*. The son of a Great Lakes ship captain, Holmes had sailed since boyhood on both salt and fresh water and had more than a decade of experience on boats large and small. True, some of that experience was of an unusual nature, although that didn't stop James Corrigan from hiring him for the 1900 sailing season. But as a Great Lakes shipping magnate he was aware that on November 13, 1896, Captain Holmes had been in command of the wooden steamer *Wallula*, carrying a cargo of iron ore, when she foundered at the Conneaut harbor. Attempting to make port in the midst of a severe gale, the *Wallula* had missed the pier, grounded on the beach, and caught fire. The crew had escaped without injury, but the freighter was badly damaged. Then, too, there was the much-told story about Holmes's subsequent career. Shortly after the *Wallula* disaster, Holmes turned up in New York City, where he became involved in a scheme to smuggle arms and ammunition to Cuban rebels fighting against the Spanish regime. During his last run to Cuba he was nearly captured, barely escaping from Havana as the authorities closed in. Holmes and his crew managed to escape their Spanish pursuers in an open boat, but one of them was killed and Holmes was wounded before he brought that boat to safe harbor, 800 miles later in Vera Cruz. Additionally, Holmes had fought in some obscure naval hostilities between Santo Domingo and Haiti and once set a world's record with a 72-day sail from China to New York City. Clearly, the 27-year-old Holmes was no run-of-the-mill skipper, and it is likely that Captain James Corrigan admired the streak of panache in the youthful adventurer.

The *Idler* tragedy proper began as just a pleasant summer vacation. The James and John Corrigan families were close that it was perfectly natural for them to take an early summer lake excursion together. So sometime in the last week of June, members of the two families boarded the *Idler* where it was anchored in the Cuyahoga River. Captain James's vacation guests included Ida Belle, 45; daughters Nettie Belle Rieley, 24, Jane, 22, and Ida, 15; John Corrigan, 55; his wife Mary (née Breyley), 51; their daughter Etta Irene, 18 ("Tet" to her intimates); John's married daughter and son-in-law, Mr. and Mrs. Edward Gilbert; and Nettie Rieley's 1-year-old baby daughter, Mary.

The Corrigan summer voyage was strictly a pleasure cruise to the St. Clair Flats and Port Huron, near the southern tip of Lake Huron. The *Idler* party spent several days cruising, fishing, and sightseeing in the Flats area, but the wind was too calm for much real sailing. They continued on to Port Huron and then headed home. The *Idler* was not due back in Cleveland until the afternoon of July 7, but it began to shed passengers as soon as it reached Port Huron. The first to depart was Captain James, who hurriedly entrained there for Cleveland, where he hastened to consult his physician about an ear problem. Then, on Thursday night, July 5, John Corrigan and Mr. and Mrs. Gilbert also left the boat, she and her husband to attend a social function and John Corrigan to pursue a business matter in Buffalo. Although Mrs. James Corrigan remained behind, she may have had a premonition of the fate awaiting her. Shortly after the *Idler* left Port Huron she turned to Mate Biggam and said, "Biggam, I feel as though something were going to happen, and I wish I were at home."

The *Idler* left Port Huron between 3 and 4 p.m. Friday afternoon and sailed down the Detroit River, passing Detroit about 1 a.m. on Saturday, July 7. Before departing the *Idler*, James Corrigan had advised Captain Holmes to have the yacht towed through the unpredictable waters of western Lake Erie. Holmes, ever attentive to his master's voice, did just that, attaching the *Idler* to the steamer *Australia* with a tow line as both vessels entered Lake Erie. But the towing arrangement lasted but a few hours, as the intermittent jerking of the cable made the ladies aboard the *Idler* sick. At the behest of Mrs. James, Captain Holmes dropped the towing cable as the *Idler* passed Bar Point and ordered all hands to make sail.

All augured happily for the final leg of the journey home. The early-morning weather was fair, and the *Idler,* making 10 to 12 knots that July morning, was expected to reach Cleveland at 2:30 p.m. But the wind and sea began turning foul about 10 o'clock in the morning. An hour later, as the yacht responded to a rising northwest wind, Holmes ordered the spinnaker (a large, triangular sail that balloons out and acts as an airfoil when sailing downwind) taken down. But even as the weather gradually turned dirtier, Holmes kept a nearly full load of sail up, including mainsail, foresail, forestaysail, inner and outer jibs, and jib topsail. As Holmes later stated, he had little concern for the weather, as he had sailed the *Idler* through many a worse sea and in the teeth of winds up to 35 miles per hour.

Sailing conditions were still tolerable when sailor Jacob Antonson took the *Idler*'s wheel at 12 p.m. But within half an hour, menacing clouds began to accumulate to the northwest. Virtually all the sailors aboard sensed a nasty Lake Erie squall coming, and Mate Biggam eventually nerved himself to say something to Captain

Holmes. Biggam's estimate was that the coming storm would pack winds of up to 35 miles per hour, and he and his sailors thought the yacht was carrying too much sail for such an onslaught. But even by the despotic standards of Great Lakes captains, Holmes was an autocratic ruler who never brooked nautical advice from his inferiors. Cautiously approaching him, Biggam asked if the crew could take in some of the lighter canvas, at least, say, the main topmast staysail, main topsail, foretop, and jib topsails. Holmes, by his own later admission, agreed to the main topmast staysail but vetoed the rest. And he would dispute to his dying day that he then added his opinion of the coming storm, "Keep it on and have a little excitement! I don't think it will be severe enough to do any harm." No one else aboard the *Idler* heard Holmes utter this foolishly nonchalant remark, and no one—including Mrs. John Corrigan, who was close enough to have heard their conversation—ever testified in support of Biggam's damning assertion.

But Biggam wasn't the only one concerned about the *Idler*'s generous spread of canvas as the squall closed in on the *Idler*. About the same time as the mate's alleged conversation with Holmes, the fishing tugboat *Helene* passed by the *Idler*. Captain Peter Murphy of the tug got a good look at the *Idler*'s generous spread and didn't like what he saw. Passing within earshot, he hailed Holmes and warned him that he'd better take in most of his sail, as a nasty blow was coming. Not far away, the captain of the *Effie B.*, a fishing tug, also noted with alarm the full canvas on the *Idler*, although he was too far away to give warning. Turning to a member of his crew, he remarked, "That fellow will have his hands full in a few minutes if he doesn't take in some of his canvas." Another critical observer of Holmes's complement of sails was Captain George Normand of the fishing tug *F. E. Smith*, which also passed within sight of the *Idler* just minutes before its fatal storm arrived.

Perhaps it was the steadily rising wind and the increasingly choppy waves, or maybe just the warning from a professional peer. But shortly after the *Helene* passed, Holmes took the wheel of the *Idler* and ordered her crew to don oilskin gear and prepare to take in sail. He also commanded that the eight deadlights (skylights) in the ceilings of the lower deck containing the cabins be closed. The crew on the main deck had gotten just as far as the jib topsail when the storm struck in its first, awful fury. The *Idler* was then about 16 miles north and slightly to the west of Cleveland harbor, and it was exactly 2:10 in the afternoon.

The squall, which hit Cleveland some minutes later, was a nasty gale, even by the brutal standards of Lake Erie. It was a sudden blow, with the wind accelerating from around 15 or 20 to between 60 and 65 miles per hour in just a few seconds. Maintaining that high velocity for a full minute, it subsided slightly, only to explode a few minutes later in a second, sustained gust of equal amplitude. It was estimated by observers in downtown Cleveland to be the most violent storm ever to hit the city, causing considerable damage and picking up 18 tons of grit off Summit Street to hurl at buildings and hapless pedestrians. It also spelled doom for all but one of the *Idler*'s female passengers.

Most of the ladies were below in the main cabin when the first powerful gust surprised the *Idler* and its captain—striking from the northeast instead of its previous northwest direction. Hitting the *Idler*'s nearly full complement of sails, the wind flipped the yacht over on its side, pushing the mainsail and the railing on the starboard side under water and forcing tons of water through the open cabin deadlights. Visibility diminished to only six or eight feet, and within seconds the yacht and its passengers descended into utter chaos.

Captain Holmes was at the wheel when the first gale struck. Calling Jacob Antonson to take his place, he struggled down the steps to the companionway and into the main cabin, where he found Mrs. James, Mrs. Rieley, and her baby. With the aid of cooks Hackett and Welch, he managed to put life preservers on the women. But they refused to obey his command to come topside, where he hoped to secure them in the upper rigging of the ship. Failing to persuade them, he turned to Mrs. Rieley and held out his hands to take baby Mary. But she refused to relinquish her, saying, "No! When I go, the baby goes!" Defeated by the obduracy of the Corrigan women, Holmes stumbled back to the deck to try and save the other passengers and his crew.

The situation on the *Idler*'s main deck was much improved by the time of Holmes's return. With a lull in the ferocious wind, the yacht had nearly righted herself and some members of the crew had managed to get themselves into the bow end rigging, from whence they were trying to pull Mrs. John Corrigan, Jane, and Etta up to them. Holmes ordered more sail taken in, but the yacht was still too much on its beam ends for the sails to answer to the ropes. The main deck was awash, and as a cork couch floated by, Etta grabbed it and pushed her mother atop it. As Mrs. John floated away on it, Etta, for reasons that will never be known, went below to join the hysterical but passive group in the cabin. Back on deck, her cousin Jane had fainted when the first gust struck the yacht. Holmes was trying to revive her when the second tempest smashed into the *Idler*, flipped her over again, and swept Holmes, Jane, and several sailors into the raging waters. A moment later, the *Idler* went down, sinking slowly into the mud at the bottom of Lake Erie, 58 feet below.

Even as the *Idler* began its fatal descent, Holmes found Jane in the water and, with the help of sailor Olaf Neilson, pulled her and himself onto the *Idler*'s deck and tried to drag her with him to the relative safety of the rigging at the bow end. As she regained consciousness, she started crying to Holmes, "Will no one save Mamma?" "It is all we can do to save ourselves," replied Holmes. Seconds later a monster wave washed them off the deck again, and he lost Jane in the water. Groping frantically with his hand, he seized her by the hair and swam with her to a piece of floating fender (insulation attached to the side of a boat to cushion impact). For a few moments she managed to hang on to his neck, almost choking him. Then she sank for the last time. Holmes, too weak to go after her again, watched in horror as she disappeared and drowned.

Ida May almost made it. On deck when the first blow overturned the yacht, she descended to the cabin, where she vainly begged her mother to come up. Returning to the deck, she was swept into the water but pulled out before the second gust hit. Lifted into the rigging by Captain Holmes and the two Neilson brothers, she was hurled into the water a second time before Olaf managed to get ahold of her. And by this time, real help was in sight. The two fishing tugboats steaming near the *Idler*, the *F. E. Smith* and the *Effie B.*, had been no more than three miles away from the *Idler* when it first capsized, and their crews saw the yacht sink. The latter boat arrived in time to throw a line to the exhausted Olaf, who was still holding Ida with one of his arms. Fatally, however, as the tug began to draw in the rope it caught Neilson's arm. Powerless against its strength, he watched as the rope pulled his arm away from Ida May and she sank for the last time.

It was all over by 2:45 p.m. Arriving at the site of the wreck, the crews of the *F. E. Smith* and the *Effie B.* fished Holmes and the rest of the *Idler* crew from the lake or the topmost part of the bow rigging, still standing a few feet above the surface of the water. Carpenter William Summers, by his own reckoning, had been the luckiest person aboard. Unable to swim a stroke, he was pulled, half drowned, into the rigging by Mate Biggam. The mate, for his part, would claim that after the second gust knocked him off the boat, he remained under water for three minutes before struggling his way to the rigging.

Most miraculous, however, was the survival of Mrs. John Corrigan. Watching in horror from the cork couch to which she clung, she saw

CAPT. CHARLES HOLMES

Idler's Captain Charles Holmes, *Plain Dealer*, July 20, 1900.

the *Idler* go through its final death throes. Its lifeboat was smashed to pieces by the second gust, but sailor Charles Johnson succeeded in cutting loose a smaller dinghy from the deck as the yacht sank. He soon hauled Jacob Antonson into it, and they then rescued both Holmes and Mrs. John Corrigan. Minutes later all four were picked up by the *F. E. Smith*. The crew in the *Idler* rigging was extracted by the *Effie B.,* using a life buoy to bring them out, one by one. Anticipating the reaction of most Clevelanders to the disaster, the two tug crews did not fail to notice that while all of the *Idler*'s crew survived, only one of its seven female passengers was saved.

Crew of the Ill Fated Yacht Idler.
From Photo by Plain Dealer Photographer.

The *Idler* crew, *Plain Dealer*, July 10, 1900.

The two tugboats steamed around the wreck for a few minutes but, finding no more survivors, steamed toward the Cleveland harbor. Their arrival there at 4 p.m. set off a predictable firestorm of criticism and blame. Sailors and nonsailors, celebrities and nonentities, the attributable and the anonymous—all weighed in loudly and authoritatively on just what had occurred on the lake that afternoon. A good sample of expert nautical opinion came from Chicago yachtsman Captain John Prindville. Calling the *Idler* "the best boat of her inches that ever floated on salt or fresh water," he judged her the safest boat extant "when properly handled." His comments were echoed by Commodore Percy W. Rice, who said:

> I could not believe the news of the accident when I first heard it. It did not seem to me possible that the *Idler* could have gone done in a storm such as we had Saturday. I have known the *Idler* for years. I saw her once go through a storm on the Atlantic that wrecked many other vessels, some of them large steamers, and the *Idler* went through it without the slightest damage. This was twenty years ago about, and the storm was one of the most severe that ever visited the Atlantic coast.

Soon joining the angry chorus against Holmes's seamanship were the captains of the *Effie B., F. E. Smith,* and *Helene,* all three offering damning catalogues of just which sails had been aloft when the *Idler* sank. But more inflammatory and emotional were the statements of James and John Corrigan, reeling from the tragedy that had destroyed their families. John Corrigan was the more measured in his remarks, stating to a *Plain Dealer* reporter:

> If the boat had been properly handled the accident would never have happened. A person sailing a yacht should be on the lookout for trouble all the time. Squalls come up very suddenly, but you can always see them far enough away to prepare for them by dropping sail. It is no time then to be particular how sail is taken in, but time to act. I can't understand how the accident occurred; the yacht is a large craft and perfectly safe. I would not be afraid to sail across the Atlantic in her.

His brother James, who suffered the loss of almost his entire family, expressed himself with greater brevity but more anger when he returned Saturday evening from a view of the wreck, where he had gotten a good look at the telltale set of its sails. Speaking to the same *Plain Dealer* journalist, he said: "I consider criminal negligence on the part of Captain Holmes as being the cause of the disaster. . . . If Holmes had been trying to capsize the boat he would not have done it in any different way."

Captain Holmes, for his part, kept a low profile, going into seclusion at the Bethel Hotel as soon as he reached Cleveland. His rescuers on the *F. E. Smith* disclosed that his first query to Captain Normand after his rescue was to ask how many of the female passengers had been saved. When told only one had survived, he muttered, "Why in the devil didn't I drown, too!" Claiming to be dangerously ill, he put himself under the care of Dr. J. P. Smith, who immediately banned all visitors.

James Corrigan was not a successful industrialist for little reason. Some men might have collapsed under the loss of so many loved ones, but Captain James was made of sterner stuff. Repressing his shock, anger, and grief by an act of will, he immediately began to organize his response to the *Idler* disaster. His first task, the recovery of the bodies, began at once. Little more than an hour after receiving word of the sinking, he was aboard the tugboat *William Kennedy,* steaming toward the site of the *Idler* wreck. Accompanied by the tug *George C. Lutz,* the two vessels arrived at the scene at 5:45 p.m. The waves were still too vigorous to allow access to the wreck, so the tugs placed warning lights on a tethered raft and in the *Idler's* rigging before returning to Cleveland at 7 p.m.

Just eight hours later the tugboat *Ben Campbell* arrived at the scene. Along with Captain James, it carried Cleveland's best-known professional diver, Walter Metcalf, whose equipment and crew would allow him to search the flooded cabins of the submerged *Idler.* But the sea remained too rough, and the *Ben Campbell* returned to Cleveland. The *William Kennedy* was likewise stymied on a further venture that Sunday, and the tug *Joe Harris* was almost swamped by the waves when it ventured out on Monday.

With the weather turning fairer, the *Lutz* brought Metcalf's crew back to the wreck at 4:15 a.m. on July 10. Connected to his oxygen source by a 100-foot hose, Metcalf descended a 60-foot wire ladder to the *Idler's* deck at 4:56 a.m. Entering the main cabin below, he labored for almost an hour to clear it of debris that floated below its ceiling—furniture, clothing, linens, and fixtures—and obstructed his search. Finally, at 5:42, a tug on a rope signaled to his helpers above that he had found something. Pulling on the rope, they brought up the corpse of Mrs. James Corrigan. Brought aboard the *Lutz,* it was covered with a piece of sail torn from the ruined yacht's rigging. Breaking away from those who tried to restrain him, James Corrigan rushed to his wife's body, crying just two words, "My God!" He remained with her until the *Lutz* returned to Cleveland six hours later.

Metcalf had found Mrs. Corrigan's body buried under three mattresses in the companionway leading to the cabin. She was wearing a life preserver, her dress remained intact and there was no hint in her countenance that death had come to her with extraordinary suffering. She was still wearing two diamond earrings, a crescent-shaped diamond pin at her throat, and one diamond and two emerald rings on her left hand.

An hour later both Metcalf and his assistant, Fred Schwab, descended to clear more debris from the cabins and sleeping berths. Diving a third time at 7:20, Metcalf found Mrs. Rieley's body at 8 a.m. Lying in the top sleeping berth on the starboard side of the aft cabin, she, too, wore a life preserver, and her dress and jewelry were intact. But her face wore an expression of terrible agony, and her hands remained outstretched in death, as if she were still trying to protect her baby as the deadly waters closed in. There was no trace, however, of baby Mary.

At 9:40 a.m. the doughty Metcalf went down again. Just twelve minutes later he pulled the rope, and the corpse of Etta Corrigan surfaced. She was found in an adjacent sleeping berth, one hand still grasping a hank of her hair and her face contorted with the terror of death. Diver Schwab made one final but fruitless search that morning, and then the *Lutz* returned to Cleveland with its grisly cargo.

A novel feature of the discovery of the three corpses was the speedy transmission of the news to Cleveland. Among the passengers on the *Lutz* that morning were Andrew Kappenhagen and Fred Lehr, accompanied by their brood of twelve carrier pigeons. News bulletins detailing the events of that memorable morning were written on tissue paper and placed in small tubes the size of quinine capsules. The capsules were attached to the left legs of the pigeons, who then went winging their way southeast to Cleveland. To cite just one example of their efficiency, the pigeon carrying the bulletin announcing the recovery of Mrs. Rieley's body was released at 8:05 a.m. It arrived in Cleveland at 8:25, the bird covering the 16 miles in just 20 minutes.

That same Tuesday morning saw the commencement of James Corrigan's other two tasks, the obsequies for the dead and the investigation of the causes and circumstances of the *Idler* disaster. Etta Corrigan's body was quickly removed to Saxton's undertaking establishment and by evening reposed in a snow white casket at her father John's home at 71 Cutler Street. The bodies of Mrs. James Corrigan and Mrs. Rieley were removed to Harris's morgue for funeral preparation and then returned to their Willson Avenue home.

With three of the bodies still missing, search efforts were renewed on Wednesday, July 11. Captain James's first impulse had been to blow up the *Idler* with dynamite, but he soon realized that he must first find the bodies of his missing daughters and granddaughter. To that end he began recruiting search parties to patrol the southern shores of Lake Erie in quest of the missing corpses. But there remained the possibility that the bodies might still be inside the *Idler*, so he decided to have the yacht raised and towed into Cleveland, where a more thorough search could be made of its interior. Early Wednesday morning the tugs *William Kennedy* and *Tom Maytham* and the wrecking scow *Jupiter* arrived at the wreck site. The plan was to lift the *Idler* enough so that chains could be wrapped around its keel, allowing it to be pulled to the surface and thence to Cleveland by the powerful tugboats. All went well for the first couple of hours after the chains were placed, but at 9:06 the cable attached to the chains was severed by the *Idler*'s bobstay (a chain providing support to the prow's projecting bowsprit), and the *Idler* settled back into its Lake Erie mud bed. The work was immediately renewed but had to be suspended at 8 p.m. due to foul weather, which would continue through Thursday.

Etta Corrigan's funeral was held at 3 p.m. Wednesday afternoon at her parents' home. Her mother, who had been in seclusion, heavily sedated, and under treatment for shock since the disaster, managed to make a brief appearance, pale and audibly sobbing. The short, private services were conducted by the Rev. J. W. Malcolm of the First Congregational Church, and Etta's body was afterwards conveyed to its final destination in Woodland Cemetery. The following day, services for Mrs. James Corrigan and Mrs. Rieley were held at the Corrigan residence on Willson Avenue. There, in the main parlor, the two caskets were flanked with dual floral tributes, a green wreath symbolizing the death of an adult and a white wreath denoting a young woman's demise. The Reverend S. P. Sprecher of the Euclid Avenue Presbyterian Church conducted brief services. The crowd of mourners was so large it filled the yard outside and spilled into the street.

Meanwhile, both semi-official and official investigations of the *Idler* tragedy gained traction. James Corrigan's house lawyer, Harvey D. Goulder of Goulder, Holding & Masten, open his unofficial probe at 8:30 a.m., Tuesday, July 10. Summoning the crew of the yacht and the captains of the rescue tugs, Goulder began taking depositions from them behind closed doors. His probe did not elicit any testimony from either Mrs. John Corrigan, ostensibly excluded because of her traumatized condition, or Captain Holmes, who claimed dispensation on the grounds of ill health. Several days of that same week were consumed by Cuyahoga County coroner John C. Simon, who dithered at length over whether he had the jurisdiction to conduct an inquest into the six *Idler* deaths. The gist of his difficulty was the question of whether the *Idler* had sunk within the nautical boundaries of Lorain or Cuyahoga County—or even in Canadian waters. It was Assistant County Solicitor Frederick L. Taft's opinion that the wreck lay within Lorain County, an opinion shared by the Lorain County coroner. Eventually, however, Taft discovered that the site lay less than two miles east of Cuyahoga County's western limit, and Simon's inquest, after several delays, opened on Wednesday, July 18, at 9:30 a.m.

By then the *Idler* had been towed back to Cleveland and pumped out. The tugs *Kennedy* and *Dreadnaught* began pulling it south at 7 a.m. on Friday, July 13, and by 6 p.m. Saturday it was beached in shallow water just 1,000 feet north of the Division Street water pumping station. Just before it was grounded, the *Idler* inflicted its last casualty, its bowsprit staving in the side of the wrecking scow *Jumbo* and causing her to sink. At dawn on Sunday a suction hose wide as a man's waist was run from the dredge *Ohio* to the *Idler,* and water began to flow out of her hold. About 2 p.m., someone noticed an object caught against the hose's strainer, and the pump was stopped. It was the corpse of baby Mary Rieley, badly decomposed. After it was removed for burial, diver Metcalf and his crew entered the hold, searching for the two missing corpses even as the final four feet of water were drained out.

Metcalf and his men didn't find the bodies—but an ugly episode soon distracted the searchers from their work. As the divers encountered various objects and bits of debris, they handed them through the skylight openings to a work crew above, who were under orders to lay them out carefully on the deck for further inspection. Suddenly, Captain Richardson of the *Ohio* noticed that two of the objects, a small bag and a woman's jacket, had been separated from the other objects and tightly folded together. He brought them to James Corrigan's attention, and their investigation revealed a cache of jewelry, cash, a pocketbook, and some personal objects—including baby Mary's shoes—inside the bag. It was only too obvious that one of the deck workers had put it aside for later abstraction, but the culprit was never found.

Perhaps even more disgusting than the attempted robbery of the dead was the behavior of several hundred Clevelanders, who thronged the Cleveland shoreline to gawk at the *Idler* after she returned to Cleveland. Such voyeurs were so numerous and aggressive that they actually interfered with the search and salvage of the ruined yacht, many of them cutting themselves ghoulish souvenirs from the *Idler's* sails and rigging. Several enterprising tug owners further capitalized on the situation by charging ten cents a head to take the most curious for a closer look at the death ship.

Coroner Simon's inquest at the county morgue finally opened at 9:30 on Wednesday, July 18. None of the crew subpoenaed to give testimony was represented by an attorney, and much of Simon's previous knowledge of the case, he freely admitted, came either from newspaper accounts or the secret testimony gathered by Harvey Goulder's probe. Mate Biggam was the first witnesses, and there was little in his testimony that he had not already blurted out to newspaper reporters. But this time he was on the record and repeated the assertion that Captain Holmes had ignored his advice to take in more sail, and Biggam insisted "absolutely" that Holmes had said that he wanted "a little excitement." Biggam also insisted that it was he who had begged the women to come out of the cabin and offered to take Mrs. Rieley's baby. The real meat of his testimony, however, came at the end, when Coroner Simon solicited his professional opinion as to why the disaster had occurred. Biggam did not hesitate with his answer:

From my experience of sailing the lakes I should have had all sail in before the squall struck us with the exception of the forestaysail.

Etta, Ida May and Mrs. James Corrigan, *Plain Dealer*, July 8, 1900.

According to my judgment we had out too much sail for the appearance of the weather. . . . I should say that the yacht *Idler* was perfectly seaworthy in all respects. In my opinion, had the yacht been stripped of canvas she would have been all right.

Biggam finished his testimony at 11:45 a.m. Even before the next witness, Olaf Neilson, began his afternoon testimony, an order, previously drafted by Coroner Simon, was issued for the arrest of Captain Holmes. After U.S. District Attorney John J. Sullivan signed it, Marshal John J. Keeley delivered it to Holmes at his 212 Abbey Street boardinghouse and read him the warrant charging him with manslaughter under the provisions of the United States Revised Statutes, Section 5344:

Every captain, engineer, pilot, or other person employed on any steamer or vessel, by whose misconduct, negligence, or inattention to his duties on such vessel, the life of any person is destroyed, and every owner, inspector, or other public officer, through whose fraud, connivance, misconduct, or violation of the law, the life of any person is so destroyed, shall be deemed guilty of manslaughter, and upon conviction thereof before the District Court of the United States shall be sentenced to confinement at hard labor for a period of not more than ten years.

Taken before U.S. Commissioner Harrison J. Uhl for arraignment, Holmes was formally charged with manslaughter and bound over to a federal grand jury for the October term. He was then removed to the Cuyahoga County Jail.

Holmes quickly made bail, the $1,000 bond signed by his personal physician, Dr. Smith. But it was clear that the captain, still suffering from the psychological and physical shocks of the sinking, did not appreciate the gravity of his position. Nor did he comprehend the animosity felt toward him by James Corrigan, who held him totally responsible for the death of his loved ones. Holmes's naive obliviousness was clear from his first comments to reporters, when he walked out of jail late Wednesday afternoon. Employing a most unfortunate choice of words, he said:

This charge does not amount to a hill of beans and cannot be corroborated. The excitement will soon blow over. Of course, Mr. Corrigan feels bad about losing his family, but he will remember when this all blows over, how careful I have always been.

The perilous dimensions of Holmes's position became clearer to him the following day. He had previously entertained hopes that Captain Corrigan would defend him, but that Thursday morning's Cleveland *Plain Dealer* reported that James Corrigan had insisted on Holmes's arrest after hearing the testimony gathered by Harvey Goulder the previous week. Then, at noon, Holmes was rearrested and jailed after Dr. Smith rescinded his bail commitment, which he had only intended to be temporary. During a subsequent jailhouse interview, he pointed out that he *had* gone down with his ship, and he made strenuous attempts to poke holes in Biggam's reported testimony. Mocking the mate's implausible claim that he'd been under water for three minutes, he wondered aloud why the burly Biggam simply hadn't forced the women to leave the cabin. More plaintively, he noted that he had lost $295 when his wallet went down with the *Idler*. Eventually recovered, it only contained $5 when it was returned to him.

While Holmes fought incarceration, Coroner Simon's inquest ground on through the rest of Wednesday. But the testimony of Olaf Neilson, Severn Neilson, and Jacob Antonson added nothing to the record except more evidence that Captain Holmes had done little to prepare for the storm until it was far too late. That same day, James Corrigan commissioned the *Lutz* to start dragging the lake at the wreck site for the missing bodies of Jane and Ida Corrigan. The device employed was a huge equilateral triangle, to the bottom of which were attached hooks that combed the lake floor in eight-foot paths as the *Lutz* steamed in circles. The dragging continued for several days with no results, as did repeated attempts to raise the bodies by exploding large quantities of black powder in the water. The blasts were conducted by Colonel Conrad Beck, who tried various amounts of explosives—in 200- to 500-pound lots—at various depths to no avail. Meanwhile, James Corrigan continued to fund pedestrian sleuths to roam the Lake Erie beaches from east to west, and north to the Canadian shore. He also placed newspaper notices offering rewards for the discovery of his daughters' bodies. A typical notice was this sample from the July 25 edition of the Cleveland *Plain Dealer:*

A liberal reward will be paid for the recovery of the bodies of the Misses Jane and Ida Corrigan, drowned off yacht *Idler*, near Cleveland, July 7. Wire any information to James Corrigan, Perry-Payne Bldg., Cleveland. O.

Before the two missing bodies were found, James Corrigan would spend at least $10,000 on search efforts and gravely compromise his health in his nearly sleepless quest for his daughters' remains.

On Saturday, July 21, Holmes again posted bail, the $1,000 bond signed this time by attorney Ernest M. Shay. Coroner Simon's inquest resumed two days later with the interrogation of carpenter William Summers and sailor Charles Johnson. Both of them mostly echoed the previous testimony, but Summers's recollection of the state of the *Idler's* deadlights when the squall hit the yacht further muddled that already tangled question. Virtually all of the *Idler's* crew and Mrs. John Corrigan had already made statements, either to newspaper reporters or under oath at the inquest, that at least *some* of the *Idler's* deadlights were open when the yacht first turned over, allowing a fatal influx of water into its cabins. But none of these witnesses could agree on just how many or which of the deadlights had been open. And now, on July 23, came carpenter Summers to tell the inquest jury that not only was Holmes correct in his claim that he had ordered the skylights closed well before the first blast—but that Summers knew for a fact that they had in fact been closed:

> The deadlights were closed a quarter of an hour before but I don't know who closed them. The reason I know they were closed is because I picked up the brass gratings on the deck and put them in the boatswain's box. They were on deck because they were forced out of place by the closing of the deadlights down below.

Charles Johnson followed Summers on the stand, only to contradict him, testifying that he saw two open deadlights on the starboard side after the first blow.

The mystery of the deadlights was never cleared up. In subsequent inquest testimony on August 1, cook Charles Hackett insisted that it was he who had implemented Holmes's order to close the deadlights before the storm hit. He swore he had closed them all, except one in a locked lavatory. And when Holmes himself testified before Coroner Simon on September 14, he simply repeated his claim that he had ordered all the deadlights closed before the storm. In that same testimony, however, he said that he saw water coming in through several of the deadlights during the several minutes of chaos following the first gale. The deadlights mystery will never be resolved, although the preponderant evidence suggests that whether or not Holmes ordered the deadlights closed before the storm, at least some of them were open when it arrived. Indeed, the core of Holmes's defense of his actions was that the *Idler* would have survived the squall had it not been fatally compromised by the influx of water through the open deadlights. Such a defense not only explained the disaster but also shifted the ground of the argument away from Holmes's failure to anticipate and prepare for the coming storm by taking in sail.

Hackett's testimony also contradicted both Holmes's and Biggam's testimony about the life preservers. According to Hackett, it was he and cook Welch who actually put the preservers on the women in the cabin, not the captain or the mate. More interestingly, Hackett swore that Holmes had initially resisted advising the women to don the preservers after the first gale hit, warning that it would only alarm them unnecessarily and assuring Hackett that he had "been through a hundred like this."

With the conclusion of Hackett's testimony and pending Holmes's inquest appearance, the focus of events returned to the dead and the search for the missing bodies. On July 31, Mrs. Reed Frazier, a former housekeeper at James Corrigan's summer

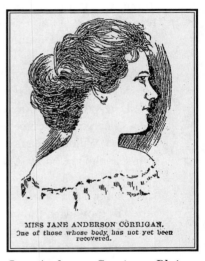

MISS JANE ANDERSON CORRIGAN.
One of those whose body has not yet been recovered.

Jane Anderson Corrigan, *Plain Dealer*, July 11, 1900.

Wickliffe residence, was arrested in Lorain. While going through the dead Jane Corrigan's effects, her family discovered that some of her dresses had gone missing. The evidentiary trail led to Mrs. Reed, and the dresses were found in one of her trunks. Meanwhile, through the dog days of August, James Corrigan prosecuted his relentless search for his dead daughters, running daily reward offers in Cleveland newspapers and paying scores of men to comb the beaches of Lake Erie. Success finally crowned his efforts on Wednesday, August 29. About 4 p.m., H. J. Latimer of Cleveland, a passenger on the steamer *City of Detroit,* was standing on her hurricane deck when he spotted something that looked like a body in the water. He informed the captain, who dispatched a crew in a small boat to retrieve what proved to be the body of Ida Corrigan. Her corpse was in bad shape, but her hair color, a diamond ring, a locket, and gold stickpin quickly clinched the identification. Latimer, as it happened, was not only the Corrigans' near neighbor on Willson Avenue, but had also served in the Fifth Army Regiment with Ida's brother James during the Spanish-American War. The classy Latimer refused to accept the offered reward from James Corrigan. There was no funeral for Ida and her remains were taken to the receiving vault at Lake View Cemetery to join those of her mother, sister, and niece all awaiting the discovery of Jane's remains before final burial.

Captain Holmes's long-delayed inquest testimony on September 14 added nothing to the record but more fervent denials that he had acted irresponsibly before or after the first squall hit the *Idler.* Two weeks later, on September 28, the corpse of Jane Corrigan washed ashore at Willoughbeach in Lake County, just east of the border with Cuyahoga County. At about 6:30 in the morning it was spotted in the surf by fisherman John Campbell, who lived in a nearby lakeshore cabin. Jane Corrigan's body was badly decomposed, and one arm was torn away. But her brown shoes and tan skirt were intact, and a single but distinctive button completed the identification. Two weeks later, on October 9, the bodies of Mrs. James Corrigan, Ida May, Jane, Mrs. Rieley, and her baby were finally interred in the Corrigan family plot at Lake View Cemetery. While 2,000 mourners listened, the Rev. Sprecher spoke briefly, and then the earth closed over the mortal remains of most of James Corrigan's family.

The discovery of Jane Corrigan's body solved one mystery but only amplified another. Several of the *Idler* survivors, including her aunt, had stated that when last seen on the afternoon of July 7, Jane had a small chamois bag lightly attached to her neck by a silk cord. It contained $1,000 worth of uncut diamonds and other jewelry—but there was no trace of bag, cord, gems, or jewelry on her body when found. James Corrigan immediately hired Jake Mintz, Cleveland's most celebrated private detective, to investigate, and the efficient Mintz did not disappoint. Five days after Jane's corpse was found, Charles R. Samuels, 38, of 193 Stearns Street, was arrested on a Pittsburgh street by Mintz operative Aaron Goldsmith. When apprehended, Samuels had on his person some 14-karat gold link buttons bearing the incriminating initials *JC* (Jane Corrigan). Samuels would not or could not account for the valuables still missing, which included the $10,000 worth of uncut diamonds; a large turquoise ring encircled by 16 diamonds and valued at $1,800; a

diamond and sapphire ring worth $600; a diamond ring with five jewels in a cluster valued at $400; nine miscellaneous rings valued at $800; two watches, one valuable and having the initials *J.F.C.* engraved on the back; a gold and blue enamel bracelet valued at $225; an opal and rhinestone brooch worth $200; and a bar pin with five perfectly set diamonds valued at $500 for the diamonds alone.

Samuels, it developed, had been one of a crew of Russian sailors hired by James Corrigan to search the *Idler* in the Old Riverbed. The inept thief's downfall had begun some weeks be-

Mrs. Charles L. Rieley, *Cleveland Leader*, July 9, 1900.

fore, when his curious neighbors began gossiping about his family's sudden and unwonted prosperity. And the only reason that he still had the incriminating buttons was because none of the prospective buyers were willing to wear the buttons of a dead person. Taken before Pittsburgh magistrate Samuel Brown, a weeping Samuels fell to his knees and begged for mercy from James Corrigan. It was reported later that not only was the magnanimous Captain James disinclined to prosecute but that he had offered financial support to the Samuels family.

Following the closure provided by the last burials, the remaining aftershocks of the *Idler* tragedy occurred almost without much public notice. Captain Holmes's manslaughter trial, scheduled for October, was initially delayed by the necessity of appointing a new

U.S. district judge to hear his case. Then came several pleas for continuances, all requested by Holmes's counsel and all granted. Eventually, Coroner Simon got tired of waiting, and on November 10, he directed Deputy Coroner West to issue the *Idler* inquest verdict. West's terse ruling of death by drowning pertained only to the death of Ida May Corrigan and did not attach blame to anyone.

All was ready for Holmes's manslaughter trial when the new federal court term commenced in January 1901—but the good captain was nowhere to be found. Judicial officials remained patient until April 24, when an exasperated Judge Francis J. Wing brusquely ruled Holmes's $1,000 bond forfeit and demanded that the captain's attorney, C. G. Canfield, produce the missing defendant. Canfield failed to find him—but then Holmes surfaced on his own just a month later in New York City and promised to return to Cleveland. Holmes's excuse for his absence, however implausible, was apparently true and worthy of the inveterately intrepid seafarer. It seems that the previous fall, having to support his wife and two children, Holmes had shipped out on a tramp steamer to India. The ship had been lost at sea, and Holmes, marooned on a desert island for three months, had only just returned to the United States to discover that he was a fugitive from justice. An unappeased Judge Wing slapped him into jail and rescheduled his trial for the October term.

That trial never occurred. Holmes did spend three months in jail before he was bailed out on August 17 by Cleveland mayor Tom Johnson and West Side realtor John Curran. Mayor Johnson defended his unexpected intervention in the case with his usual simplicity, telling Holmes, "I think you are an honest man and I didn't want to see you in jail any longer." Cuyahoga County sheriff Barry, who had hosted Holmes for 90 days, added, "There goes the nicest man we have had in jail for a long time." The *Idler* case was again called in the October term but, owing to the illness of Holmes's attorney, Robert S. Avery, had to be postponed again to the February 1902 term.

By the time that term opened on February 18, Judge Wing and U.S. District Attorney John J. Sullivan had had more than enough of the *Idler* case. Citing in particular the difficulty of locating the relevant witnesses after an interval of a year and a half, Sullivan nolled the manslaughter indictment, and the *Idler* prosecution was over.

The real reasons for the decision not to prosecute Captain Holmes remain unknown to this day. There *was* great difficulty in procuring the chief witnesses, especially the most important one, Mate Biggam, who apparently went to heroic lengths to elude federal subpoena servers; they ultimately lost his trail in Louisville, Kentucky. There was also the possibility, considerably discussed by Cleveland journalists, that a trial exposition of the *Idler* case might discover that Captain James Corrigan—in law the de jure master of the *Idler*—had at least as much legal liability for its fate as Captain Holmes. That possibility was angrily denied by Corrigan's attorney, Harvey Goulder, who also expressed surprise and incredulity—probably feigned—at Sullivan's decision to drop the case. Sullivan, for his part, insisted that the decision was his own, and made after careful consultation with Judge Wing. And so Captain Holmes went free at last.

The most likely explanation for the abrupt end to Holmes's prosecution was that James Corrigan had simply lost his appetite for recrimination. The *Idler* case had already dragged on for 19 months, and there was little to be gained in pursuing further vengeance. A full-bore manslaughter trial would probably require not only his appearance on the witness stand, but also that of his still traumatized sister-in-law, Mrs. John Corrigan. Not to mention the possibility, given the conflicting testimony of the available witnesses and the reality that the July 7 squall was one of almost unprecedented fury, that Holmes might well be acquitted.

The subsequent destinies of most of the surviving principal actors in the *Idler* catastrophe were tragic. Following his release by the court, Holmes went on a treasure-hunting expedition to the West Indies. Next came a spell of newspaper work, followed by more treasure hunts, one to the South Pacific for treasure wrecks and one to the Yukon for gold. When the United States declared war on Germany in 1917, Holmes enlisted in the U.S. Navy as a boatswain and was eventually promoted to ensign rank before losing his life on the collier *Cyclops*, which disappeared in the Atlantic during the spring of 1918.

That same fatal destiny pursued the surviving members of the Corrigan family. On December 24, 1908, James Corrigan died at his Euclid Avenue home from peritonitis, a complication of a three-month bout with appendicitis. Two and a half years later, his brother, John, was killed near Los Angeles when his automobile was hit by a Los Angeles Pacific Railway streetcar at a traffic crossing. His wife lingered on until April of 1927, forever haunted by the tragedy that took her daughter, nieces, and sister-in-law.

JAMES CORRIGAN,
Who accuses Rockefeller.

Cleveland Plain Dealer, July 13, 1905

Captain James Corrigan.

James W. Corrigan Jr., the sole surviving child of Captain James, had an interesting, if truncated life. Considered just a frivolous playboy by his father and his social peers—with considerable justification—James Jr. was shocked to discover, upon his father's death in 1908, that the terms of his will left most of his bequest to his son in trust and—most hurtfully—gave control of the Corrigan-McKinney Steel Company to Price McKinney. Eight years later, James Jr. further damaged his dubious social position with marriage to flamboyant Chicago divorcée Laura Mae McMartin. The final straw for Junior came when McKinney changed the name of the firm to the McKinney Steel Company. After that, it was all-out war, and Corrigan finally triumphed in 1925, seizing control of the company stock and changing the name back. On April 3, 1926, Price McKinney shot himself to death with a Luger pistol. (Nine years later his son, Price McKinney Jr., 24, would also die by a bullet, "accidentally" fired while cleaning his rifle.) But Jimmy Corrigan didn't have long to enjoy his triumph; he and Laura remained Cleveland society untouchables until he unexpectedly dropped dead of a heart attack at the entrance of the Cleveland Athletic Club in January 1928. He was only 47. Permanently frozen out of Cleveland society, his widow Laura Mae would endure to become a social lioness in Europe, where she became renowned for her hospitality and philanthropy. She died in January 1948, twenty years to the day after her husband passed away.

There was yet one more chapter to be written in the terrible annals of Corrigan family woe. John Corrigan's granddaughter by his son, John A. Corrigan, married patent attorney and socialite Charles Wesley Williams on August 18, 1936, following the 1948 death of Laura Mae Corrigan.

Mrs. Williams inherited a million dollars from her aunt's estate. Twelve years later, life seemed superb for the Williamses and their four children at "Hounds' Hill," their 110-acre Hunting Valley estate on County Line Road. (In one of the frequent ironies flowing from the few degrees of separation at the upper levels of Cleveland society, the Williamses had bought Hounds' Hill from the estate of Mrs. Corliss E. Sullivan, whose first husband had been Price McKinney.) Its 24-room castle-like mansion was impressive enough, but its structural charms were dwarfed by the splendors of its first-floor library, which contained a celebrated rare book collection valued at more than $500,000. But sometime in the early hours of March 21, 1960, a fire broke out in that library, gutting part of the house and taking the lives of Charles Wesley Williams and Margaret Corrigan Williams. The two Williams children in residence at the time, Marcia, 14, and Michael, 10, survived the fire, Marcia heroically saving her brother's life. The Corrigan curse had struck for the last time.

Chapter 4

"I DIE AN INNOCENT MAN!"

The Gruesome Death of William Beatson

James Parks traveled far and took considerable pains to commit the crime that put him on a Public Square gallows in 1855. Born James Dickinson in Bolton in the West Riding of Yorkshire in 1814, he lived mostly at Clitheroe, Lancashire, until his early twenties. Brought up as a farmer and reared in the tenets of the Church of England, he learned the craft of a weaver and eventually embraced the Chartist political agitation that swept England in the 1830s. He would later claim that he was involved in the printing and distribution of radical newspapers outlawed by the British government. But whatever his political ideals, he found himself unable to better his condition and grew weary of working 12 hours a day in the heat of the harvest sun. He probably didn't care, either, for English jails, which he apparently sampled after some episodes of poaching in the late 1830s. He was also said to have served time for his activities there as a "resurrection man," robbing graves. For these and sundry other reasons he left Lancashire in 1838 for a better life in the United States. The latter part of that year found him working as an overseer in charge of 40 girls in a weaving room at Bristol, Rhode Island.

Whatever wages Dickinson earned at his new job were inadequate to his striving spirit. Sometime after quarreling with a man named Jim DeWolf, he learned that the mausoleum of DeWolf's father contained a silver coffin and other costly items. Conspiring with a man named Gardner, Dickinson contrived an audacious scheme. Rowing across Narragansett Bay through a driving thunderstorm in a skiff, Parks and Gardner entered the cemetery grounds, scaled the high mausoleum walls, and broke into the DeWolf family vault. Blowing the coffin lock with gunpowder, they tore off the shroud and frisked the corpse for jewels, "an outrage hellish in conception and revolting to humanity in its execution," as a *Cleveland Herald* chronicler aptly put it. Alas, the only valuable found was the inscribed silver plate on a child's coffin, which the thieves wrenched off and broke into pieces. Dickinson, no mental giant, sold the silver fragments to a man named Ellis Gifford, When Gifford found a child's name on one of them, he went to the police. Under arrest, Dickinson's story was that he had gotten the silver from a man named Dodds; when that explanation proved dubious, he said his source was a fellow named McCarthy. Confined to the Bristol jail, he was allowed visits from his wife, with whom he had a relationship derisively described in a subsequent newspaper account as "pro tem." The "wife" soon furnished him with a pistol, and Dickinson forthwith escaped from jail. Although he didn't scruple to fire a shot at his pursuers, his bullet missed, and in September 1842, he was sentenced to a four-year term in a Providence prison.

Dickinson subsequently claimed that he educated himself in the prison library, reading widely in the history of Greece, Rome, and the East Indies, and reading the Bible three times through. But whatever wisdom he derived from the Good Book must have soon dissipated, for immediately after his release he returned to a life of crime. Years later, facing death on the scaffold, Dickinson would excuse his relapse by citing the ineradicable taint he carried as a former jailbird. Decent men, he said, shunned him, unwilling to work at the side of an ex-convict and leaving him no choice but a dishonest livelihood. There may be some truth in this, as evidenced by the rueful regrets Parks expressed on the scaffold just minutes before his death:

Ah, there is where the circumstances that environed me, my eleven years in prison, my blackened character, flashed across my mind, and determined me in what I did. I had swerved from the path of duty and had lost what Solomon speaks of, in that good proverb, *"a good name."* "A good name is better than riches." Ah, how true! So long as your good name is yours, it will be a rock of defence against a thousand assailants, and without it, a single man shall put you to flight.

Inevitably, Parks fell in with some ex-convicts in New Jersey, and they purposed to rob a Mr. Kempton of Manayunk, near Philadelphia. Entering his home at night, they locked his servants in a closet and put a pistol to Kempton's head. Dickinson's disguise on that occasion as an Indian did not deceive Mr. Kempton, however, and he soon found himself serving another four-year stretch, this time in Pennsylvania's Eastern Penitentiary.

By the early 1850s Dickinson was out of jail and, under the name of James Parks, running a notorious dive on Pittsburgh Street in Cleveland, the Jenny Lind Saloon. He is also said to have run a disreputable rooming house for railroad hands in Berea at this time, but Parks's supposed infamies during his Forest City residency remain murky. It is alleged that he recruited a depraved female named Ann Carpenter to be another "pro tem" consort—and then murdered her when her presence became inconvenient. It was later said, too, that he was arrested on a charge of adultery and that he murdered a man. Summit County sheriff Samuel Lane, the first historian of Parks's misdeeds, states only that he was arrested on various misdemeanor charges during his Cleveland stint and enjoyed a mephitic reputation.

Late in 1852, Dickinson returned to England. There he married a cousin, Bessie Dickinson, said by one chronicler to be a damsel of "humble birth but unstained reputation." Time would certainly tell about the latter assertion. The path that led to a hangman's noose opened up considerably on February 13, 1853, when Parks and his new bride left Liverpool for the United States on the ship *Constitution*. Also on the vessel was William Beatson, a sometime butcher, thief, and all-round confidence man from Yorkshire. What exactly happened during that fateful voyage was never documented in court or elsewhere, although it is instructive that both Dickinson and Beatson traveled under aliases, the former calling himself "James" and the latter "Besan." And it is said that during that Atlantic crossing a number of passengers were robbed of considerable cash—a man named Thornton was relieved of 60 sovereigns—and that James Parks likely knew that Beatson was the thief. An even more likely explanation, of course, is that the two Yorkshiremen were working together as a criminal team.

Landing in New York City on March 12, the newly wed Parkses journeyed to Cleveland, where they established their bridal bower at Riley's, a private boardinghouse on River Street. A few days later, an armed gang of thieves, inadequately disguised as black men, entered the Ohio City home of Joel Scranton and removed its valuables. It was believed but never proven that Dickinson was the robber chieftain. Then, on April 12, William Beatson showed up at the Parks domicile, flush with liquor and cash, and anxious to see his erstwhile shipboard friend. Beatson claimed that his impressive bankroll came from the sale of a farm, but the real story was far more interesting than that feeble canard. It seems that a fellow *Constitution* passenger named William Gee had often boasted of his comfortable solvency. Arriving in Buffalo, Gee deposited $600 in the Buffalo Savings Bank. Soon after that Beatson looked Gee up and quickly devised a clever scheme to relieve him of the sum. Visiting the bank, Beatson introduced himself to bank officials as Gee's brother and flourished a letter allegedly written by the absent Gee. Gee, the letter stated, wished to withdraw his funds, needing the money to purchase a farm, but was unable to receive the money in person, as he had been kicked in the head by a horse. It was a plausible enough story, and Beatson promptly exited the bank with a check drawn on another bank, the Oliver & Lee Company. Arriving at the latter, Beatson was asked to sign a receipt for the money. Shyly explaining that he could not write, the wily Beatson made his "mark" and departed with $600 in gold coins.

It is likely Parks didn't care how Beatson had obtained his newfound wealth, as he seemed thrilled to see him and was buying drinks without limit. On April 13, the morning after Beatson arrived in Cleveland, the two men commenced the epic bender that would

James Parks, the Murderer of Wm. Beatson,
Plain Dealer, June 4, 1855.

culminate in sordid death for both of them. Parks drinking beer
and Beatson swilling brandy, they were seen in a number of saloons, inhaling liquor without surcease and carousing noisily. John
W. Richardson, keeper of the U.S. Hotel on River Street, served
them drinks there about noon. He would recall at Parks's murder
trial that Beatson was already quite tipsy but that Parks remained
relatively sober. Two hours later, Beatson aroused the ire of barkeep
James Burton at his Pittsburgh Street Eagle Saloon. After several
brandies, Beatson began boasting about how much money he had
and started flourishing $50 and $20 gold pieces. Burton, who feared
his drunken customer might be robbed on the premises, told him
to stash his money or leave his saloon. Sometime later, Parks and
Beatson departed to seek further liquid refreshment, telling everybody they met that they were going to Pittsburgh, Pennsylvania.
Elizabeth Faulkner was one of the bartenders who served the two
men late that afternoon of April 13. After Beatson babbled about his
Pittsburgh trip, Parks told her that he would accompany the gravely
inebriated man to protect him. Eventually, fearing that the slurring

and staggering Beatson would be arrested for public drunkenness, Faulkner threw them out on the street, advising Parks to walk Beatson around the streets of Cleveland until he was sure that all the trains for Pittsburgh had departed. (The effect of Beatson's drunken diction may have been exaggerated by the inability of many of his auditors to understand his pronounced Yorkshire accent.)

They never made it to Pittsburgh. Securing Beatson's traveling chest, the still-imbibing twosome embarked on "the cars" (as the newfangled railroad was then called) at 7:30 p.m. Conductor C. C. Cobb would later recall that Beatson was so drunk he could barely proffer his ticket. Shortly after the train left Bedford, Parks found a pretext to leave his companion and went to the baggage car, where he rifled Beatson's chest. Finding no money in it, he contrived another plan to rob him. As they reached Hudson, he aroused the befuddled Beatson and hustled him across the depot to an Akron-bound train. Minutes after it departed, Parks realized his "mistake" and they left the train at Cuyahoga Falls, hoping to resume their trek to Pittsburgh from there. But the Pittsburgh train was delayed by a downed tree near Macedonia and, after some time spent huddled in the driving rain, they headed for the nearest inn, the American Hotel run by A. W. Hall near the falls of the Cuyahoga River.

Parks and Beatson stayed in Hall's tavern room for about an hour, drinking ale and smoking cigars, while Parks bragged about the considerable cash his "brother-in-law" carried on his person. Hall would recall that Parks made many "witty and jocose" remarks that evening, and that he also spent much time trying to persuade Beatson to walk the seven and a half miles back to Hudson with him to catch another train. Perhaps it was his fervency; perhaps it was his focus on his companion's wealth. But whatever Parks's demeanor, drunken or not, it was enough to make Hall suspect that he intended to rob Beatson on the darkened road to Hudson. The fatal moment arrived at 11:02, when Hall refused to furnish the two men with any more alcohol, and they departed, walking slowly and tipsily north on the road toward Hudson. Beatson was so drunk that he forgot his overcoat.

They never got to Hudson. Perhaps the last person to hear, if not see, them was Mrs. Eunice Gaylord of Cuyahoga Falls. A little after 11 p.m., she heard two men outside her door arguing about directions. They were walking in single file about 15 feet from her house, and from her house the last words she heard were one of them saying, "No," to which his companion replied, "We will go up and around."

About 7 o'clock the next morning, two boys named Alley and Waters discovered large pools of blood about half a mile from the American Hotel and close to where the railroad crossed both the road and the Little Cuyahoga River. Searchers soon arrived on the scene to find, under the abutments of the bridge, a vest button, a cane, human brains, and a great deal of blood splashed head-high on the abutments. There were two sets of muddy footprints leading under the bridge—but only one set leading out toward the river, toward which something heavy and bloody had been dragged. In the nearby Pennsylvania & Ohio Canal they found a suit of men's clothing cut to pieces and a man's cap on a stump in an adjoining field. The clothing was soon identified as belonging to the man who had been so drunk at the American Hotel the previous night, and the hue and cry was out for his erstwhile drinking companion even before William Beatson's headless, naked corpse was discovered floating in the Cuyahoga River the following morning.

Meanwhile, where had that erstwhile drinking companion gone? Parks's trail was first marked by a canal boat driver, who saw him walking by the towpath about midnight. Another driver saw him three hours later, and at 8:30 on the morning of April 14, at a stable two miles from Akron, he hired a rig from Hiram Cory to take him to Ohio City. That was about nine hours after Beatson was last seen alive. Parks explained his blood-covered clothing to Corey with the story that he had fallen off a canal boat coming from Pittsburgh and bloodied his nose. Later that afternoon, Parks surfaced in Ohio City, inquiring for an Englishman named Clark, and he spent the next two days in Cleveland before departing for Buffalo, followed two days later by his wife and one of her brothers. There he was arrested by Joseph Tyler at an English grocery on Monday, April 18 and brought back to Cleveland, followed two days later by his wife Betsy and John Dickinson. The canny Tyler, who had traced Parks by shadowing the eastward flight of his wife and brother-in-law, had also brought along a handbill featuring Parks's description, which he triumphantly flourished when Parks denied his identity. Surely, Parks's appearance on this dramatic occasion must have been the last word in Victorian melodrama:

> [He] is an Englishman, thick set, about 5 feet, 6 inches high, had on a low plush black cap, black sack coat, black pants, black satin vest, had lost one or more of his upper front teeth and is apparently 35 years of age.

Parks' "Wanted" handbill had included the helpful detail that his left pant leg was covered with blood from the knee down, but the conclusive detail was the missing tooth, which Tyler shrewdly verified by sticking his hand in Parks's mouth. Tyler's lack of delicacy would pay off later when he collected the $500 reward by the Summit County commissioners for Parks's capture. That same day Betsy Dickinson and her brothers John and George boarded an eastbound Lake Shore Railroad train. The next day they were taken off the train and arrested in Rochester with more than $1,000 in gold and currency on their persons. The "humble" woman of "unstained reputation" admitted no wrongdoing, insisting angrily that she had righteously fled a city where such unjustified accusations could be made against a member of her family. Brought back to Cleveland by Sheriff Seward and Cleveland police chief Mike Gallagher, Parks attracted crowds of curious spectators at every stop westward along the Lake Shore line.

Following his indictment for first-degree murder in July, Parks's trial commenced at Akron's Summit County Courthouse on December 26, 1853. Ably defended by lawyers George Bliss, Christopher P. Wolcott, John A. Pleasants, and W. S. C. Otis, Parks was prosecuted by Sidney Edgerton and William H. Upson with the Honorable Judge Humpreyville presiding. Parks's defense, as a *Plain Dealer* scribe later put it, was "most remarkable, almost unprecedented." Claiming that he and Beatson had decided to veer off the Hudson road and take the more direct route of the railroad tracks, Parks swore that Beatson had met an accidental and unexpected death when the two of them fell 12 feet in the dark through the widely spaced wooden planks of a railroad bridge spanning the road. (In fact the planks were no more than 12 inches apart.) Although injured himself by the fall and entirely innocent of Beatson's death, Parks, still haunted by his jailbird past, was convinced that no one would ever believe that he had not plotted and wrought his companion's demise. So there, in the darkened, rainy gloom of that April night, the panicked ex-convict stripped off Beatson's clothes and cut off his head to make identification as difficult as possible. He then took to his heels, hoping for the best and fearing the worst.

There were no eyewitnesses to back up Parks's melodramatic story, and it is probable that his past irreverence in the matter of corpses—the DeWolf mausoleum—may have told against him. So, too, did the testimony of expert medical witnesses, who found the injuries to Beatson's ill-used corpse incompatible with a single fall of 12 feet: a total of four wounds made with a knife, a pistol, a stone, and one unknown weapon. It was further established in court that some of the injuries were inflicted while Beatson was still alive. Nor could the grisly fact that the victim's missing head was never found—Summit County sheriff Dudley Seward had part of the Ohio canal drained and searched for it to no avail—have favorably swayed the jury of 12 men in Parks's favor. They must have also, doubtless, taken a suspicious view of the considerable amount of cash found in the possession of Parks's wife and brothers-in-law when they were apprehended at Utica, a golden windfall whose provenance neither Parks, his wife, nor his brothers-in-law could satisfactorily explain. Ultimately, the jury, who visited the murder scene before deliberating, accepted the prosecution's assertion that Parks had simply lured Beatson to a remote locale to murder and rob him. It is possible, too, that the jurors resented the prolixity of defense attorneys Wolcott and Bliss, each consuming *10 hours apiece* in their final pleas to the jury.

Not content with his denials to Judge Humpreyville at his sentencing, Parks spent his next few weeks in the Summit County Jail composing a feisty pamphlet in defense of his actions on the night of April 13. He took particular pains to excuse his treatment of Beatson's body, specifically the severing of his head:

If anybody thinks that it was not hateful to my feelings, they are very much mistaken. I conceived that that necessity of the case was in a great deal excusable; as much so as it is to dispose of the dead in the various ways that they do, in order to prevent them from injuring the living; and I shall here state, with all due respect to the feelings of others, that I think it does not matter what is done with a dead body, providing it does not injure the feelings of living friends.

After all, what was corpse abuse among reasonable people? Or as Parks put it:

The previous tyrannical conventionalism of society imposed the task upon me; I never sought for it, and did not like it. I may have sinned.
    Nay, I *have* sinned, but I have suffered, have repented, but I could not be forgiven. When will society cease to hunt a man down for one error? After punishing him with a penalty ten times greater than his office, they are not satisfied. How often is the law made the weapon of the vilest malignity and its penalties the most revenge!

Truly, on the basis of that statement alone, it could be said of Parks, as one Cleveland journalist did:

The man appears to have been an unusual character. He had traveled far and in strange places, and evidently might have developed into a strong and forceful character had it not been for his lack of ambition and his careless life.

Parks didn't spend all of his leisure hours in his Akron jail cell in flowery composition. Treated with great leniency by Sheriff Seward, Parks schemed with his brother-in-law George to effect his escape. Their plan was to smuggle Parks a saw—"not more than three-quarters of an inch broad"—and tools with which to make copies of the jail keys. But their letters were intercepted, and Parks soon found himself confined more closely. He then adopted a policy of surly noncooperation, which Deputy Sheriff George W. Mariner terminated with one good punch.

Duly convicted and sentenced to hang, Parks won an unexpected, indeed freakish, reprieve when his verdict was overturned by the Ohio Supreme Court. Parks's attorneys had appealed the verdict on several evidentiary grounds and also argued that one of his jurors, Frederick Newburgh, had expressed a conviction of Parks's guilt prior to the trial. But the Court ignored these arguments in granting Parks a new trial, instead just noting fussily that the jury's announcement of its verdict had only been "Guilty"—instead of the prescribed "Guilty of murder in the first degree." With a change of venue to Cuyahoga County to avoid severely inflamed local prejudice, the same evidence was presented to another 12 good men and true in March 1855 with the same result. With Judge Samuel Starkweather presiding, Samuel Williamson prosecuting, and lawyers Hiram Griswold and Amos Coe defending him, Parks's second trial was highlighted by the rhetorical forensics of County Prosecutor A. G. Riddle (later a U.S. congressman and intimate of James A. Garfield), whose closing speech against the accused drew the admiration of a worshipful *Cleveland Leader* reporter:

His argument was logical, his diction gorgeous, and his eloquence splendid. His reasoning was close and convincing, like that of Choate; his eloquence sublime, subduing, like that of Prentice. He possesses the powers to charm with eloquence and to ensnare the mind with his reasoning.

In spite of Riddle's persuasiveness, the jury took five hours to convict Parks on the first of the four capital counts against him, that he had murdered William Beatson by a stab in the neck with a knife. But it couldn't have been much consolation to Parks that the jury cleared him of the remaining capital charges. This time the jury foreman was careful to state "Guilty of murder in the first degree," and Judge Starkweather scheduled Parks's execution for the first Friday in June 1855.

Bitterly protesting his innocence, Parks schemed to the end to avoid his fate. A week before his scheduled execution, the head of a broken key was discovered in an inner door of the Cuyahoga County Jail cells. Interrogation of the prisoners disclosed that Parks had tried to bribe a fellow prisoner to obtain a key to expedite his escape. When pecuniary inducements failed, Parks threatened to kill the man unless he cooperated, and only the unexpected breaking of the key in the lock aborted the desperate plan. Then, the day before his scheduled execution, Parks tried once more to cheat the hangman. After remarking that he would soon see the recently deceased Czar Nicholas I of Russia and tell him just what he thought of Cleveland, Parks suddenly shouted, "This mortal man must die; you can't save me now!" and slashed his throat with a three-inch knife. Although he succeeded in gashing his jugular vein badly enough to spew "great jets of blood" about his cell, jail physician Dr. Robert Strong managed to stop the bleeding and preserve his patient for judicial death. Not that his patient was grateful for the reprieve: "God damn your miserable soul; let me alone!" is what Parks is reputed to have said as Strong and jail turnkeys struggled to subdue and pinion the suicidal prisoner. It is more than likely that Betsy Dickinson was the culprit who smuggled in the knife, although she was never prosecuted.

Parks conducted himself better on his last day, June 1, 1855. After asking Dr. Strong, a practicing phrenologist, to examine the bumps on his head, he donned a clean linen shirt. Insisting on his complete innocence to the last, he finished a final cigar and walked calmly from his cell to the scaffold at 11:54 a.m., accompanied by Sheriff Miller S. Spangler, Deputy Bosworth, and U.S. Marshal Jabez Fitch. Outside the jail, the Cleveland Grays maintained order as thousands scuffled for a look at the proceedings. The scaffold, built by J. M. Blackburn and placed in the jail hall facing Public Square, was a platform eight by five feet, about eight feet high and surmounted by an eight-foot frame for the gallows proper. It would be used to hang six more men in Cuyahoga County over the next 24 years, not to mention several from other counties. There, after a restorative glass of wine, Parks sat in a chair with a rope around his waist while he was permitted to speak to the crowd of 40 persons assembled in the jail yard, the fortunate few culled from the many thronging Public Square. Parks had flirted with the notion of taking chloroform to help him face the ordeal of his hanging, but there is no evidence that he did.

Parks's oration was described by commentators as short—but that must have been only by the heroic standards of the age, as it seems to have lasted for over an hour. After fulsomely thanking his lawyers and various law officials, he swore that he had been misrepresented by the press, insisting one final time that his version of Beatson's death was accurate in every detail and that "as I stand before my God, I speak the truth." Speaking of his aged parents in England, he begged that they not be informed of his disgraceful end and spoke with feeling of his infant child and dear wife: "I had never known her virtues had it not been for my sad misfortunes." At this juncture, so moved was his crowd of witnesses, that the proceedings were interrupted so a collection could be taken up for the impending Widow Parks. It yielded $44.60, and Parks continued in his understandably lachrymose vein:

> I assure you that I do not deserve this fate. No man has a kinder disposition, no one whose life is freer from cruel acts. . . . I leave the world at peace with all mankind, without censure upon any one.

Concluding his remarks about 1 p.m. with the words "I prepare to meet my God," Parks sipped another glass of wine while his hands and feet were bound and the rope secured around his neck. Granted permission to give the death signal, he waited patiently while a white cap was placed over his head, and then, at 1:04 p.m., he dropped his handkerchief, crying, "I die an innocent man!" A second later, the drop opened, and he plummeted six feet down through it like a stone.

There was no evidence of struggle or pain, and when the corpse was cut down at 1:40 p.m. Drs. Strong and Cleveland found that the neck had been cleanly broken by the drop. In deference to his last wishes, Parks's body was removed from the view of the gawking crowd, given a fresh shave, prepared for burial, and turned over to his grieving widow. Along with the legacy of $44.60, Parks left the following literary legacy, a poem he confided to a friend. Suffice it to say that it bears comparison with the jailhouse effusions of Dr. John Hughes (see the author's "In the Name of Violated Chastity" in *The Corpse in the Cellar* for the history of this eminent Cleveland murderer), Charlie McGill ("Shootin' and Shootin' and Shootin'" in the same volume), or even the seemingly inimitable Joseph "Specs" Russell:

> Sweet bud of the wild wood—emblem of all
> That remains in this desolate heart
> The fabric of bliss to its center must fall
> But patience shall never depart.
> Through the wilds of enchantment all vernal and bright
> Were the days of delusion when fancies entwined
> They are vanishing phantoms of love and delight
> That abandon my soul like a dream of the night
> And leave but a desert behind.
>
> Be hushed my dark spirit—for wisdom condemns
> When the faint and the feeble deplore,
> I'll be strong as the rock of the ocean that stems
> A thousand wild waves on the shore;
> Through the perils of chance and the scowls of disdain,
> May my front be unaltered and courage elate;
> Nay, even the name I have worshipped, in vain
> Shall bear not the sight of remembrance again;
> To bear, is to conquer my fate.

As always in such cases, Parks's execution elicited misplaced compassion in the bosoms of those whom H. L. Mencken once acidly characterized as "little old ladies of both sexes." One of them was Miss Louisa Reeder, accurately described by the Cleveland *Plain Dealer* as "a lady of lively sensibilities and rare abilities as a writer." She ended her anguished poetic meditation on the appropriate religious note expected by her Victorian readers:

> Tell him how fast the sands of time,
> Are speeding in the glass,

And then how dark the valley's gloom,
Through which his soul must pass,
And bid him e're he enters it,
To breathe a prayer above,
And though his crime's a fearful one,
We know that GOD is Love.

Only two more comments need be appended to afford a balanced measure of the pathetic James Dickinson Parks. One is his own self-serving lament, a final apologia written just before his execution and intended as his manifesto to a misunderstanding and murderous world:

When I meet Christ in the Kingdom of Heaven, he will congratulate me, for my case is parallel with his, with only a little exception. There were only two false witnesses against him; and there were some twenty that were false witnesses against me: but I attribute that to the alteration of the statutes and the increase of population since Christ's time; for when he was tried they hunted the whole kingdom and could find but two . . . . They set up over Christ's head his accusation written thus: "This is Jesus, the King of the Jews"; but they will set up over my head, I suppose, my accusation, written thus: "This is James Parks, the murderer." But it may all be true of Christ; but it is a lie concerning *me.*

The other comment came from the editorialist of the *Cleveland Herald* on the day after his hanging. Noting Parks's protestations of innocence in the face of overwhelming circumstantial evidence and his inability or unwillingness to explain his motives, the editorialist opined sourly on his conduct in the shadow of the gallows:

A desire for notoriety, an itching desire to have his name continually in the papers, has characterized him for the last two years. That his nature was brutal, every circumstance shows, while no action indicates the talent of the "accomplished villain," or any sympathy for humanity.

Actually, the last word belongs to Betsy Dickinson, who surely proved a hard woman to circumvent. After her husband's prosecution, she sued Cuyahoga County officials, demanding that the money taken from her in Utica during her April 1855 flight be returned. Her lawsuit dragged on for years, Cuyahoga officials arguing that the money really belonged to either Beatson's heirs or even the long-forgotten William Gee. But when the case was finally settled in September 1861, the money, nearly $1,000, was returned to the persistent Betsy Dickinson.

Chapter 5

OHIO CITY SHOOTOUT

The 1875 Murder of Michael Kick

Dedicated with awe and esteem to retired
Cleveland police officer Joan Patrici

More than 100 Northeast Ohio police officers have been killed in the line of duty since 1853, and most of their deaths are easy to explain. They died because evil men were willing to kill them, in hot blood or cold. That was a truism when John Howley slit watchman John Osborne's throat in 1853 and no less valid when Cleveland police officer Derek Owens was gunned down on February 29, 2008, while investigating four men drinking beer in an abandoned garage on Cleveland's East Side. Be that as it may, it is nonetheless true that many of those police murders were avoidable deaths. Some of those policemen died, if only in part, because they or the men commanding them made mistakes. The death of Patrolman Michael Kick in 1875 was just such a tragic but unnecessary death.

It all began on the morning of Sunday, May 9, 1875. L. A. Benton, a prosperous downtown jeweler, was in the habit of going to his Superior Street shop at the corner of Seneca Street (West 3rd Street) every Sunday morning. His purpose on this weekly errand was to wind his stock of pocket watches, lest they be damaged in running down. Benton saw nothing amiss as he entered the store that morning and, after locking the door behind him, went to his safe. Just as he pulled the door open, a man appeared behind him, sporting sandy whiskers and a black mask pulled over his face. Demanding that

Benton surrender to him, the man menaced him with a large bowie knife. Showing more courage than wisdom, Benton seized a nearby hatchet and swung at the robber. The latter dodged and struck Benton a terrific blow on his right arm. Even as the hatchet fell from the jeweler's grasp, another assailant came up behind Benton and hit him on the back of his head with some heavy object, cutting his scalp severely and bruising his skull. Seconds later, Benton was felled by another terrific blow and lost consciousness as he fell to the floor in a pool of his own blood.

Benton was out for at least two hours. When he regained consciousness, he was alone, and most of his more expensive wares (diamond rings, gold chains and some forty watches)—not to mention the diamond pin that adorned his bosom—had vanished with his assailants. Weak from loss of blood, Benton painfully crawled the hundred feet to the unlocked door of his store. Minutes later he was found there by Assistant Cleveland fire chief Harry Rebbeck, who summoned medical aid and some policemen from the nearby Central Police Station on Champlain Street (now the site of the Tower City complex). Superintendent of Police Jacob Schmitt's men eventually deduced that the thieves had entered Benton's store through a coal chute grating on Seneca Street and then simply waited for him to arrive. With no particular clues to follow, however, the police simply rounded up the usual suspects (three suspicious persons found on nearby streets) and hopefully awaited further developments.

They were not long in coming. That very night the same gang broke into N. G. Burns's school store at 190 Prospect Street and removed $16 worth of shoes. Minutes later, they smashed the front windows of Bent's Cigar Store on the corner of Prospect and Brownell Street (East 14th Street) but left without any valuables. The next night they resumed their larcenous spree, hitting several residences in the city, including that of a Mr. Sheldon on the corner of Franklin Avenue and Duane Street (West 32nd Street), where they purloined a lady's gold watch and bracelet worth $100. Early the next morning, Tuesday, May 11, the gang broke into the home of Mr. A. Bishop on the Heights (Tremont, then called "University Heights") and stole some expensive clothing.

Sometime that Tuesday, Cleveland police captain E. B. Gaffett at the 4th Precinct station on Detroit Street (just east of Pearl Street, now West 25th Street), became aware of a group of six suspicious strangers who had been hanging around for some days at John Ritenspacher's Wacht Am Rhein saloon at 490 Pearl Street (on the south side of the street near the corner of Columbus Street). Having no apparent occupation or visible means of support, these half dozen strangers habitually disappeared from the saloon around sunset, only to return by the dawn's early light. Acting on Gaffett's suspicions, Chief Schmitt ordered Detective Theobald Laubscher to put the Wacht Am Rhein under surveillance. Donning civilian clothes, 4th Precinct patrolmen George Floyd and Michael Kick began their stakeout of the saloon that night.

Tuesday and Wednesday nights passed uneventfully. By day the six suspects passed the time in the saloon drinking, dancing to the music of itinerant Italian street musicians, and flirting with teenage girls, two of them daughters of the complaisant John Ritenspacher. But each night,

A BOLD VILLAINY.

Benton's Jewelry Store Robbed in Broad Daylight,

And Six Thousand Dollars Worth of Goods Taken.

The Proprietor Terribly Injured in Its Accomplishment.

One of the most daring, and so far successful, robberies ever perpetrated in Cleveland was committed yesterday forenoon in the jewelry store of Mr. L. A. Benton, on the corner of Superior and Seneca streets, the parties committing it getting away with some six or seven thousand dollars worth of jewelry and inflicting severe and dastardly injuries on the person of Mr. Benton. The full particulars of the robbery, and the attack which accompanied it, were furnished to a LEADER reporter by the sufferer immediately after the attack was discovered.

Cleveland Leader, May 10, 1875.

as the Forest City sun waned, the men would leave the saloon in two trios, only to return in the wee hours of the next morning. By Thursday afternoon, Laubscher was convinced that the men under surveillance were the gang responsible for the Benton outrage and the other burglaries. That afternoon he persuaded Chief Schmitt to authorize a reinforcement of six uniformed officers. Schmitt's orders were clear: Laubscher's six officers were to remain out of sight at a location near Clark Avenue, several blocks south of the saloon, until they received a signal from Floyd and Kick to come up and join them in pursuit of the suspects.

That was the plan. Why and how it went wrong is still murky—

but the plan soon fatally miscarried. It was a little before 8 that evening when Floyd and Kick saw the six suspects exit the Wacht Am
Rhein. This time three of them were carrying paper bundles under
their arms. More confusingly, they exited Ritenspacher's saloon in
three groups of two, rather than two threesomes. Worse yet, Laubscher's six officers failed to pick up the signal flashed by Kick and
Floyd as they left their stakeout to follow the sextet walking rapidly
north on Pearl Street. It would seem that Laubscher was largely to
blame for the confusion. Some minutes before the six men left he
had conferred with Floyd and Kick but had then returned to the six
officers at Clark Avenue. He did so, he later insisted, because he
was apprehensive that the officers would get tired of waiting and
return to the 4th Precinct station. As the next day's Cleveland *Plain
Dealer* editorialized, it "seems singular that officers on so important
a mission and under command of some detailed chief should leave
their posts without orders"—but such was Detective Laubscher's
public justification.

At some point the six suspects became aware that they were
being followed by Kick and Floyd. Floyd's subsequent, if unlikely,
story is that he and Kick successfully deceived their quarry until the
moment hostilities erupted. In any case, Kick and Floyd followed
the men at a discreet distance up Pearl Street and then turned with
them as they turned left and west up Franklin Avenue. There was
no sign of Laubscher's six men as the pursuers and pursued reached
Franklin Circle (West 28th Street), but Kick was persuaded, errone-
ously, that they were coming up fast in support. The six suspects
began to pull away fast, and a decision had to be made before they
got away.

The arrival of Patrolman William Hildebrand precipitated the
tragedy. By this time, Laubscher realized that Floyd and Kick had
left the saloon in hot pursuit, and his six officers, including Hildebrand, ran as fast as they could up Pearl Street. As they passed
Bridge Avenue, however, Hildebrand decided to take a shortcut,
and he arrived at Franklin Circle well ahead of his companions.
There he encountered Kick and Floyd. The three officers held a
hurried conference and decided to arrest the suspects immediately.
"Let's tackle 'em," said a confident Kick, and the trio moved in to

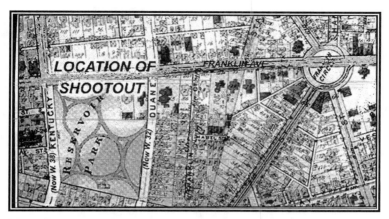

Map of the area where Patrolman Kick was fatally shot.

confront their prey in front of the Kentucky Street Reservoir on Franklin Avenue.

Given the relative correlation of forces, the outcome of the confrontation was predictable. Drawing their revolvers, Kick, Floyd, and Hildebrand called on the six men to surrender themselves. They replied by calling the officers "vile names." Seconds later, they brought out their bowie knives and revolvers, and shooting commenced in earnest.

There were at least a half dozen shots fired by each side. Kick was hit almost immediately by a bullet from the gang's apparent leader. Entering his body just below the heart, the bullet passed through his large and small intestines before stopping in his stomach. He fell to the street while both his fellow officers and the six robbers continued blasting away ineffectively with their weapons. Within a minute, the battle was over, as the robbers fled into nearby residential yards and Floyd and Hildebrand rushed to Kick's side.

It was a miracle any of the six suspects was caught. As Floyd and Hildebrand were deciding where to take the wounded Kick, Laubscher's other five men arrived and quickly dispersed in pursuit of the fleeing men. One of the pursuers was 4th Precinct patrolman John C. Miller. He was walking in front of the home of Dr. E. W. Robertson near Franklin Circle when the firing began. He had just noticed two men on Robertson's porch and was about to interrogate them when the first shots were heard. One of the men on the porch muttered, ""I'll bet that's Jim!" and then he and his companion vaulted a fence and set off running. It was while pursing this duo that Miller encountered a third man on Woodbine Street who fired at Miller unsuccessfully before the officer subdued him. Taken to the 4th Precinct station, Miller's captive initially stated that his name was James Moore, his age 26, and his nationality Canadian, and that he was a stonecutter newly arrived in Cleveland. After Floyd and Hildebrand identified him as one of the six men involved in the Kentucky Street Reservoir shootout, however, "a few vigorous measures" extorted his confession that he was one of six burglars in a gang that had come from Chicago.

Vigorous methods notwithstanding, Moore probably considered himself fortunate to be in police custody, as by the time he was jailed a mob from the aroused Ohio City neighborhood had gathered by the precinct station, and there was loud talk of hanging Kick's killers from the most convenient lamppost or tree. Several other men on the near West Side were also hauled into the station that night, but none of them were successfully implicated in the shooting melee at the Kentucky Street Reservoir.

Meanwhile, the dying Kick had been put in a carriage and taken to Dr. Robertson's office near Franklin Circle. Although in severe pain, he remained conscious, and when the police dragged "Moore" into Robertson's office at 11 p.m., he was able to identify him as one of the six suspects—but not as the man who shot him. Robertson's prognosis was swift and gloomy—Kick had only a few hours, at best a couple of days, to live—and Kick's family was summoned to his bedside for the inevitable.

Who was this Michael Kick, the victim of desperate criminals and his own poor tactical judgment? Like many of Cleveland's finest in that era, the 34-year-old Kick came from Germany. Born in Wurttemberg in 1841, he had come to the United States as a young man and lived in St. Louis until the Civil War. Enlisting in the 15th Army Regiment of the Missouri Volunteer Infantry, Kick served as his unit's color-bearer through 27 battles, many of them the fiercest of the war. After the war, he came to Cleveland and joined the police when it was organized as a metropolitan force in May 1866.

During the following decade Kick served the department honorably and was known as a valiant and honest officer.

Removed from Robertson's office to his own home on Myrtle Street (West 42nd Street), Kick lingered until Saturday, when he died at 2:40 p.m. of his internal wounds. Before expiring, he told his minister, the Reverend August Krause, that he was ready to leave this world. His funeral, two days later, was held with services at home, at the United Brethren in Christ Church on Orchard Street, and at his grave in Monroe Street Cemetery. The obsequies, conducted in German by the Reverend Krause, were an impressive spectacle, highlighted by a police parade from the precinct house to Myrtle Street, a standing-room-only throng at the church attended by department brass, and a large contingent of Odd Fellows in full regalia. Kick left a wife, Francisca, and four young children.

Meanwhile, the manhunt for his killers proceeded. Just minutes after the shooting at the reservoir, police officers raided Ritenspacher's dive on Pearl Street and subjected its residents to more "rigorous measures." Ritenspacher proved uncooperative, as did several of the dubious young women arrested with him. But after "James Moore" was brought there from his cell, Ritenspacher's daughters identified him as James Hyland, and Kick's probable killer as his brother, William Hyland. The police also discovered a great deal of stolen property in the saloon, most of which was traced back to the spate of burglaries that followed the Benton heist. The trail of the five fleeing burglars was eventually picked up in Elyria, but by that time the fugitives had hopped a westbound freight train and disappeared. Meanwhile, to the chagrin of the Cleveland police, the city's property crime wave continued unabated. On the night after Kick was shot there were several more burglaries, including a particularly shocking one at 41 Scovill Avenue. There, eight residents at the home of Jacob Stephen and George Menger were chloroformed by burglars while they slept. They groggily awoke the next morning to discover that their house had been emptied of valuables.

Between Ritenspacher's daughters and the captured Moore, Jacob Schmitt's men extracted enough information to send out a wanted circular for Kick's murderers on Monday, May 17. It announced a reward of $500 for apprehension of two of the gang,

William Hyland and Henry Hill, both of whom were charged with Kick's homicide. In those pre-Bertillon days, Hyland was described as "about five foot five or six inches high, sandy or reddish hair, curley [*sic*] if not cut short, freckled face, smooth, and about twenty years of age." Hill was more vividly sketched as "a short little fellow, smooth face, about twenty-three years of age, black hair, cut short, dark eyes. He has a peculiar walk, as if suffering from a broken or deformed leg."

Patrolman Michael Kick.

It would be gratifying to record that the assassins of Michael Kick were soon hunted down and made to pay the supreme penalty of the law. But such was not the case. On May 20, James Hyland, the only gang member captured, was bound over to the Cuyahoga County Common Pleas Court on a charge of burglary, bail being fixed at a then-astronomical $8,000. The sum might as well have been $1 million: three weeks later, on June 13, "James Hyland"— if that was truly his name—escaped from the notoriously porous Cuyahoga County Jail in a mass jailbreak of no fewer than 16 prisoners.

Hyland and the surviving members of his gang eventually gravitated to San Francisco, where they resumed their criminal ways. On April 19, 1876, the Cleveland Police Board was notified that the San Francisco authorities had captured and convicted all six of the Kick murder suspects on various charges and sentenced them to hefty prison terms. In light of this communication, the Cleveland Police Board nolled any further prosecution of the supposed murderers of Patrolman Michael Kick. And that was the end of the matter, except for the passage of a Police Board resolution expressing sympathy to Kick's bereaved family and a poem written by Sergeant William Thompkins of the 7th police precinct to memorialize his fellow officer:

LINES FROM A BROTHER OFFICER
This deed of darkness stands almost alone
For which no human sacrifice can e'er atone;
The victim, a man untainted, without blot,
The crime and sequel ne'er to be forgot.
Justly avenged, indeed, it never can;
Poor satisfaction had we—man for man.
The slain a man in image of his God;
The fiend a wretch reeking with human blood.
Kick lived to adorn the position that he filled,
Courteous to all and kind to the self-willed,
True to his duties, e'er guarding well his post,
At his death do mourn a numerous host.

Michael Kick's name is inscribed on the National Law Enforcement Officers' Memorial Wall in Judiciary Square, Washington, D.C. (Panel 52, West Wall, Line 4). There is no trace of his bloody martyrdom in Cleveland, and no more is known of his life or death. Since his long-ago demise there has been unproven speculation that the men responsible for his death were cohorts of the infamous "Blinky" Morgan, who later, in 1887, murdered Cleveland police detective William Hulligan in Ravenna. (For the history of this legendary outlaw see the author's "Bring Out Your Man!" in *The Maniac in the Bushes*). But in 1881, there was one additional echo to the Kick murder. Life had been deteriorating for Detective Theobald Laubscher for some time before he went missing on Halloween morning that year. Always conscientious, the methodical Laubscher had become noticeably brooding and obsessive in the weeks before he failed to return home on October 31. No doubt one of the subjects of his morbid preoccupation was his fateful decision to leave the Wacht Am Rhein stakeout on the night of May 13, six years before. As is usually the case with troubled policemen, his colleagues were not surprised when he turned up missing, and the search for his body began at once. They found him at the foot of McCart Street, just outside the city limits on the Lake Erie shore of West Cleveland, then a suburb containing most of the area west of Gordon Avenue (West 65th Street). Laubscher had shot himself in the head with his service revolver. He left a wife, six children, and an unblemished reputation as a brave and conscientious officer. Like Michael Kick, he had come from Germany, where he had been imprisoned for his actions during the revolutionary upheaval of 1848. Escaping from a Bavarian prison, he had come to America and served bravely in the Civil War before donning Badge #1 of the Cleveland police force in 1866. The tribute rendered him at the time of his death by Cleveland Police Department deputy superintendent James MacMahon, might well serve as an epitaph for all the psychologically overstressed policemen of any era, including ours:

> I was looking for something like this a long time back. I could see that his mind was becoming clouded and that he was not the man he used to be. He overtaxed himself with business. He allowed people to rap him up all hours of the night with the most trivial matters. He took the responsibility of the entire force on his shoulders. I often cautioned him to shake off the weight of responsibility that he carried, but he was of that peculiar temperament that he could not.

Chapter 6

CLEVELAND'S FIRST DISASTERS

I. The Perils of Ben, and His Startling Escape

Unsurprisingly, little is known of Cleveland's black residents before the Civil War. Indeed, more ink has likely been spilled chronicling the area's white abolitionists and their admirable activities—the Wellington slave rescue episode comes to mind—than the free and slave African Americans who make infrequent but tantalizing appearances in the annals of the Forest City. An exception to this rule, however, is Ben, almost invariably identified as "Ben, an escaped slave" in the handful of historical accounts in which he appears. He deserves more mention, for he had starring roles in both Cleveland's first disaster and Cleveland's first anti-slavery adventure.

The personal odyssey that brought Ben from the slave states to Northeast Ohio during the first decade of the 19th century is unknown. But it is a fact that he made his entrance on history's stage on a spring Friday in 1806. A canoe carrying a Mr. Hunter, his wife, their child, a young black boy, and "Ben, an escaped slave," was upset in Lake Erie by a northwest squall, just off the cliffs of the future suburb of Lakewood. All the passengers initially escaped to shore, where they desperately clung to rocks at the foot of the cliff. But the cold, wet tempest continued for several days, and the children died on Saturday, the mother expired the following day, and the father on Monday. Only Ben survived, desperately clinging to the upper part of a tree that had half fallen into the water. Found there nearly naked on Tuesday by French traders from Detroit, Ben was barely conscious by the time he was rescued, and his limbs were so badly frostbitten that he eventually lost all of his toes. That mutilation and the effects of rheumatism induced by his ordeal reduced him to the status of a half cripple, hobbling for the rest of his life. But he was alive, and it was also his unpredictable and ironic fate to be taken by his rescuers to the inn of Cleveland resident Lorenzo Carter, pioneer Cleveland's most prestigious citizen and, notwithstanding Moses Cleaveland's undeserved repute, the true founder of the Forest City.

At first glance, Major Carter must have seemed a most unlikely benefactor for Ben, or any black person at all. Although an outspoken advocate of "liberty," Carter was a creature of his times, and his only recorded opinion on blacks was the succinct comment: "I hate negroes and do not want them about me." But Major Carter was one of those conflicted persons who find it easy to hate people in the abstract but difficult to mistreat when encountered as individuals. The upshot of this not uncommon cognitive dissonance was that he not only willingly took Ben into his abode but lavished tender care on him as he painfully recovered throughout the spring, summer, and fall of 1806. Nor did Major Carter pay any mind to the strictures of a draconian Ohio law passed by the state legislature just two years that minced no words about the Buckeye State's abhorrence for just such persons as Ben, the escaped slave. It provided that:

> No black or mulatto person shall be permitted to settle or reside in this state unless he or she shall first procure a fair certificate from some court within the United States of his or her actual freedom; and every such person shall have such certificate recorded in the clerk's office in the county in which he or she intends to reside

Additional laws passed that same year mandated substantial fines for any white scofflaw foolish enough to employ, "harbor or secrete" any black lacking such a certificate.

Although it would be inaccurate, at best, to say that Ben had landed on his feet, all went well for him until October 1806. One fine day that month two men from Kentucky stopped by Amos Spafford's house in Cleveland (at what would later be the southeast corner of Superior Street and Vineyard Lane, now approximately where the Detroit-Superior Bridge has its eastern terminus). They told Spafford that Ben was an escaped slave, and one of them claimed to be his owner. Spafford sent them to Carter, who frankly admitted both his tender treatment of Ben and his hatred of blacks. But Carter also told the alleged owner that he virulently detested slavery and would not willingly abet sending Ben back to involuntary servitude. Ben's owner blandly reassured Carter that he had no intention of coercing the slave, as he was certain that Ben loved him and had only been lured to freedom by bad counsel from a wicked companion. All he wished for was a face-to-face meeting with Ben, after which he was convinced that he would voluntarily return with him to Kentucky.

Lorenzo Carter, *Plain Dealer Sunday Magazine*, November 2, 1907.

After several meetings with the two slave catchers, Carter finally agreed to let Ben get close enough to talk to them. The plan was to have Ben stand and speak on the west side of the Cuyahoga River (a wooded plot later owned by Joel Scranton) while his owner stood across him and talked on the east side (not far from the end of Huron Street). Their ensuing dialogue, at least the part overheard by Cleveland eyewitness Ashbel Walworth, went better than one might have expected and was entirely civil on both sides. Ben even agreed with his master's claim that he had "always used you well, and treated you as well as the rest of my family." Sadly nothing more is known of the rest of conversation except its astonishing result. It came the next morning, when a pacific Ben and the two Kentuck-

Sketch of the Cuyahoga River mouth and Lorenzo Carter's
Cabin, *Plain Dealer*, June 16, 1907.

ians mounted horses at Carter's tavern and set off for the return to
Kentucky. Even more surprising than Ben's unexpected decision,
perhaps, was Carter's apparent indifference at the prospect of his
protégé reentering servitude.

Or perhaps not so surprising. Major Carter was a wily man,
and whether he took a direct hand in what next ensued may be
confidently surmised if not utterly proven. James Geer and John
Thompson, two of the Carter tavern's more notorious layabouts,
were also privy to Ben's situation and decided to do something
about it. So sometime that afternoon, as Ben and his captors trotted
down the Carter Road, about three miles out of Newburgh Mills,
two men, armed with rifles and with faces masked, came out of the
woods and accosted them. The dialogue was brief, one sided, and to
the point. One of the masked men said to the erstwhile slave, "Ben,
you damned fool, jump off of that horse and take to the woods!"
Ben didn't wait for further instruction. Leaping from his horse, he
scurried into the woods, while the two slave catchers, unpursued,
galloped away.

Little certain is known of Ben's subsequent fate. Sometime that following winter, one of Major Spafford's sons and a brother of Nathan Perry Jr. got lost in the woods on the west side of the Cuyahoga River. Stumbling through the forest, who should they meet but Ben, who told them he was living like a hermit in a sylvan hovel, probably in what is now either Brecksville or Independence township. After swearing the two hunters to secrecy, Ben bid them farewell and disappeared back into the woods. He was never heard from again, although it was generally assumed that he eventually found his way to permanent freedom in Canada. An alternate legend states that he remained in Brecksville for the rest of his days, which would easily make him the township's earliest non–Native American resident.

II. A Tragic Voyage

Early Cleveland was a rustic place with simple needs and a basic economy. So in 1808, when rumors that Lake Erie yellow catfish abounded in the mouth of the Maumee River reached the Cleveland settlement (which would not gain even village status until 1814), the response was quick and enthusiastic. Captain Joseph Plumb of Newburgh took the lead, outfitting a suitable bateau (a small, shallow-draft, flat-bottomed sailing craft of variable size) and recruiting a crew to accompany him on a fishing expedition. The company included Stephen Gilbert (husband of Chloe Spafford Gilbert, daughter of pioneer Cleveland surveyor and mapmaker Amos Spafford); Spafford's son Adolphus; a young man of Newburgh named White, age 18; mail carrier William Gilmore; and Captain Plumb's two sons, 16 and 14 years old. Also aboard was a passenger Mary Billinger, 45, en route to her new home just east of the Lorain River mouth, where she was slated to become a housekeeper for Nathan Perry, a 20-year-old farmer, ferryman, and Indian trader.

Boarding the bateau in Cleveland on April 18, the crew sailed to the Rocky River, where they anchored and spent the night. Inventorying their fishing gear, they realized they had forgotten to pack seine tackle. Without it, their fishing expedition would flop, so

White and Plumb's two sons were forthwith sent back to Cleveland on foot to retrieve it. The plan was that if they speedily returned, they would sail from the Rocky River with the rest of the crew; if not, they would reunite at Perry's Black River store. As fate would have it, they were tardy in their return, and they got back to the Rocky River only to discover that the bateau had left without them. Disappointed, tired, and hungry, they commenced the long trudge to the Black River.

As the weary trio trekked west that afternoon the wind began to pick up. Soon after that, a storm broke, and they watched and cowered from the shoreline cliffs as it churned the lake into a terrifying maelstrom of wind and waves. The tempest abating, they continued on, climbing an old Indian trail that followed the cliff line west past Dover Point (now in Bay Village). Suddenly, as they looked to the right, they saw some objects floating in the lake. A closer view disclosed this flotsam as some empty casks, an oar, and other mundane objects. Their first reaction was to laugh, as they were unable to conceive that the bateau had suffered any mishap. But the laughter died on their lips as they took the next curve in the path and caught sight of the bateau. It was 70 feet below, wrecked on the rocks where the cliff met the lake, a site almost inaccessible from the path above. Beside the bateau was Captain Plumb, nearly more dead than alive. The only survivor of the wreck, he was nearly frozen and too weak to stand, much less walk.

But he could talk, and Captain Plumb's dreadful tale was quickly, if painfully, told to his auditors above. The day had waxed fine and fair after their Rocky River parting, and a light morning breeze had boded well for their passage around the perilously rocky waters off Dover Point before halting ashore to await White and the Plumb boys. And they had nearly passed the Point when a vicious lake squall suddenly hit them from the north, about a mile from shore. The first gust simply flipped the bateau over, hurling all of its passengers and cargo into the lake. The last anyone saw of Mary Billinger she was helplessly floating away on the bed she had brought for her new home.

Clinging to the steering oar, Plumb eventually heaved himself up onto the stern of the overturned boat. Wrapping his legs around its sides, he gripped his heels around the gunwales and held on for dear life as one titanic wave after another smashed over him. Eventually, he was joined on the capsized bateau by Gilbert, Gilmore, and Adolphus Spafford. All of them were washed off the overturned craft several times, only to struggle back to its precarious safety. At Gilbert's suggestion, they all stripped themselves naked, the better to swim to shore if chance allowed. But the relentless waves continued, and Gilbert saved Spafford once but was too weak to help him when he washed away a second time. Abandoning hope of reaching the bateau, Spafford swam to a floating cask and with it drifted westward, never to be seen alive again. Shortly after that, Gilbert let go of the bateau and made a desperate attempt to swim for shore. He never made it there alive.

Losing strength as the waves continued to pound, Gilmore realized he would be the next to die. Facing eternity, he spoke to Plumb of his parents and his old New England home and begged him to collect some fees due to him for carrying mail between the Vermilion and Huron Rivers. He also asked him to sell his rifle, his ax, and whatever other possessions remained and send the money to his aged father. Gilmore was still talking when a colossal wave yanked him off and down to death. Sometime after that the overturned bateau finally grounded herself and its last exhausted passenger on the beach.

Half dead or not, Plumb was still in command, and he ordered White and his 16-year-old son to go to the Black River and fetch back Nathan Perry and Quintus F. Atkins, Gilmore's associate mail carrier. They immediately departed, leaving Plumb's younger son to look after the Captain and keep watch from the high cliffs for rescuers. It was a wise division of labor, for the 14-year-old Plumb son soon proved his sterling mettle and pluck. Recalling that a whiskey chest from the bateau had washed ashore, he guessed that a dram or two of it might revive his father. The only problem was how to get it—as it remained below on the beach, a sheer drop of 70 feet. So, shimmying up a tall but thin ironwood sapling, the intrepid teenager waited until it bent far over the cliff, slid its entire length down to the end . . . and dropped the additional 30 feet to the beach. Unhurt, he procured the whiskey, and its restorative power and a vigorous body rub eventually revived his father. All that moonless night they watched and waited as the waves continued to pound the narrow strand of beach.

Meanwhile, White and Plumb's older son had arrived at Perry's Black River home about sunset, April 19. Although they expected to find Captain Plumb dead upon their return, they still needed to recover his body, so Perry's first task was to find a suitable length of strong rope. For lack of a better alternative, he finally pulled a long fishing line out of the river and stripped it of fishhooks. Leaving Perry's huge black dog, Bonaparte, to guard the Plumb boy, Perry, White, and Atkins lit hickory torches and began their nocturnal 18-mile trek back through the forest. Arriving at the Dover Point cliff at midnight they found the younger Plumb boy gone. Their first fear was that he had been eaten by wolves.

Still, they had to try. Bellowing to compete with the noise of the lake surf, they lit more torches and scoured the cliffs for several hours. Finally, they heard a faint voice coming from down below. So they lit a fire and cut a forked tree, stripping it of its bark and then anchoring it to the side of the cliff as a rope guide. Fastening a torch to the rope, they carefully lowered it down until it dropped onto the beach. Seconds later, someone picked it up, and by its flickering light they could see Captain Plumb and his son below.

Using the anchored rope as a hoist, the trio at the top first pulled up the whiskey chest, followed by other flotsam from the bateau that had drifted onto the beach. Next they drew up young Plumb and his father after him. The latter was their supreme labor, as the captain weighed at least 220 pounds, and their hands were woefully blistered by the time they hauled his body to the top of the cliff.

The next morning brought more necessary and disagreeable tasks. The first priorities were to bring back the older Plumb boy from Perry's home and to find the missing, or at least their corpses. To these ends Perry and Atkins trekked westward. Scanning the coast as they walked, they soon found Stephen Gilbert's body on the beach and William Gilmore's corpse not far away. Laying them together on the sand, they covered them with a large coat and weighted it down with stones. Two miles farther west, they discovered Adolphus Spafford dead, his head and arms still on the beach, the rest of his body in the water. Dragging him ashore, they covered him with a flour sack and more stones and marked the spot with a pole. Four more miles brought them to Mary Billinger's body. Covering it with some of the bedding she had intended for her new home, they set up another marker and continued on their way west.

Carrier Atkins's lot was not an easy one. Technically, he was employed by Nathan Perry, and he had to perform whatever work assigned to him by the enterprising young man. Retrieving the bodies was a burdensome enough task, but it was his bad luck that day, as they were walking along the cliff path, that Perry spied one of his own chests on the beach below, one he had commissioned Mary to bring to her new home. It must have been rather unpleasant for Atkins, whose already blistered hands were now further tortured by the agony of hoisting Perry down to the beach and then pulling both him and his precious chest back up.

Captain Plumb, his younger son, and Mr. White had, perhaps, the more unenviable task, which was to take the terrible news back to Cleveland. Its impact was devastating to the residents of that small, compact society, especially the Spafford-Gilbert clan, which had lost both husband and son. A sailboat from Cleveland later retrieved the bodies from their improvised beach cairns and brought them back for burial in the old Ontario Street Cemetery, now covered by the southern end of the old May Company store. Stephen Gilbert and Adolphus Spafford were eventually reburied in the Erie Street Cemetery, where their graves may be seen to this day. Mary Billinger's body was not found until some time later, when it was taken by canoe to the Black River and buried on the east bank by Nathan Perry Jr., his father, and Quintus Atkins. An early Cleveland historian would note that 11 of the first 18 deaths during the first 12 years of Cleveland's existence were by drowning.

Chapter 7

MURDER ON THE SHAKER ROAD

The Strange Deaths of John and Josiah White

There are some Cleveland murder stories so wonderfully macabre that they would be worth making up if they weren't true. The Shaker Road murder is one of them, rivaling in melodrama its later suburban rivals, the William Lowe Rice assassination, the Lakewood Kaber murder, and the interminable Sheppard case. And it all happened back in 1843 . . .

Josiah White was not a popular man. The owner of a commodious inn near the Shaker North Union Colony (between what are now Shaker and South Park Boulevards), he had settled there even before those peculiar religious visionaries emigrated to the "Valley of God's Pleasure" in 1822. A sullen, unpleasant man, he rebutted repeated Shaker offers to buy his property and more often than not failed to respond to even the most casual "Good morning." Still, he seemed to prosper during the third and fourth decades of the 19th century and it was easy see why. Cleveland was already a major market town with a population of some 6,000 as the 1840s rolled around, and White's inn was strategically located just nine miles away from it on the road that led to all towns eastward, including Gates Mills, Burton and Hudson. Farmers and drovers coming to Cleveland to market their produce or livestock found it convenient to spend the night there, coming or going—especially going, as White's tavern served sufficiently hard liquor to slake the thirsts of his hardworking and cash-heavy customers. And this success was achieved despite the disquieting rumors about White and his inn in circulation by the early 1840s. Some of them stemmed from his reckless gambling. Josiah liked his cards and dice, and as the years went by, he lost more and more money to his nightly guests.

By 1843, Josiah faced financial ruin and foreclosure, although his dire situation was unknown to most of his neighbors. It wasn't just the gambling, although it became more frenzied as he sank ever deeper in debt. It was the manner of his play, which eventually triggered rumors of loaded dice and cards that were marked. Worse yet came uglier gossip regarding guests complaining that they were being robbed of small amounts of money while they slept in the White inn guest rooms.

The arrival of John Wilmont at White's inn on the evening of September 6, 1843, provoked the final act in the White tragedy. A well-to-do farmer and cattleman, Wilmont had driven his herd to Cleveland and sold it the previous day. Flush with cash, he spent a little of his money in the city but still retained most of it in the money belt around his waist when he arrived at the inn.

Wilmont was a hearty fellow, and he had begun drinking before he left Cleveland on the morning of the 6th. Too tired to go on, he decided to spend a night at the inn and return to Gates Mills on the 7th. Stabling his horse, he went into the tavern and ordered a drink from White. Wilmont probably thought little of it as he plucked at his belt, momentarily disclosing its contents as he opened it up to get a coin for his drink. But White thought much of it, although he said nothing as he showed Wilmont to a second-floor bedroom and bade him a good night.

Exhausted and tipsy, Wilmont placed his money belt under his pillow and soon fell asleep. He would later recall that he had slept for about two hours before he was abruptly awakened by a noise at the window. Getting his pistol out, he stealthily made his way to the window and looked out. Peering down, he could just make out the form of a young man who was attempting to get to the inn's upper story by way of a porch pillar. He eventually succeeded, pulled himself up on the roof, and then, using a piece of iron, tried to pry open the window. The still sleepy and hung over Wilmont was much bewildered as to his course of action. He didn't want to shoot

Plain Dealer Sunday Magazine, July 15, 1906.

an apparently unarmed man, but he didn't want to be robbed, either. So he sidled over to a clothes press against the wall and hid himself inside it, with its door cracked just enough to keep the room under surveillance and his pistol at the ready.

Wilmont was completely unprepared for what happened next. Instead of moving toward the bed, the young man sat down on a chair, stripped off his shoes and clothes, folded the latter carefully, and placed them on a second chair. Then, without further prelude, he leaped into the bed, pulled the sheet over his head, and quickly fell asleep. Within minutes he was snoring loudly.

Inside the clothes press, the cautious Wilmont was still wondering what to do when he heard footsteps ascending the stairs to the second floor. The footsteps continued to his door, followed by the noise of someone trying the door with a key. The attempt failed, as Wilmont's key was on the other side and could not be displaced. Then, as Wilmont watched and listened, something snapped—apparently a secret hinge that made it possible to open the door even when locked—and a dark figure entered the room. The figure stood motionless for a minute, as Wilmont struggled vainly to hear something it was muttering under its breath. Then, as Wilmont gaped in shock, the figure turned around to reveal the person of Josiah White. He held a butcher knife, and after a moment's further hesitation to calm his shaking hand, White brought the knife down and stabbed the sleeping man under the sheets in the heart. Wilmont promptly fainted dead away.

Wilmont never knew how long he was out, but when he awoke both White and the sleeping man had vanished. Staggering out of the clothes press, he crept to the bed, hoping that it had all been but a grotesque dream. Then, in the moonlight, he saw the pool of blood at the center of the bedsheets. Throwing his clothes on, he ran to the window, dropped to the roof, then to the ground, and starting running as fast as he was able. Leaving his horse behind in his panic, he didn't stop running until he got to Doan's Corners (East 105th Street and Euclid Avenue), four miles away. Awakening its residents, he blurted out his horrible story and demanded that White be apprehended before he had a chance to flee. His listeners were at first dubious, but they eventually put together an armed posse and started toward White's inn to sort things out.

What they encountered there was dreadful even beyond the gothic surmises suggested by Wilmont's horror story. As they neared the inn, they could hear the unmistakable sounds of a man in anguish, sobbing and crying. Drawing closer, they recognized the voice of Josiah White. And what he was sobbing was these words: "Jack! My son! Come back to me, Jack! I didn't mean to do it! Before God, I didn't, Jack! Speak to me, for God's sake, speak!" In that instant the posse members realized the awful truth: Josiah White, intending to murder Wilmont for his money, had mistakenly killed his own son.

The denouement was quick and violent. Trying the inn door, the posse found it locked and bolted. Pounding on it with rifle butts, they shouted, "Let us in or we'll break down the door!" An instant later, Josiah's livid face appeared at a window, then disappeared. The posse had almost smashed the door to pieces when it suddenly opened to disclose Josiah White with a pistol in his hand. Two men leaped for him, but it was too late. Putting the pistol to his head, he blew out his brains and fell lifeless into their arms.

The story behind John White's unintentional murder was a simple one. Drinking heavily in Cleveland the very night that Wilmont came to his father's inn, Jack had arrived home late, tipsy and quite fearful of alerting his father to his condition. Thinking that Wilmont's room was unoccupied, he scaled the porch pillar, opened the second-floor window, and flopped into bed for the night. Josiah had not realized it was his son that he'd killed until he dragged the corpse out to the back of the inn for clandestine burial. It was believed that he spent some hours weeping by his son's body before the posse showed up.

That was the end of the infamous White inn on the old Shaker Road. The Shakers, sympathetic to all human frailties, buried the Whites in their own cemetery. Following the inevitable foreclosure on White's property, the Shakers purchased it and kept it until 1889, when they resettled their Cleveland-area believers in Lebanon, Ohio, and other locales. The old White inn was still used as a general store into the late 19th century and then stood vacant for some years until it was torn down. Eventually, like the rest of the future Shaker Heights, it was acquired for development as a garden suburb during the first decade of the 20th century by the Van Sweringen brothers.

Chapter 8

FIREMAN'S FIREMAN

The George Wallace Legend

Like most large American cities, Cleveland has produced its share—probably more than its share—of firefighting heroes. But surely none was braver or more revered than George Alexander Wallace, its legendary chief. And no wonder, for his exemplary character and courage were matched by a longevity and physical toughness that never faltered throughout an incredible career that began in 1869—just four years after the American Civil War—and ended in 1931, only a year before the election of Franklin D. Roosevelt. Over his six decades plus of service the Cleveland Fire Department evolved from a virtual social club of enthusiastic "fire-eaters" into an elite cadre of highly trained specialists, and no one epitomized or personified that transformation more splendidly than the "Old Man in the White Helmet" himself. Joining a small corps of 73 men using horse-drawn equipment and hand-pumped water engines, Wallace spent the next half century and more struggling to make the Cleveland Fire Department what it was by the time he left it: a technically sophisticated force of 1,034 men using the most modern equipment available. Along the way he became a Cleveland legend (a global one among firefighters), and both the oldest and longest-serving professional fireman in the world.

Born in Erie, Pennsylvania, on February 22, 1848, Wallace took his names from fellow birthday boy George Washington and Alexander the Great. During the many birthday interviews that became an annual fixture in Cleveland newspapers during the 1920s and 1930s, Wallace would pridefully recall that his birthplace had previously served as Oliver Hazard Perry's military headquarters in

1813, the house where the Commodore planned the naval campaign that culminated in his stunning victory over a British fleet at Put-in-Bay. Shortly before his death in 1940, Wallace was contacted by a breathless Pennsylvania reporter who informed the aged firefighter that he had discovered a secret underground chamber at Wallace's old Erie home, presumably a clandestine lair used by Perry for su-persecret conferences. An amused Wallace gently told him that the subterranean lair was only his mother's water cistern, which the aged chief well remembered from the days when it was his task to pump it out during his mother's wash days.

In 1854, when Wallace was six years old, his parents, George and Margaret Hendrickson Wallace, moved to Cleveland. Although he left school when he was 14, George acquired a pretty solid primary education during several stints in Cleveland's rudimentary primary schools, including terms at a facility at Alabama (East 26th) and St. Clair Streets, the old Rockwell Street School, and the Eagle Street School. Wallace would always associate the latter with his most vivid recollection of the Civil War. Shortly after the outbreak of hostilities in April 1861, Wallace, 13, was outside the school with his classmates, watching as a company of new Union Army recruits marched up Woodland Avenue toward their campground at Woodland and Sterling Avenue (East 30th Street). Supposing it an amusing lark, George and his companions suddenly shouted, "Hur-rah for Jeff Davis" as the boys in blue strutted by. An instant later the enraged soldiers broke ranks and began chasing Wallace and his fellow miscreants down the street. The panicked youngsters took to their heels in all directions. Even in his 90s, Wallace could remem-ber his terror as he hid under a school desk, cowering with terror as the school building shook under the feet of the pursing soldiers.

Adolescent boys will always find interesting places to hang around, and George Wallace was no exception to the rule. Dur-ing his youth in the 1850s, three most alluring social magnets for restless young males were the livery stable, the railroad depot, and the volunteer fire station—and it was the last which early capti-vated George Wallace for life. He learned soon after his arrival in Cleveland that the ringing of the bell of the First Baptist Church at the corner of Champlain (now covered by the Terminal Tower

complex) and Seneca (West 3rd Street) meant there was a fire some-
place and that all of Cleveland's hundreds of volunteer firemen
were going into action. Rushing to their particular firehouses, the
men of the various engine companies (Eagle No. 1, Forest City No.
2, Saratoga, Phoenix, Cataract, Red Jacket) and hose units (Alert
and Protection) would hastily trundle out their hand-pumped water
engines and drag them with ropes to the scene of the fire. Almost
invariably, the firemen were accompanied, and often outnumbered,
on their journey by an excited, screaming mob of men, women, and
children, all anxious to view the free entertainment of a public conflagration. Throughout his lengthy life and career, Wallace would
often recall that his youthful attraction to fires was a love at first
sight that endured forever. As he told an interviewer in 1912:

> I have always been an enthusiastic fireman; there is some ex-
> citement about it that attracted me in the first place and made
> me choose it as a life work and business, and the excitement
> and liking have continued and held.

It wasn't just the primitive and obvious thrills of leaping flames,
perilous hazards, and death-defying deeds that drew young Wallace
to the firefighting life. He also recognized, even as a teenager, the
special bonds of bravery and sacrifice that cemented firemen into a
brotherhood apart. He may, too, have been initially lured by a more
concrete benefit incident to hanging around the firehouse. Each volunteer unit held a monthly meeting, which was usually followed by
enthusiastic attention to the contents of a beer keg. Young George
was delighted to discover that he could usually count on a couple of
glasses of free beer after the volunteers had drunk their fill. It is not
known whether Wallace ever joined in the more boisterous antics
of his volunteer patrons and role models. When mere roistering
failed to suffice, such companies sometimes battled in the streets
with their rivals. During one such set-to, men from one unit burned
a rival firehouse at Water and Frankfort Avenues to the ground.

Not all of Wallace's youthful encounters with firemen were of
a benign nature. One night during the early days of the Civil War,
a structure on Ontario Street caught on fire. As it contained the of-

fices of *The Spy,* a scandal sheet published by a Mrs. Frederick that contained scurrilous gossip about prominent Cleveland citizens, it was probably an arson job. Be that as it may, George and one of his chums were in the vicinity when the first chimes of the Baptist Church bell informed them of a fire in the offing. Running to the nearest firehouse before any volunteers arrived, the two teenagers took it upon themselves to roll out a pumping engine—they weighed between one and three tons—and try to pull it down the street. But it was too heavy, and they were soon interrupted by a real fireman, a gigantic tinsmith, who shouted, "Get out of here!" and gave each of them a hearty kick. "That fellow almost kicked me humpbacked!" Wallace would recall six and a half decades later. But the burly tinsmith, too, was unable to move the engine, and when he begged the boys to help they jeered at him and ran away.

In 1863, the year after George quit school, Cleveland's volunteer fire companies were abolished, and a professional city department was organized. Too young to become a fireman, George took a job as a brakeman on the Cleveland & Toledo Railroad (later part of the Lake Shore & Michigan Southern line). But his first passion remained firefighting, and his long-deferred dream came true on June 1, 1869, when Wallace joined the Cleveland Fire Department as a 2nd Class Fireman at the No. 2 Firehouse on Champlain Street.

Wallace's real initiation into his profession came just two days later, when he manned a hose at a fire in the Farnam & Searles oil refinery works on Canal Street. In 1931 he dismissed it casually as "not much of a fire," but the old firedog was being characteristically modest. The blaze, in fact, was a huge gasoline fire that destroyed the entire (uninsured) oil works and spilled a large quantity of burning oil into the canal and thence to the Cuyahoga River—not the last time that watercourse would be in flames. Wallace, in his blasé dismissal of the Canal Street conflagration, may also have been comparing it to his next big fire, which occurred only a month later, on July 15. Ignited by the gas lamp of a careless Atlantic & Great Western Railroad (later Erie Railroad) employee, a fire in an oil tanker car on the tracks spread to 42 other tank cars, which burned right down to the wheels for a loss of $50,000.

Wallace soon proved himself a born fireman, and his superiors

Chief George Alexander Wallace.

were quick to recognize his dedication and talent for the work. In 1873 he was made captain of Hook & Ladder Company No. 4. Only a year later, he was promoted to captain of Hook & Ladder Company No. 1. (It is worth noting that Wallace's chief task as captain was to insure that his engines always had a full head of steam. This necessitated his being on duty at all times, especially as his underlings were wont to while away the hours of waiting for an alarm by drinking in conveniently located saloons.) It was during his tenure as the number-one captain that he first came to the notice of many Clevelanders. In 1881, during the public obsequies for assassinated president James A. Garfield, Wallace led the men of his company in draping civic buildings in black, and he supervised the building of the catafalque that supported Garfield's casket while it rested in Public Square. Wallace also attained modest local fame as a champion walker, a popular public sport in the early 1870s. On March 30, 1872, the Cleveland *Plain Dealer* reported that George Wallace, "driver of fire engine 5's hose cart," had announced that he would dare to walk from his engine house on Phelps Street to the Fire Department headquarters on St. Clair near Bank (East 6th) Street in just 35 minutes. He further boasted that he would do so while pushing a wheelbarrow.

One wonders, though, how the young fireman had time for such stunts. When Wallace joined the force in 1869 there were *no* days off. After working for three months he requested some time off and was grudgingly granted it—four hours. Some years later the time-off policy was relaxed, with each fireman taking the tenth day off of his cycle. The catch was that if his company made a fire run on his day off, he would forfeit his next day off. Wallace would long rue the day he took a tenth day off and went out of town. When he returned the next day he discovered that his company had made three runs during his absence, and he didn't get another day off for forty days.

During these apprentice years Wallace discovered that the Cleveland journalists who covered the fires he fought likewise worked under the special constraints of their own profession. One day, after fighting a very minor factory fire, he was surprised to read in the *Cleveland Leader* account of the blaze that it had had caused $100 in damages. Confronting the author of the story, newspaperman J. H. Maddy, he insisted that the loss had been no more than $50. "It's like this," explained the abashed Maddy:

> I didn't get to ride to the department [to the fire] and had to hire a horse and buggy. Under the rule of the office, the loss had to be $100 or more in order to entitle a reporter to hire a rig, so you see I really had to make my estimate the limit to get under the wire.

Although Wallace would protest many times that he was "no politician," he made important and useful friends during his climb up the ladder of promotion. One of them was former fireman Nicholas Weidenkopf. Wallace failed in his first bid for the rank of Fifth Assistant Chief in 1881. His second and successful attempt came two years later, when Weidenkopf, now on the Cleveland Board of Fire Commissioners, championed his promotion. It took Wallace another ten years to make Third Assistant Chief, and he remained stuck in that position into the new century. Then, on March 4, 1901, Mayor John H. Farley appointed him chief of the entire department.

In Wallace's later glory years it would be charitably forgotten that Farley's choice did not elicit unanimous approval at the time. It was true that Wallace, by virtue of his 32 years' service, had a solid claim on the job by right of seniority, and from its earliest days the Fire Department had promoted solely on that basis. But the practice of promotion on the basis of civil service tests was gaining increasing favor as the Progressive movement gained traction— most of the executive positions below chief were subject to it, and Farley was honest enough to admit that Wallace would probably have not made the cut if he had submitted to a competitive exam. Wallace, for his part, never made any secret of his opposition to deciding a fireman's fate on the basis of a written exam. Experience, he believed, was the most important qualification for any firefighting job, and it is only fair to say that Wallace himself was the most impressive evidence of the truth of that belief. Moreover, Wallace had oodles of something else, a character trait he thought to be the most important quality in any fireman who aspired, as he did, to be a hero. As he once stated:

> People talk about courage, the heroism of firemen. Why, courage is nothing but pride. Nobody is brave who isn't proud. The man without pride is no good. It is pride that makes men ambitious and willing to labor and suffer in order to achieve.

Wallace never lost the pride that made him appear, in the words of an admirer, a "lion" among men. He also never forgot that the best firemen were also motivated by pride, and he followed an inflexible rule of never reprimanding a fireman in the presence of his peers. They in turn rewarded him with a degree of loyalty and obedience that was the envy of all other fire departments, and that allowed him to say, even at the end of his illustrious career:

> I have never known a fireman to flinch from obeying instantly when ordered into dangerous or uncomfortable duty.

Instead, my hardest trouble is keeping them from getting into unnecessary peril.

Experience and pride are crucial perquisites for a great fireman. But what earned Chief Wallace the nearly idolatrous admiration and affection of his men, and what made them unquestioningly risk death at his behest, was his leadership by example. During his 30 years as chief there wasn't a single major fire in Cleveland at which Wallace was not present, and, more often than not, at the point of maximum danger. Newton D. Baker, former Cleveland mayor and U.S. Secretary of War, astutely identified the core of Wallace's charisma when he spoke at his 1931 retirement fete:

There are two kinds of leadership—the "go on" and the "come on" type. Wallace was of this type. He never sent his men where he wouldn't go himself. There hasn't been a fireman in Cleveland in the last 50 years who hasn't looked at the most dangerous spot expecting to see Wallace there.

Along with his pride, courage, and leadership came Wallace's firm commitment to discipline, a by-the-book zeal that many a rookie fireman had reason to remember during Wallace's reign. In his younger days, Wallace had been a bit lackadaisical about spit and polish, but his epiphany came sometime after John Bennett became chief in 1875. One day as he was walking through the No. 1 Firehouse Bennett noticed that Captain Wallace was wearing—horrors!—a non-regulation pair of "light-colored trousers." Reproved for his garb in the presence of his company, Wallace was so incensed that he told the chief that he, too, was wearing non-regulation clothing and that he had no right to humiliate Wallace in front of his peers. The brash captain never forgot Bennett's next words, uttered in a calm but steely tone:

Captain Wallace, I want you to understand that you are not here to tell *me* what to wear, but I am here to tell *you* what to wear, and I tell you now, sir, that *you* are violating the rules of the department!

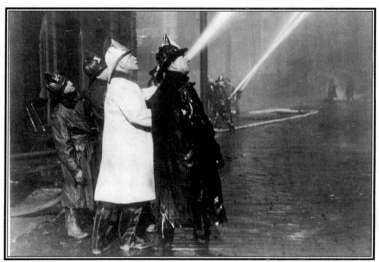

Wallace at the scene of a fire, circa 1930.

Thinking it over later, Wallace decided that Chief Bennett was right, and he henceforth followed his authoritarian example, except that he confined his dressing downs to private conferences.

Throughout his 30 years as chief, Wallace's larger-than-life institutional and public profiles were much amplified by his deliberate cultivation of a colorful style and flamboyant persona. Always the easiest person to recognize at a Cleveland fire, he wore an all-white uniform and white helmet. Unusually open to journalists, he often, during his years in subordinate positions, earned their enduring goodwill by readily providing them with needed copy and even giving them free rides to fire scenes, thus saving them precious carfare. One thing these journalists, or anyone else who ever witnessed Chief Wallace directing a fire scene, never forgot was the superhuman volume and masterly eloquence of his profanity. It is well known that journalists, or for that matter firemen, are not easily impressed by "colorful" language, but the sound of Wallace in full profane cry was an incomparable spectacle. Especially, as one Cleveland *Plain Dealer* scribe recalled, if any imprudent Forest City journalist interrupted Wallace while a fire was in progress:

When the flames leaped high and the smoke billowed, the bellow of the late Fire Chief George A. Wallace could be heard four city blocks. Though it is inconvenient (and probably libelous) to quote the peppery old gentleman too literally, the tenor of his remarks was to the effect that somebody better get that so and so hose up to the top of that so and so ladder pretty so and so quick or he, personally, would give them such a so and so kick square on the so and so that they would never forget it, by something or other. Newspapermen now grown gray or bald or both, shudder when they remember how they finally screwed up their courage to such a heroic point that they dared to ask a question of the old man in the white helmet. The essence of his reply was that he was fighting a so and so fire; he had no time to answer a lot of so and so questions; the reporter had better get his so and so out of there—and pretty so and so quick.

Or as an impressed *Cleveland Press* reporter once put it, "He is one of the most accomplished cussers in the nation, not excluding mule-skinners."

Not the least remarkable aspect of Wallace's long career was the fact that he was never seriously injured in the line of duty, despite dozens of minor injuries and countless brushes with death. Ignoring—as he invariably did—the hundreds of bruises, scrapes, burns, cuts, and sprains he sustained over 62 years (somewhere in the neighborhood of 22,600 days), he took only 13 days of sick leave during that period. Typical of his "minor" mishaps was an incident that occurred at the burning of the Giles Livery Stable on Long Street (now covered by the Terminal Tower complex) on June 13, 1895. The hottest part of the fire was in an enormous loft containing tons of hay and straw. After beating the flames back into the building, Wallace led a crew of hosemen up a ladder and into the loft, where they extinguished the fire in 15 minutes. They were just preparing to leave when the whole floor collapsed, hurling them down to the foundation and covering them with fire debris. Wallace had only a sprained ankle to show for that near-deadly experience. He had an even closer call during the Erie Building fire on April 19, 1924. While coming to the rescue of firemen trapped by flames, an explosion knocked the 76-year-old chief down a flight of stairs, accompanied all the way down by a shower of shattered glass. Stunned, bruised, and bleeding, he staggered to his feet and brought his men out alive. Five years later, the day after the Cleveland Clinic disaster, Wallace shyly approached Cleveland safety director Edwin D. Barry and told him he might have to take a few days off. Intrigued, Barry did some sleuthing and was astounded to learn that his self-effacing octogenarian chief had fallen twice while inside the lethal gas-filled Clinic building and had pulled one victim from the bottom of an elevator shaft. After discovering the facts, Barry ordered Wallace to go to a hospital. Serenely insubordinate, Wallace simply returned to his regular bed at Firehouse #14 at Chester Avenue and East 12th Street. The next morning he showed up at his City Hall desk as if nothing had happened.

George Wallace probably fought more fires than any professional fireman *ever*, alive or dead. Of his personal top five, the worst was the 1908 Collinwood School fire, which took the lives of 172 children. Wallace was present there mainly as a witness, for by the time his Cleveland force arrived at the outlying village school there was little to do but pour water on the smoking ruins and bring out the dead. His next worst fire, and the most dangerous of all, was the Flats lumber fire of May 25, 1914, which incinerated 20 million feet of wood, knocked two bridges out of commission, killed one man, and came very close to engulfing the entire city of Cleveland. Thirty-five of the 150 men who battled the 1914 blaze had also stood with Wallace when he fought two other serious Flats lumber fires in September 1884. The first of those arson blazes, on September 14, nearly burned the city down and brought firefighters from as far away as Columbus and Sandusky. The glow the 1884 fire created was so intense that newspaper photographers Louis Baus and William Zapf would long remember that they could read newspapers by its terrible light—a mile away. Third Assistant Chief Wallace battled that blaze for 72 hours without rest, and by the time he stopped, his face, as a reporter described it, "seems to have been boiled in wax, judging from his complexion and his voice is *non est.*" Next in gravity came the Standard Oil fire of 1883, which unleashed a river of burning oil that threatened to burn everything between Kingsbury Run and the mouth of the Cuyahoga River. At the bottom of Wallace's list was the 1929 Clinic disaster, probably because the fire there on May 15 was a subordinate factor in the deaths of 128 patients, physicians, and nurses, most of whom were killed by toxic gases. (For the Clinic fire see "Breath of Death" in the author's *They Died Crawling*; for accounts of the other four blazes see "Cleveland's Burning!" in *The Maniac in the Bushes.*)

Wallace's achievements were not restricted to his out-front leadership style and model of personal courage. It was during his administration that the Cleveland Fire Department became a truly modern force. Wallace was one of the first firemen in the country to realize that fire *prevention* was even more important, if less exciting and dramatic, than fire *fighting*. His repeated mantra was that seven-tenths of all fires were caused by simple carelessness. It was to remove that cause that in 1896 he helped organize the first municipal fire prevention bureau in the nation. During his tenure as chief, his officers conducted thousands of inspections of schools, theaters, factories, stores, and dwellings, a service that helped save an incalculable number of lives and also reduced insurance costs. Wallace also always kept himself abreast of new developments in firefighting methods and equipment. As newer and better equipment became available he made sure his "boys" had it, and even as he faced retirement he was dreaming Tom Swiftian dreams of what the future held for his profession:

The next great change? To my mind, it's going to be a new type of fire engine, bigger and with heavier trucks. It will be operated by electricity, carrying wire cables to connect with high-tension wires built into the hydrant. This engine will pump water through five or six sets of hose, instead of two or three, and will have more pressure for any of them than it now has for the two or three. What does this mean? It means fewer engines, fewer firemen, less apparatus. It means it will not be necessary to fill a whole street with engines and wagons and trucks, tying up traffic, while you are fighting the fire.

Truly, George Wallace had come a long way from the reactionary who, three decades before, had fiercely resented the replacement of fire horses by gas-powered vehicles. Occasionally, in his old age, he would suffer a momentary twinge of nostalgia for the olden time, muttering "Horses need affection."

Inevitably, time caught up with even the seemingly ageless and invulnerable Wallace. A severe case of conjunctivitis, probably acquired during his 1929 Clinic ordeal, worsened the next year and put Wallace in a hospital bed for a couple of days. Rumors that he was about to retire, some of them deliberately floated by Cleveland city officials, increased in frequency as the 1920s waned and the Depression decade began. Finally, on January 15, 1931, after reading a newspaper editorial suggesting he step down, Wallace confronted Safety Director Barry and asked him point blank if he wanted his resignation. Barry, who apparently thought the department needed a younger chief but who also greatly revered Wallace, handled the situation with sublime tact. Assuring Wallace that he wanted him to stay on as long as he wished, he went on to warn him that his advancing age made a crippling injury or even death in action more and more likely. And, should a grave injury or accident happen to Wallace, Barry continued, the citizens of Cleveland would never forgive city officials for allowing it to occur. He then offered Wallace exactly the retirement package he had hoped for: the rank of Chief Emeritus at his full chief's pay of $6,000 per year; the continued use of his quarters at Engine House No. 14, where he'd lived since his wife Emma's death in 1921; the right to wear his trademark white uniform and helmet; an advisory position; and a gold badge as a symbol of his continuing status and authority. Barry kindly added that Wallace would still be allowed to chase fires and to curse the firemen—but he was expected to stay out of harm's way.

It was a deal almost too good to be true—and thus it proved to be. Wallace's official sendoff, an elaborate fete attended by 10,000 well-wishers at Public Hall on March 1, 1931, was an appropriately fulsome tribute to the only fire chief most Clevelanders had ever known. The festivities included a parade of both ancient and contemporary firefighting apparatus, from the most modern fire en-

Sketch of George Wallace at a Cleveland fire, *Plain Dealer Sunday Magazine*, April 21, 1912.

gine truck to a 90-year-old hand-pulled model borrowed from the Seville Fire Department; a dazzling exhibition by firemen of their skill with ladders and other firefighting tools; and, of course, too many speeches. Many lovely things were said about Wallace, probably the best of them being Newton D. Baker's concluding paean:

> It is given to few men to live so many years. It is given to almost no man to live the years half as usefully as he has lived them. When I congratulate Chief Wallace, I do it mostly because he is and has a right to be a supremely happy man.

Baker then presented Wallace with a gold badge upon which was inscribed a simple but heartfelt tribute to the man his peers worldwide had come to revere as "America's Grand Old Firefighter":

Presented to
George A. Wallace
by members of the
Cleveland Fire Department
in esteem of his leadership as chief

The crowd then sang "Auld Lang Syne" and suddenly, after 62 years, George Wallace's work was over.

The Grand Old Man soon found out how short the memories of Clevelanders could be. The very next year the Fire Pension Board, hard pressed to cut expenses during what had turned into the Great Depression, cut Wallace's $6,000 pension down to $3,695 per year. A few months later, in December 1932, the Board announced it had voted to reduce it further to $1,800. (By way of comparison, consider that his annual pay as an assistant chief in 1894 was $1,900.) Perhaps because he had suffered a bad fall at his house three weeks before, the news that his pension had been slashed by more than two-thirds sparked an upsurge of public outrage, abetted by newspaper editorials and the angry words of retired safety director Barry, who led the drive to restore Wallace's pension. Thanks in large part to Barry's efforts, the amount was eventually raised to $3,900.

Wallace's last years were grim. Confined more and more to his home at 1862 East 75th Street, he rarely summoned the energy to leave it, much less chase his beloved fires—although he had a working alarm installed in his home to let him know whenever one occurred. One by one, all the companions of his early career died before him, the last being Jake Kahill, who had died in 1927. His son, George S. Wallace, who had served as clerk of the Cuyahoga County Courts, had passed away in 1930, leaving only his brother, Stanhope, to survive and mourn George A. Wallace when he answered his final alarm on August 4, 1940. Ninety-two years old, he was at last carried off by the malady he had assiduously courted during all those decades spent fighting fires in frigid weather: pneumonia. Mourning with Stanhope was Edward C. Sasek, who had served as Chief Wallace's driver for two decades and then as his faithful companion during his final decade.

Every hero has his flaws. If George Wallace had a big one, it was probably his apparent conviction that he was an indispensable man. As Charles de Gaulle remarked, the graveyards are full of indispensable men, and it has been 70 years since George Wallace joined their company. But it is also indisputable that Cleveland has not had a heroic leader of his stature since he last shook its firmament with his mighty oaths. (It has had plenty of other heroes, of course, all of them policemen and firemen who have died in the line of duty.) Indeed, it is fair to say that the city's annals, since his time, have been cluttered with, as Henry Adams might say, nothing more than damaged reputations. But if you would yet aspire to be a hero, you could do no better than to study George Alexander Wallace's life of unflinching and unstinted dedication to the public good.

Chapter 9

THE LAST DAYS OF CLEVELAND

The 1925 Adventist Hysteria

NOW IS THE END—PERISH THE WORLD! . . . Well, it's
not quite the conflagration I'd been banking on. Never mind,
lads, same time tomorrow—we must get a winner one day.
                —Peter Cook, "The End of the World,"
                comic sketch, *Beyond the Fringe*

Most Clevelanders, like the author, probably think of California
as the quintessential land of nuts, cults, and credulous loonies of all
persuasions. But Cleveland, alas, even from its early days, has not
been immune to what 19th-century author Charles McKay anato-
mized in 1841 as the "extraordinary popular delusions and the madness of crowds." No doubt coincidentally, Northeast Ohio suffered
its first virulent outbreak of just such popular madness two years
later, when the Millerite movement reached the Cleveland area.
William Miller was a self-taught New England Bible enthusiast
who convinced himself, sometime before 1818, that his "scientific"
analysis and numerical manipulation of biblical dates foretold the
end of the world and the Second Coming of Christ, sometime in
1843 or 1844. Miller liked to remain cagy about the exact date, but
he eventually conceded the millennium was likely to occur sometime between March 21, 1843, and March 21, 1844. As the 1830s
gave way to the 1840s, Miller's prophecies attracted thousands of
believers, especially in New England but also, alas, in the homes
and farms of its satellite Western Reserve. Persuaded that terrestrial
concerns would soon be meaningless, serious Millerites prepared

for the end by shedding their property and possessions and congregating on hillsides, many of them appropriately garbed in flowing robes, to await the coming Rapture. When March 21, 1843, came and went without incident they did some hasty recalculations and announced a revised date of April 23.

Dawn of that fateful spring day in Cleveland found a small but fervent band of the Millerite faithful inside their downtown tabernacle, a round brick structure, 60 feet in diameter, which stood on Wood Street (later East 3rd) between St. Clair and Rockwell. Its windowed cupola, atop the one-story structure, would allow them to see the predicted portents in all directions. Although they received initial encouragement that morning from a fiery and miraculous glow in the eastern sky—originating miles away in Chagrin Township, where Earl's mill was burning to the ground—their Last Day passed without further tumult, and the ensuing disappointment left only a steadfast remnant to await a subsequent, new and revised millennial deadline, which duly passed on October 22, 1844. One journalist wag on the *Cleveland Herald*, after noting that the main event of the day had been the arrest of two Millerites for bizarre behavior, suggested that the Cleveland Millerites' mistake had been in not selecting April 1 as the Day of Days. But some still believed, and splinters of the Millerite movement in Cleveland and elsewhere would survive and eventually lead to the formation of the Seventh-Day Adventist church. But for most Clevelanders, the end of the world had been canceled for good. The memory of Miller's failed prophecies ebbed with the passing years, and the tabernacle, after successively serving the worship needs of a Wesleyan Methodist sect and the Old Plymouth Congregational Church, was demolished during the 1860s.

Cleveland's more recent and more sensational brush with millennial frenzy originated, appropriately enough, in . . . Hollywood, California. It was there, on December 18, 1923, that prophetess Margaret W. Rowen had her first vision foretelling the end of the world. Rowen was no stranger to the millennial movement, having been formally expelled from the mainstream Seventh-Day Adventist Church for divers doctrinal irregularities in 1916. She had since organized a Reformed Adventist variant of her original faith with her as its chief and replaced its end-time imprecision with more specific dates and predictions. Beginning on February 6, 1924, stated Rowen, there would come a year of seven plagues. Then, on February 6, 1925, there would be a resurrection of both the righteous and the damned. All the righteous would go straight to heaven, while the wicked remained on earth for a thousand years of punishment. Finally, at the end of the thousand years, the New Jerusalem would descend upon the earth, and the wicked would be utterly annihilated. Rowen also claimed to have seen such interesting sights as Lucifer's ejection from heaven, the creation and fall of Adam and Eve, and various principal incidents in the life of Christ. Her voluminous publications broadcast the details of her various visions and prophecies, along with much moralizing on the more mundane subject of Sunday blue laws, which she found woefully in abeyance.

As the countdown toward the 1925 Armageddon proceeded, Mrs. Rowen's predictions, broadcast through her Reformed Adventist publications, became increasingly dramatic and specific. The February 6 resurrection would bring no less a personage than Pontius Pilate to rule over the thousand-year realm of the damned, while Christ spent the same interval leading the blessed or "perfect-in-soul" on a tour of the solar system. His advent would be announced by a great light in the western sky, which the saved would follow as He drew them up to heaven.

Most Clevelanders first learned of Rowen's alarming prophecies on December 7, 1924. Led by Reverend Carl F. Woertz, pastor of the Reformed Seventh-Day Adventist Church at 3298 Fulton Road, a line of eight automobiles paraded that day from Rocky River through downtown Cleveland and all the way to East 55th Street. While forty shabbily garbed believers brandished signs reading "Christ Comes Feb 6. 1925" and "Saturday Is God's Sabbath," the Reverend Woertz bellowed repeated warnings through a megaphone: "The end is upon you!" Hymns were also loudly sung as the parade progressed, alternating with impassioned public prayer. Interviewed afterwards by amused journalists, Woertz and his followers explained that they had worn old clothing because they had feared, mistakenly, that their message would be ill received. More assertively, the Reverend Woertz insisted that "God's law is our only law. When man's law conflicts with our religious beliefs we will break it." He went on to boast that he had already sold his home and all his possessions in anticipation of the End, as had followers Andrew Hoffer and "Brother" Kinter. The money realized, he said, would go to fund the publication of Rowen's warnings, a sacrifice made for the benefit of the unenlightened.

Despite immediate and impassioned disavowals from the mainstream Seventh-Day Adventist Church in Cleveland and others around the country, Forest City journalists knew they were on to a good thing, and they stepped up coverage of Woertz's tiny and obscure congregation as 1924 waxed into 1925. Thanks to such efforts and the work of other journalists around the country, the Fulton Road believers soon had comforting evidence that they were not alone in their convictions. Robert Reidt of East Patchogue on Long Island, New York, it was reported, had sold all of his property, not excepting his stock of winter potatoes, and was prepared to head for the hills, or at least move his family to a higher elevation in Port Jefferson to enjoy the Second Coming. Similar actions by believers in Boston, Los Angeles, Baltimore, and Takoma Park, Maryland, were also reported. A true believer in the latter town patiently explained:

> According to the Bible, the end of the world will be accompanied by a falling of the stars and a darkening of the sun. Both of these phenomena are at hand. We are preparing for the end. We may assemble for a final meeting of prayer but we plan nothing fanatical. We hope only to be calm and at peace with God.

Back in Cleveland, Reverend Woertz heaped more fuel on the publicity pyre with a letter to the editor of the Cleveland *Plain Dealer*. Bad times—*very* bad times—were coming soon:

> The United States is on the brink of a world war a thousand times greater than the last. The war will originate in Asia Minor over religious differences. All nations will be drawn

into the fight and those not killed in actual fighting will die in a great famine and pestilence by Feb. 6, 1925, when the world will end.

Meanwhile, activity at Woertz's Fulton Road church, near Carlyle Avenue, intensified. During the last week of January the pastor announced that new conversions were running at a rate of five a day and that his faithful were preparing 300,000 Rowenite handbills for distribution, a truly last-moment effort to get the word out. The handbills, appropriately titled, "A Last Call and Warning to You," would be handed out on street corners and in streetcars, and shoved into mailboxes and automobiles. The handbills, Woertz gloated, had already resulted in "many conversions."

Not all Clevelanders were as credulous as Woertz's followers about the claims he spouted regarding his congregation's growth and influence. There was actually no evidence, excited newspaper coverage notwithstanding, that his sect ever amounted to more than half a hundred persons, including children. And his religious competitors were having none of it. The Reverend W. W. Bustard, pastor of the Euclid Avenue Baptist Church, mildly demurred in commenting on Woertz's bloodcurdling predictions, saying that the evangelization of the world would likely precede Christ's return. The Reverend W. F. Schwartz of the mainstream Seventh-Day Adventist Church on Hough Avenue was, understandably, more critical. If Christ were really coming as soon as Rowen predicted, he argued, Satan would be ready for him:

> Satan would have discovered the landing place of Christ and would have constructed a great amphitheater there. He would be busy selling seats in his final attempt to cheat the righteous.

More darkly, Schwartz went on to tell of one such venture already under way in Australia, where some demonic promoter had already built a stadium for 60,000, with seats at a pricey $500 each.

Unsurprisingly, Woertz's most vehement opponents were found in the ranks of the mainstream Seventh-Day Adventist Church.

N. H. Ashton, President of the Ohio Conference of Seventh-Day Adventists, reacted to their Cleveland parade by denouncing them as false Adventists and "fanatical people." Fearful that the general populace would confuse Woertz's cult with the mainstream Adventist church, Ashton begged Cleveland's newspapers to make the distinction clear to their readers.

During the last days of January, a Cleveland *Plain Dealer* reporter dropped by the Fulton Road church to interview some of its zealots. Noting that previous predictions of Christ's Second Coming had notoriously flopped, he asked one of the men folding handbills why he was so certain the end was perilously nigh. "We are sure," he retorted robotically. "This time we were told of the end by the word of God. He spoke to Mrs. Margaret Rowen at Los Angeles. She, you know, is the prophetess of our Reformed Adventist sect." And how about the prophecy that Pontius Pilate would show up as early as January 26, an appearance the former Fifth Prefect of Judea had failed to make? "No," the believer blandly corrected the journalist. "He couldn't rise, being a sinner." He continued:

> Pilate will not rise, even when Christ comes. Those who rise will be those who died in him. The sinners will lie in their graves for 1,000 years, while their sentences are being passed in heaven. At the close of 1,000 years they will rise and receive their sentences.

The Reformed faithful, the Fulton Road believer went on to say, would be drawn by a "translating" star—visible only to the faithful—to one of several gathering places in the United States, one of which would have room for 144,000 saved souls when the final trump blared. That particular group, he explained, would be made up of those who had sinned little, if at all. When pressed to disclose the location, he modestly demurred, saying only, "That's up to God."

All good things come to an end, even newspaper-abetted campaigns of contrived hysteria. On the night of February 4, the Fulton Road faithful huddled together in their church for their last prayer meeting. Mrs. E. H. Frey and Mrs. Helen Roberts, the congregation's most prominent lay leaders, had previously announced that

Millerite Tabernacle on Wood Street, c. 1850s.

there would be no more meetings before the End but yielded to temptation when they saw the crowd gathered outside the church. Some had come to jeer but most remained politely silent as the small group in the church prayed, sang, and offered personal testimony about the coming Rapture. The services passed without untoward circumstance, save for a young child who squirmed and romped playfully while the adults carried on. When the service closed, an irate believer reproved the child's mother, chiding, "That child is not filled with the Lord. It would not have misbehaved if it were filled with the proper spirit." Proving that a soft answer turneth away wrath, the mother mildly rejoined, "It was merely showing in the only way it could how joyful it is at the coming of Christ." The man and mother then shook hands, and Mrs. Frey ended the meeting by announcing one "final" meeting the next night.

This much-anticipated event occurred on February 5, as hundreds of curious Clevelanders stormed the Fulton Road church, anxious to hear more details of the impending millennium, now scheduled for exactly 12 a.m., February 7. The congregation inside the church and an excited crowd outside—some craning their necks through the windows, others lining the street for several blocks—listened intently as Mrs. Frey exhorted the faithful one last time to hold firm to their beliefs and ignore the scoffers. Explaining that there would be no more meetings, she gave them their final boarding instructions for Heaven:

> Gather at your hearthsides and pray tomorrow, and at midnight Christ will appear from the constellation Orion. He is coming from God and will be on time. A great square will surround Orion. In the square will be a hand. From the nail print in the hand a beam of light will point the direction in which Christ wishes you to go. Forget everything else and follow where the beam directs, and God will take care of you.

Building on Frey's fervor, speaker Helen Roberts followed to remind her audience that that very day's sunset had shone with a suggestive "blood red" tint and that the moon outside the church had an "ominous look." Falling to her knees, she pleaded with her auditors:

> Hold to the faith of Noah! Even when the appointed day for the flood had passed, he believed, in spite of the jeering unrighteous outside the ark. [Even as Roberts spoke, a police flying squad was struggling mightily to control the mob of jeering unrighteous outside.] And on the seventh day came the rain. Then the scoffers besieged the ark, even as they besiege us tonight, but it was too late.

"Are you ready to met your Savior?" she wound up. "Yes, praise His name!" her believers shouted back. "Are your grapes ripe?" "Yes!" "Is your wheat shocked?" "Yes!" "Are you prepared for the end?" "Yes, God speed the coming! Bless Him, Hallelujah!"

Properly, the climax of the evening's events focused on the original source of this religious mania, which was the supposed vision of its Hollywood founder, Margaret Rowen. After reading from some of the prophetess's sacred texts, Mrs. Frey offered her own enthusiastic personal endorsement of the California Cassandra:

> I have been with her for hours while she was in vision. She never took a living breath the while. As she goes into the

trance life leaves her, she raises her hand and cries "Glory!" three times. Then her soul wings to the pearly gates. Gabriel touches her and Christ leads her to the tree of life, from where God speaks to the world through her. Although ordinarily she speaks in broken English, God's words through her are perfectly pronounced. Mrs. Rowen inhales seven times and life returns to her. Only God can take and restore life, so her messages are divine.

Sadly, it was all downhill for the Reformed Adventists from the moment Frey concluded her testimony and her congregation dispersed. Even as February 6, the next and "last" day dawned, fatal fissures began opening in the Reformed Adventist firmament. First came word from Margaret Rowen's mother, Mathilde Rowen, in Philadelphia, who held forth in the morning's *New York Times*. Sourly maintaining that Margaret simply ought to be "spanked," she presented a perspective much at odds with the near idolatrous views of Mrs. Frey and Helen Roberts about her daughter. Apologizing for Margaret's antics, she made it clear that she was speaking for most of the much mortified Rowen clan:

> It isn't my fault she is acting this way. Before I left her in Hollywood three years ago she had managed to change the views of her husband's three children. She did not change me, however. I was as good a Methodist when I left there as I was when I went to California fourteen years ago. We hadn't been there very long before my daughter started having visions after she attended some meetings in a tent on a vacant lot. I felt sorry about the children. When they would see a dark cloud in the sky they would come running to me and say, "Granny, does that mean the world is coming to an end?" They'd look all worried like, and I'd have to comfort them. She is not four feet tall and she is almost as wide.

Margaret, it was further reported, had not even sent any farewell messages to her mother or brother. When queried about that, her brother simply sniffed, "Huh—we're not the elect."

All of this family backbiting, of course, would not have mattered, had Margaret's prophecies only come true. But midnight arrived at the end of February 6, and neither the end of the world nor Christ's Second Coming duly occurred. Indeed, when the decisive instant arrived, the Fulton Road church was empty and locked, and its leaders, the Reverend Woertz, Mrs. Frey, and Mrs. Roberts, had vanished. Rumor had it that Roberts and Frey, alleging death threats, had quietly fled to a hillside in Bedford, where they planned to stand and wait—for seven days, if necessary—for the imminent Rapture. An alternate rumor had it that they and the Reverend Woertz were California bound to a rendezvous with Mrs. Rowen. A suspicious clue that they had might have covered their bets, however, came on the morning of February 8, when a "For Sale" sign appeared on the door of the Fulton Road church.

Frey and Roberts may have believed the best ringside seat for the End was Bedford, but it is indisputable that the real epicenter of Cleveland's 1925 millennial frenzy was Garfield Heights. As the evening of February 6 waned toward midnight, 15 carloads of the faithful gathered there on a muddy hill at the back of Charles Ford's Turney Road home. Few were willing to talk to reporters after the Great Disappointment, some silent from sheer humiliation or disappointment, others with more worldly fears of legal reprisal from those who had sold their homes and worldly goods during last-minute panic sales. Many, though, were merely cranky from having stayed up all night to no purpose, their response to journalists' questions being a curt "Let us sleep!"

It was much the same with the various Reformed Adventist church congregations around the country. As February 7 began, midnight found Robert Reidt in his Long Island home, surrounded by curious neighbors, inquisitive reporters, and some opportunistic members of the Ku Klux Klan, who anticipated the expected Coming by burning a cross on his lawn. Dawn found him obviously downcast by the night's non-event, but he valiantly maintained his public front. "But it's coming," he still assured reporters, "it may even now be on its way." Adding insult to injury, an unsympathetic *New York Times* reporter, perhaps cranky from his all-night vigil with Reidt, described him as a "rotund little German, his chubby cheeks obscured by a dingy stubble, his eyes wan from peering into an unresponsive eastern sky."

Some of Mrs. Rowen's followers did not take the millennial denouement so well in stride. In Wilkes-Barre, Pennsylvania, Mrs. Andrew Kort, 53, anticipated the End by hanging herself in despair several hours before its scheduled arrival, as did Walter Michlowsky, 37, of Brooklyn, New York. In Temperance, Michigan, farmer Karl Danzelsen, worried that the Second Coming would obviate his life of hard toil and the value of his $35,000 farm, shot himself to death and wounded his wife. In New York, Benjamin Lemoncelli, 23, turned himself in to the cops, confessing he was a fugitive from justice and wanted to clear his conscience before Christ arrived. And in Des Moines, Iowa, traveling salesman S. M. Morehead spent his presumed last hours riding around town on a horse and loudly proclaiming that the end was nigh. It was reported that he was attired in only a nightgown and galoshes. On a more uplifting note, Springfield, Ohio, merchants were happily surprised by the number of supposed deadbeat debtors who suddenly paid off their accounts, wishing to square themselves with the Almighty before the impending Last Judgment. Meanwhile, back in Hollywood, California, Mrs. Margaret Rowen, presumably still wearing her habitual "gingham bungalow apron," retreated into an utter and silent seclusion, refusing to talk to reporters or anyone else.

It is a strange but true fact that some people can find a silver lining even in a false Armageddon. Such was the fate of Robert Reidt, who soon smothered his disappointment enough to parley it into a brief but memorable show-biz career. He was much in need of money, as he had sold his car and most of his possessions. So on the night of February 8, less than 48 hours after the Great Fizzle, he appeared at the Patchogue Movie Theater to lecture upon his recent spiritual odyssey. The hometown crowd listened somewhat restively for about 5 minutes and then someone screamed, "Give him the hook!" and a minute later he departed under a chorus of catcalls and raspberries. Afterwards he maintained his calm good cheer, although he suffered a moment of snippiness when a reporter asked him why the worldwide pestilence he'd previously predicted hadn't occurred. "There was no pestilence because there was no persecution," he huffed. "When I start on my speaking tour the words I say will bring plenty of persecution. *Then* will come the pestilence!" When last heard from in May 1925, the ever-hopeful Reidt was reported to have booked another theatrical appearance to explain his unfulfilled prophecies.

Mrs. Frey, Mrs. Roberts, and the Reverend Woertz were not heard from again in the public prints of Cleveland, and their mostly disillusioned followers melted back into the obscurity whence they had come. The final act in Cleveland's Roaring Twenties millennial hysteria came five months later, in July, when the Harvard Mortgage Company foreclosed on Charles Ford's Turney Road home. It was reported that Ford, who had mortgaged the home to fund the last-minute evangelical effort, had waited for seven days beyond the February 6 deadline before hanging himself in despair.

During the four score and five years since the Reverend Woertz and his crazies packed up shop, echoes of the Millerite madness have resounded more on theatrical stages than within the walls of millennial sect churches. In 1959, the Cleveland Play House mounted a production of Reginald Perry's *Heaven Come Wednesday,* a play about the original Millerite frenzy set to music from "The Millennial Harp," one of its original hymnbooks. Four years later, it was successfully revived in a production at the Cleveland Heights Church of the Savior for the Festival of Religion and the Arts. Could there be other Clevelanders, besides the author, who would be delighted to see it performed again?

Chapter 10

ALL UNHAPPY FAMILIES ARE NOT ALIKE

The Ashtabula McAdams Family Values

Her mother she could never stand,
Sing rickety-tickety-tin,
Her mother she could never stand,
And so a cyanide soup she planned.
The mother died with a spoon in her hand,
And her face in a hideous grin, a grin,
Her face in a hideous grin.
—Tom Lehrer, "An Irish Ballad"

During my nearly two decades as a chronicler of Cleveland-area woe, I have frequently been asked whether one could write a book about the crimes and calamities of smaller cities and towns. Yes, I have always replied, there is usually enough malign history in even the smallest of places to warrant a hefty narrative compilation of its misdeeds. No place is so small as to have missed out on the consequences of its residents practicing the Seven Deadly Sins—especially anger, envy, and jealousy—or on the malignancy of fate, which sooner or later puts innocent people in the wrong place at the wrong time. And one could hardly do better than to enter Ashtabula County, Ohio, in evidence as Exhibit A to prove the validity of my assertion. True, this relatively rural county has never been a densely populated, urban complex like the Cleveland metropolitan area, containing hundreds of thousands of potential victims and at least hundreds of hardened criminals to prey upon them. Nor has it boasted a huge industrial and technological infrastructure with all of its possibilities for lethal failure (think Cleveland Clinic) or widespread devastation (think East Ohio Gas Company). Still, the county has had woeful episodes well worth chronicling. Practically everyone there knows about the 1876 Ashtabula railroad bridge collapse, which incinerated nearly 100 persons in a fiery holocaust on the night of December 29, 1876. Less well known but still deserving historical remembrance is the natural gas explosion that killed 20 persons, injured 18, and leveled an entire business block in the little village of Andover on August 10, 1955. Nothing there to compete with the scale of the Forest City, you might still say. But even colossal Cleveland, with all its dozens of fabled murders, cannot exceed the horror of Ashtabula's McAdams family saga. Although short, it is a shattering story and as creepy a murder as ever was told around a campfire or recounted in a book of woe.

Like many an ambitious farmer in the middle decades of the 19th century, Alexander McAdams came to Ashtabula to farm its rich soil. Arriving in East Ashtabula in the late 1830s, he constructed a house in the woods for his ever-growing family, which eventually included Alexander's wife, Rebecca, and nine children. He worked hard, and by the end of the following decade he had earned a reputation as a prosperous and respected farmer and all seemed well with him and his loved ones.

It was not. Jeanette, his eldest child, had always been the most difficult of his brood, and Alexander and his wife were probably relieved when the willful teenager moved to Cleveland. Rumors occasionally reached the homestead that Jeanette led a "wild" life in Cleveland and that she was engaged to married. But nothing certain was known, and she was welcomed back into the family bosom when she returned to visit in late February 1848. Her sister Julia, 14, was there too, although she was soon to depart to live with a family named Holdridge so she could attend school in the village. The family spent a pleasant evening reminiscing by the family fireplace while Julia hemmed a handkerchief, before they all retired to their beds. Sometime that night of February 26, Jeanette awakened her mother and told her that Julia was "very sick." Very sick she was, for despite the care of her worried parents, Julia died the next morning, just before the family physician, Doctor Coleman of Ashtabula, arrived. She is still buried in the McAdams plot in Ashtabula's Edgewood Cemetery, where her grave inscription reads:

JULIA A.
Daughter of A. and R. McAdams
Died February 27, 1848
Aged 14 years

Following her sister's burial, Jeanette returned to Cleveland. Nearly two more years elapsed before Jeanette returned to celebrate the 1849 Christmas holidays. The eve of the New Year found the McAdams family again a comfortable, happy gathering around the clan hearth. Suddenly, Jeanette's brother Arthur, 8, who had been lying next to the fire on a buffalo rug, eating an apple and playing with his dog, went into agonized convulsions. The doctor came more quickly this time, but the result was the same, and Arthur soon joined Julia in the Edgewood Cemetery, where his grave reads:

ARTHUR
Son of A. and R. McAdams
Died January 1, 1850
Aged 8 years

Jeanette stayed on to help with the funeral, while younger brother Walter hitched up the family wagon and went to retrieve their sister Abigail for the obsequies. Abigail was still home the day after the funeral and while helping her mother make up the family beds, suddenly asked, "Mother, did you know that Jeanette has a man's suit of clothes in her room?" Owing to the tumult of later events, it is not known whether Abigail's statement was true, or, if so, constituted evidence, as was deliciously rumored, that Jeanette liked to wear such male garb while sneaking out of the house to prosecute scandalous nocturnal adventures. Poor Abigail, in any case, never got a chance to find out. Several hours later, she turned to her mother and said, "I wish I had not eaten that piece of candy that Jeanette gave me." Legend has it that as she uttered these words she clutched the family mantel with her hand, leaving behind the telltale stains of . . . *a white powder.* But she said no more and, finding Dr. Coleman's ministrations unavailing, soon joined the silent company of siblings Arthur and Julia.

Apparently, notwithstanding these untoward events, Jeanette was still welcome at the family manse, for she returned home in August that same year. Not long after her arrival, her brother Walter returned home one evening after an exhausting day of hauling staves with his father. His mother was out visiting a sick neighbor, so Walter sat down to dinner with Jeanette. Soon after, Walter complained of the usual pains and went upstairs to bed. Racked with pain and fear, he eventually crawled down the stairs to his mother's bed, where, after she came home, he was attended by Dr. Coleman and a nurse. Neighbor Lucy Cook would long remember watching Walter McAdams's last hours, recalling in the pages of the *Ashtabula Beacon*:

> He died in great agony. My husband helped hold him on the bed. By this time the sight of the gray team speeding toward town brought terror to all the neighborhood, for there were no telephones, and each time a member of the McAdams family was stricken someone went with all speed for Doctor Coleman of East Ashtabula.

Walter was duly buried with his brothers and sisters, and Jeanette resumed her "fast life" in Cleveland.

Astonishingly, there still seem to have been no suspicions, even after four deaths, about footloose family visitor Jeanette. But it wasn't long after she returned in September that her brother Luther was struck down. Returning home after playing in the street with some friends, he complained of not feeling well. His nursing responsibilities devolved upon Jeanette, with the usual convulsive and fatal consequences. Several days later, while Jeanette cooked a Sunday dinner, the rest of her family attended church. Every one, including Jeanette, became ill after eating her dinner, but all survived and Jeanette again returned to Cleveland.

Plain Dealer Sunday Magazine, September 10, 1911.

Five months later, Jeanette returned home to find her mother Rebecca bedridden with a severe cold. That evening, Jeanette brought her a packet of white powder, saying it was some medicine left for her by the doctor. Mrs. Alexander swallowed the medicine and dozed off while her husband sat by the fire. When she awoke she was groaning in pain, and she died in the usual convulsive agony several hours later. Subsequently Alexander McAdams learned that Dr. Coleman had not left any medicine for his wife.

It is at precisely this juncture of the narrative that the intelligent reader will stop and say to herself: "How much of this story could possibly be true? Is it probable—or even possible—that no one, whether in the McAdams family or outside it, tumbled to the suspicious pattern and circumstances of the family deaths?" Well—the facts are these. There *was* a McAdams family and they all died at the times stated. There *was* a Dr. Coleman and a Lucy M. Cook, and you can still find all of the McAdams graves standing in the

Edgewood Cemetery. But as for the rest of the story . . . well, here it is, and you can believe it or not . . .

Legend has it that Jeanette left rather hurriedly after her mother's funeral, especially as the McAdams neighbors, if not her father, were beginning to put two and two together regarding the McAdams family's woes. But a few months later, Jeanette suddenly returned and gave her father a letter to post. Secretly opening it, he found she had written to a friend about her plans to do away with *him*. When she returned to the house he told her to leave and never return.

It is to be hoped that she didn't, although apocryphal tales about her doings continued to flourish in Ashtabula during the decades after her family misfortunes peaked. One story was that she perfected her use of male disguise and successfully served as a Union spy during the Civil War. Another tale had it that one night in later years a tramp begged for food at Alexander McAdams's door. The aged father recognized his daughter under her male attire and demanded she leave. A more benign sequel to Jeanette's story had her return to her childhood home decades later with the news that she was married and living far away. I leave it to the discretion of the discerning reader to imagine what *really* happened . . .

Chapter 11

"THEY SAY I'VE BEEN KILLING SOMEONE . . ."

The Butchery of Greenberry Hood

For sheer, wanton cruelty it would be hard to better the slaughter of 14-year-old Greenberry Hood by his adopted father, Stephen Hood. The callous murder of this young boy badly shocked the Clevelanders of 1873, and Hood became the only child killer to end up on a Cuyahoga County scaffold (unless one counts John Hughes, the pitiless slayer of child-woman Tamsen Parsons in Bedford in 1866). And the horrible details of Greenberry Hood's murder remaining shocking today, even to a public saturated by such Herod-like atrocities as the murder of Amy Mihaljevic and the drowning of the Smith boys by their mother in South Carolina. Suffice it to say that Stephen Wood was the kind of parent that makes one think Hansel and Gretel got off easy.

Greenberry Hood's last day on earth began early. Awakened July 17, 1873, at 3:30 a.m. by his father, Stephen, at the family home on Webster Street, Greenberry and his stepbrother Fred struggled into their ragged clothes and staggered downstairs to a modest breakfast prepared by their mother, Eden. They knew better than to protest their rude awakening and short commons: Stephen Hood was a notoriously violent man with a hair-trigger temper who often beat both Greenberry ("Green" to his intimates) and 17-year-old Fred. It was also known that Stephen had a special aversion for Greenberry, so he and Fred obeyed without a word when Stephen ordered them out to search for valuables in the empty lot at Payne's Pastures where

Barnum's traveling circus had just played its Cleveland engagement. (Payne's Pastures was an area then bounded by East 18th Street, East 21st Street, and Superior and Payne Avenues.)

Greenberry and Fred searched without success until daybreak, about 5 a.m., when Stephen rejoined them. Telling them that he was going fishing, he insisted they accompany him. Fred was loath to do so, but Greenberry was willing, and, in any case, the boys knew they really didn't have a choice with their implacable father. So they followed obediently along as the 32-year-old Stephen led them up to Perry Street (East 22nd), down Perry to Prospect, up Prospect to Willson Avenue (East 55th), and then south on Willson until they crossed the Cleveland city limits into Newburgh Township. Somewhere along Willson, Stephen halted at a German beer garden and bought a pop bottle filled with whiskey. Then they resumed their journey south on Willson, until the road disappeared in the wilderness of undeveloped woods that lay just south of Cleveland.

No one knows how far the threesome walked that hot July morning. When Fred Hood later tried to retrace their route for the police, it appeared that Stephen Hood had led the two boys back and forth over essentially the same ground for several hours in an attempt to both confuse and exhaust them. Fred recalled walking by a sawmill, seeing a group of laborers in the woods, and passing by a deep gully where the road from Cleveland disappeared. Finally, about 9 a.m., Stephen Hood called a halt at a point perhaps a mile and a half south of the Newburgh Township line and about a half mile from the Cleveland & Newburgh "dummy" railroad line tracks. Plopping himself down under a shady poplar tree in the woods, Stephen offered whiskey to the boys, saying, "Here, take this, it will keep you from catching cold." Fred refused to drink it, but Greenberry, probably hoping to pacify his touchy father, shared the bottle with him. Half an hour later the bottle was empty, and Greenberry was passed out on the ground. Placing a handkerchief over his face, Stephen turned to Fred and demanded that he walk back to Cleveland and purchase more whiskey from a saloon they'd passed on the way. Fred was reluctant to do so, but he gave in, lest he have to face with stepfather's anger alone.

No one knows exactly what happened while Fred Hood was gone on his whiskey errand. He thought it was only about fifteen minutes before he returned to Stephen, having been unable to locate the saloon. When he returned to the spot by the poplar tree, Stephen was waiting for him, but Greenberry was gone. More ominously, Fred noticed some spots of blood on the trunk of the poplar and on Stephen's boots, as if someone, he thought, had bled from a bloody nose. When he asked where Greenberry was, Stephen became angry, and said, "I don't know. I think maybe he is lost. Come on, let's go to town. Green's gone home." Fred then suggested that they search for him, but Stephen became even more incensed, insisting that Greenberry had gone home and forbidding Fred from hollering out his name in the woods. Reluctantly, Fred followed Stephen back toward Cleveland, watching warily as his half-drunken adopted father lurched ahead of him. Somewhere on Willson Avenue, Stephen stumbled into the Three Cent Saloon and began downing glasses of whiskey and ale. He soon passed out, giving Fred Hood the welcome opportunity to "cut" and run all the way back to his Webster Street home, just south of the Erie Street Cemetery.

When he got home about 4 p.m., Fred told his mother, Eden, and Mrs. Josephine Johnson, a woman who lived with her husband in the same house as the Hoods, what had happened in the woods. Knowing Stephen's strong animus against Greenberry, they agreed with Fred's surmise that Stephen had probably killed him in the Newburgh woods. So, when a hungover Stephen Hood returned home about an hour later in an ugly mood, Eden, Fred, and Mrs. Johnson hastily fled the house, pursued closely by Stephen as they walked up the street. Accosting Patrolman Patrick O'Day at the corner of Webster and Brownell Street (East 14th), they told him their suspicions. O'Day was skeptical, but they insisted, so he finally escorted them up to Woodland Avenue and Chapel Street, where he hailed Police Sergeant Egbert E. Morse off a horse-drawn streetcar as it passed. Pointing out Stephen, who was still nearby shadowing them, he summarized the situation to Morse in words that spoke volumes about the status of black families like the Hoods in Gilded Age white Cleveland:

> Here's a drunken darkey, who has been out in the country with his two boys and has returned home with only one of them; the boy who came back says he saw drops of blood

where he last saw the other boy and the woman fears that the man has done some harm to the boy. It's a quarrelsome family, I wish you would look into the matter.

Sergeant Morse probably knew it was a quarrelsome family: sometime during the previous year the Cleveland police had been summoned to the Webster Street house after Stephen laid violent hands on Eden. But Morse had Eden repeat her story to him, and then listened to Fred and Mrs. Johnson. Then he turned to Stephen and asked, "What have you done with the boy?" Stephen replied that he had given him to a man named Jack Leonard to take to Pittsburgh. Stephen only mumbled a few sentences, but he managed, as in his later interviews on the subject, to contradict himself. First he stated that it was "Jack Leonard," then it was "Jack Lyde," and finally it was "John Lane." "That's too thin," concluded Morse, and he arrested Stephen on the spot and hauled him to the police station at Forest Street (East 37th) and Woodland Avenue, where he was booked on suspicion of murder. (The next morning's *Cleveland Leader* would characterize Hood's post-arrest demeanor thusly: "The negro showed his ivories, look frightened and trembled.") Then Morse, Patrolman O'Day, and Fred Hood left to reconnoiter the spot where Greenberry had last been seen.

It was almost twilight when they got to the poplar tree, after a journey of several hours over the crisscross trail charted from Fred Hood's fuzzy memories. It must have been a terrible evening for the young man; tired and frightened after the events of the long day (he'd been up since 3:30 a.m.), he eventually had to be goaded forward by threats as he led Morse and O'Day in their ominous search. Just before sunset, however, as they passed by the sawmill, they saw the poplar tree and some broken branches beneath it—just as Fred Hood had described the scene. Searching around the poplar tree for bloodstains and finding none, Morse, O'Day, and Fred then fanned out from the tree in a triangular area to examine the surrounding ground. Some minutes later, Morse's foot landed on a portion of ground that "gave." Standing back, Morse noted that the area looked disturbed, and some covering debris looked as if it had been recently dragged there. "This doesn't look right," he said to

O'Day, and the officers started digging up the ground with their bare hands. The dirt was loose, and when Morse got down about 14 inches, his hand pulled out a piece of wet cloth. A little farther down, they found the dead body of Greenberry Hood and pulled it up.

DIABOLICAL MURDER!

A NEGRO KILLS HIS ADOPTED SON!

Whisky and Brutality the Cause!

A Long Search for the Body!

It is Found one Foot Under Ground!

ARREST OF THE MURDERER!

THE FULL PARTICULARS.

Cleveland Leader, July 18, 1875.

It must have been a ghastly sight in the fading twilight of that otherwise peaceful woods. The corpse was so covered with blood, all the way from the skull to the waist, that they couldn't identify any specific wounds. Greenberry was lying with his face down, his right arm twisted back, as though tied, with his left arm in a crippled position at his side. As they laid his forlorn corpse on the forest floor, it began to rain steadily.

Leaving O'Day to guard the crime scene, Morse returned to the city with Fred and sent a squad to retrieve the body. Picking up Stephen Hood at the Forest Street station, he took him to the Central Police Station on Champlain Street, where he was severely interrogated by Morse, Police Superintendent Jacob Schmitt, and Sergeant Henry Hoehn (later to become famous for his brave role in the "Blinky" Morgan affair and, eventually, be named Cleveland police chief). Throughout the third-degree session (or "sweating," as it was known to its vigorous practitioners) Hood stuck doggedly to the flimsy story he had originally told Morse and would repeat until the day he died: he had taken Greenberry to the Newburgh woods, handed him over to "John Leonard" or "Jack Lane" to take to Pittsburgh, and then returned home. He had not been drinking on July 17, he had never mistreated the boys, and he had no idea why Fred would tell such terrible and brazen lies about him. When asked why he thought he'd been arrested, he simply laughed and said, "I don't know, but they say I've been killing someone." Otherwise, his demeanor was calm and expressionless: "cool and seemed to show no emotion of guilt or fear, but only an impassive, stolid expression," said the next morning's *Cleveland Leader*, which also described Hood as looking like "a respectable, well-behaved but careless colored man."

The inquest into Greenberry Hood's death opened the next day in the basement of the Central Police Station. Chaired by Cuyahoga County coroner T. Clarke Miller, the panel called Fred Hood, Sergeant Morse, and W. J. Scott to testify. Scott had performed the postmortem on Greenberry, and a grisly business it had been. He found a wound running from the mouth back to the right ear that had fractured some facial bones, loosened teeth, and appeared to have been caused by a two-edged weapon, perhaps a thick wooden board. The groin area showed a severe contusion, as if it had been forcefully kicked, and there was another contusion and some more fractures behind the left ear. Removal of the scalp showed that several pieces of the back of the skull had been broken and driven into the brain, probably causing instantaneous death. Greenberry's fists were clenched tight and his eyes were shut, "as if death had been cruel and painful." His feet were bare, and his body was dressed in a coarse cotton shirt and shabby jeans.

Then it was Stephen Hood's turn. He was sworn in after Prosecutor Homer DeWolf warned him plainly, "Hood, you are charged with the murder of the boy Green." Hood began his testimony by repeating his story about "John Lane." He said he had met Lane by the poplar tree on the day before his expedition with the boys and arranged to have Lane take Greenberry the next day, first to Pittsburgh and then to New Albany, Indiana, where Hood's brother Andrew lived. Within a few minutes DeWolf's shrewd examination had entangled Hood in an exitless maze of irreconcilable contradictions and blatant lies. Hood tried to claim that he had first met "John Lane" in the army and had seen him several times since in Cleveland. But Hood had to admit, when pressed, that there was no one else who could verify that "John Lane" existed or that he had ever been in Cleveland, much less the Newburgh woods. Cautiously prefacing all of his answers with the conditional phrase "*If* Greenberry is killed," the desperate Hood eventually tried to make the inquest panel believe that there were two or even three men named "John Lane," none of whom could be proven to exist. His version of the July 17 events agreed with Fred's story—except for the drinking—right up to the moment he sent him to fetch more whiskey. It was then, Stephen swore, almost as soon as Fred was out of sight, that John Lane took Greenberry away. At the end of the inquest the illiterate Hood signed the inquest record with his *X,* and the panel's swift verdict was that Greenberry Hood had been murdered by his stepfather.

The Cleveland newspapers of that era could have taught Louis Seltzer a thing or two about prejudicial pre-trial publicity. Characterizing the accused as an "ignorant, beetle-browed individual," they utterly—and competitively—vilified him from the

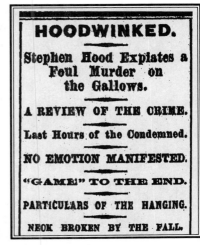

HOODWINKED.

Stephen Hood Expiates a Foul Murder on the Gallows.

A REVIEW OF THE CRIME.

Last Hours of the Condemned.

NO EMOTION MANIFESTED.

"GAME" TO THE END.

PARTICULARS OF THE HANGING.

NECK BROKEN BY THE FALL.

Cleveland Leader, April 29, 1874.

moment he was arrested until he stood on a Cleveland gallows nine months later. Although his motive for the murder was unknown, it was apparently no stretch for a *Cleveland Leader* editorialist to anatomize Hood as possessing "a depraved and ignorant nature, sunk into the lowest depths of every vile element that can enter into the composition of man and stimulated by the use of strong drink." Even before the inquest was over, the same paper insisted that Stephen Hood had murdered Greenberry "with only the mere reason that he was tired of keeping a little boy whom he had, with the sanction of the law, adopted as a son." Altogether, this "negro brute" reminded Cleveland scribes of nothing so much as . . . John Cooper. (Cooper, a casual laborer, had murdered tinsmith James Swing in his Cedar Avenue shop in 1871, probably the first intensely sensationalized black-on-black crime in Cleveland history; the story of this exceptionally brutal homicide is recounted in the author's "A Swing for a Swing" in *Death Ride at Euclid Beach.*) As one journalist put it:

[Hood] is a good match for the negro Cooper who was hanged for the cold-blooded murder of Swing. The two murderers were born to just about the same complexion, save that Hood has a tinge more of black in his color. [Contrariwise, the *Plain Dealer* would insist that Hood was "yellow" colored.] Hood is above the medium height, is stoutly built, has a broad, round head covered with a mat of close curling wool and has small, sharp eyes. His manner is dogged with an evidently assumed air of innocence.

There was obviously a lot more to Stephen Hood than the formulaic racist slurs of Cleveland newspapermen, but we have little more record of his biographical facts. Born in 1842 in Vernon, Indiana, to a free black farmer, Ephraim Hood, and his wife, Ross, Stephen had seven brothers and one sister. By the time he was a teenager he had already abandoned farming for the more romantic calling of a deckhand on a Mississippi River steamboat. He much enjoyed the steamboating life, although he had to be careful, when calling at southern ports, that he not be kidnapped into slavery. Usually he was protected by his steamboat captain, who pretended that he was Stephen's "master." But there was at least one close call in New Orleans, where Hood was jailed as a runaway slave until his captain showed up with his Indiana birth certificate. Shortly before the outbreak of the Civil War, Hood married a free black, Eden Jones, with whom he bickered and battled to the end of his life. When the first black Union army units were formed, Hood enlisted in the 28th (Colored) Indiana Volunteer Regiment. Serving 34 months as a cook, he was present at the battles of Chickahominy, White House Landing, and Halifax Court House and the siege of Petersburg, where he was wounded in the hip by a shell fragment and in the wrist by a musket ball. He was mustered out with an honorable discharge in 1865 and returned to Indiana.

It was while Hood was away in the army that Eden wrote to ask if they could adopt a three-year-old boy from the Brownstone, Indiana, poorhouse. Hood agreed, and the boy was given the name Greenberry and formally adopted by Stephen when he returned to civilian life. A couple of years later, Greenberry acquired a step, Fred, who joined the family when he was 12 (probably in 1868), after his mother and father, Stephen's brother, died. After the war

Stephen tried farming at various places and worked in a Vernon quarry before coming to Cleveland in October 1870. Up until the morning of the murder he had labored as a hod carrier for small-time Cleveland masons and contractors.

Considering the inflamed state of public opinion and his uncommunicatively surly mien, Stephen Hood received a sterling legal defense at his December 1873 trial. That was entirely due to the talent and dedication of John P. Green, the legendary African American Cleveland attorney. Green was then just at the beginning of his illustrious career, during which he would become the first black elected to public office in Cleveland, then state representative, state senator, and the "father" of Ohio's Labor Day observance before dying at the age of 95 in 1940. He and his assistant, William Clark, pulled out all the stops for Hood in their appeal to the jurymen and presiding judge Robert F. Paine. (Two years before, Paine had also presided over the first-degree-murder trial of John Cooper.) But they really had their work cut out for them: defending an accused child murderer was tough enough, but this time their prosecuting opponents were celebrated Cleveland legal lion Samuel Eddy and Homer DeWolf, who had already made a fool of Hood at the inquest.

Although it lasted four days, the testimony at Hood's trial revealed nothing more about the death of Greenberry Hood. Hood stuck to his idiotic alibi about "John Lane," despite the fact that no single fact could be discovered about this mythical personage. (John Leonard Whitfield, the 1923 killer of Cleveland police patrolman Dennis Griffin, would rely on a similar defense with a similar outcome.) Every witness who had spoken at the inquest repeated his testimony, including star witness Fred Hood, who favorably impressed everyone—except his stepfather—with his precocity in the witness box. John Green didn't dare put his client on the stand, and he had little to work with in constructing an insanity defense. Defense witness William Buckley, a friend of Stephen's, testified that Hood had suffered some ill health and that he was subject to occasional, possibly epileptic, fits. But the other defense witnesses merely offered weak testimonials as to Stephen's good character, so the burden of defense was left to Green's closing argument. And it must have been a powerful one: Green spoke for almost two hours, and it was unanimously reported that his impassioned plea frequently reduced his audience to tears.

After prosecutor DeWolf's closing argument and Judge Paine's instructions, the jury went out at 5 p.m. December 17. It returned the next morning at 9 with an announcement that they had found Stephen Hood "Guilty." Prosecutor DeWolf, mindful of the debacle at James Parks's first trial, immediately asked Judge Paine to order the jury out so they could reformulate their verdict with the proper wording of "Guilty of murder in the first degree." From the opening gavel on December 15 until the proper verdict was uttered on December 18, Stephen Hood showed no emotion or reaction to what was going on around him. His passivity was in striking contrast to his wife, Eden, who could often be seen weeping at his side throughout the four-day trial. Nor did he react much on December 31, 1873, when Judge Paine sentenced him to death. When asked if he wished to say anything before his sentence, Hood replied. "No, I have nothing much to say, only that I am an innocent man." Judge Paine then pronounced sentence in harsh words reminiscent of his sentencing of John Cooper two years before:

> It is sufficient for this occasion to remind you of the events of the seventeenth day of July last, when you enticed the little boy Greenberry Hood, whom you had adopted and upon whom you had bestowed your own name and taught to look to you as father and protector, into a lonely and unfrequented wood, and there persuaded him to partake of intoxicating liquors until he became unconscious.
>
> While in this condition you inflicted upon his head crushing blows with some heavy weapon which caused his death, and then threw his body into a hole in the ground, hastily prepared and covered it with brush, leaves and mud. It is difficult to conceive of deeper depravity than that which controlled you and nerved your arm in the commission of your terrible crime. It now only remains for me to pronounce the sentence of the law, which is, and it is the judgment and sentence of the Court, that you, Stephen Hood, be taken from

the bar of this Court to the jail of Cuyahoga County, and
that you be safely confined therein and kept in close custody
until the time of your execution, and that on Wednesday, the
twenty-ninth day of April, in the year of our Lord one thousand eight hundred and seventy-four, between the hours of
ten o'clock in the forenoon and two o'clock in the afternoon
of said twenty-ninth day of April, you be by the Sheriff of
Cuyahoga County hanged by the neck until you are dead;
and may God have mercy on your soul. The Sheriff will see
this judgment executed.

John P. Green had not given up. Hailed by Cleveland newspapers with "hearty praise" for his Herculean efforts in a lost cause,
he filed a motion for writ of error and took it all the way to the
Ohio Supreme Court. The crux of his appeal was that Judge Paine's
bailiff had allowed the jury to leave their sequestered room during
their all-night deliberations, and further, that they had entered the
adjoining courtroom to consult law books on the subject of "malice aforethought" and the legal definition of "first-degree murder."
In support of these charges Green submitted affidavits from the
bailiff and several jurymen. But the Ohio Supreme Court justices
rejected his argument, admitting that the allegations contained in
the affidavits might well be true—but that existing Ohio law pre-
vented jury members from impeaching their own verdicts. As for
the bailiff, well, wasn't he was rather to be commended for allowing the jurymen to move into Judge Paine's courtroom, which in
the chilling December cold was more comfortable and warm than
the jury quarters?

Although his stolid indifference contrasted sharply with John
P. Green's wasted eloquence, Stephen Hood hadn't quite given up
either. On March 25, Cuyahoga County sheriff Pardon B. Smith
discovered a plot to effect the escape of Hood from his death-row
cell in the county jail. That day, while escorting nine prisoners to
the Columbus penitentiary, Smith noticed one of the prisoners fid-
dling with his ankle chains. Taking a closer look, Smith discovered
that they had been neatly sawn through. Calling in more guards, he
interrogated the prisoners and finally persuaded a hardened felon

named Rover to talk. Rover confessed that it was all part of a plot to free Hood. It developed that some days before, Hood's wife, Eden, a frequent jail visitor, had brought her husband a large rice pudding. The March 26 edition of the *Plain Dealer* humorously enlarged on the pudding's virtues:

> It looked delicious. Yet we venture to say that nothing edible could have been so luscious to his palate as the pudding was satisfactory to his mind. He probably did not eat any of the dish. At least we presume he did not; it was composed of such extraordinary ingredients. The recipe she used is not to be found in any cook book. We will not pretend to give the exact quantities of the several component parts but we should judge they were in about the following proportions: One half cupful *aqua fortis* [nitric acid] in a vial. One large cupful blue putty. Four ounces steel saws. Rat-tail square, three cornered and other files to taste. Hood no doubt keenly relished such provender . . .

Sheriff Pardon B. Smith was not so amused. When he returned to Cleveland he examined Hood's cell and found that two cell bars had already been sawn through, the acid speeding the procedure and the blue putty disguising the work. Hood feigned complete innocence about it until Smith threatened to have him chained to his cell floor for the duration. Hood then surrendered his stash of saws, putty, and acid and retreated once more into his habitual silence and torpor.

Stephen Hood retained his passivity right up until the end. He showed no emotion on the day before his hanging when a reporter told him that Governor William Allen had turned down his final appeal for commutation. (A petition for such had been circulated within Cleveland's black community but had garnered very few signatures.) During his last hours, Hood received spiritual counseling from the Reverend J. P. Underwood of the African Methodist Episcopal Church on Ohio Street (Central Avenue) and additional prayerful succor from the inevitable Lathrop Cooley, who, as constant readers of these narratives are aware, was something of a fixture at death row vigils. The night before his execution he released two statements to the newspapers. One was a thank-you note to the Reverend Underwood for his attentions and a request that he preach his funeral sermon. The other was Hood's last will and testament, a self-pitying document that denied any guilt and blamed the Cleveland Police and his nephew Fred for his predicament. Claiming that Fred's testimony had been coerced, Hood charged that Sergeant Morse and other officers had threatened to send Fred to reform school unless he implicated his uncle: "I suppose they thought they would be benefited by it, as well as get their names and reputations up by bringing an innocent man to the gallows." There was actually some truth to Hood's assertion: Morse had admitted in his testimony at Hood's trial that he had employed a potent arsenal of presents and threats to persuade Fred to "tell the truth." Hood's final testament went on to offer a blanket denial that he knew anything of Greenberry's fate: "I know no more about it than a child never born." Demonstrating that his time spent with spiritual mentors like the Reverends Jones and Lathrop had not been wasted, a good half of Hood's prolix testament piously invoked God's superior judgment and foretold "a time when all truth will be brought to light."

As the hours ticked down on his fatal day of April 29, Hood stayed in character. His last meeting with his wife was at 10 a.m. that morning. They forgave each other for any wrongs done, and a few minutes later she departed in a carriage, weeping loudly. Just before he was led to the scaffold, Hood met for the last time with his son Fred. Unctuously forgiving him for his trial testimony, he told him to be a good boy and said he hoped to meet him in heaven. About the same time, Prosecutor DeWolf dropped by, and Hood thanked him for a fair trial and many kindnesses.

At 11:40 a.m. Hood was led out to the gallows. As he passed by the cells of his fellow prisoners he shook hands and cautioned some of them to "live right." Attired in his Sunday-best clothes and boots that he had himself blackened that morning, he strode to the gallows "with a firm step and calm demeanor." At the foot of the scaffold, Sheriff Smith asked him if he wished to make a final statement, but he shook his head and said, "I have nothing to say." Shaking hands all around, Hood stepped to the drop and, like John

Cooper, bounced lightly on it as if to test its solidity. His arms and legs were pinioned and the rope adjusted around his neck. Seconds later, the black cap came down over his head, and at exactly 11:54 Stephen Hood fell six feet though the very same drop traveled by James Parks and his successors. It was not a clean hanging: spectators could clearly see that the rope had slipped up toward Hood's face, and they watched in horror as he strangled in agony for the next five minutes, his sufferings clearly evidenced by convulsive shudders as he swung slowly, back and forth, back and forth, in the northeast corner of the county jail. His pulse finally stopped beating at 12:07 p.m., and the body was taken down seven minutes later. After the mandatory autopsy, his corpse was placed in a plain coffin and given to Eden Hood. Late that afternoon, spectators lined up at a second-floor room on Ontario Street to gawk at Hood's body, which was on view for anyone willing to pay admission. It was reported that Fred Hood could be seen taking admissions there for some days before Hood's corpse received more proper obsequies at the Reverend Jones's Ohio Street church.

Shortly after Hood's execution, a story circulated that he had made a "death bed" confession to a fellow jail prisoner named Stanley several days before his hanging. The gist of his admissions to Stanley was that he had killed Greenberry with a club and buried him on the spot. That is probably exactly what happened, although a last-minute confession seems incongruent with Stephen Hood's otherwise invariably defiant and unrepentant demeanor. It is possible, of course, that all reported characterizations of Stephen Hood (and for that matter, John Cooper) were simply based on the bias of uncomprehending of law-enforcement officials and racist journalists, who did not take into account the masking of personality that must have been second nature to blacks living in Cleveland during the late 19th century. They saw what they wanted to see when they looked at persons like John Cooper and Greenberry Hood, and their views were perfectly reflected in the legal and journalistic cultures of the day. And, closing on a sad note, Fred Hood was last heard of in 1889, when it was reported that he was in chronic trouble with the police.

Chapter 12

SHABBY DEATH ON SHERIFF STREET

The Murder of Louis Weik

Dedicated with love to retired Cleveland police officer Joan Patrici

Every Cleveland police murder has been a unique episode. Some random but fatal mixture of circumstances and persons has suddenly been precipitated—and a good man has fallen, a sacrifice to the safety of Forest City citizens. But not all such murders have had the fascinating melodrama of, say, the murder of John Shipp by Edward Rutheven in 1900 (for an account of the evil Rutheven see "The Black Silk Handkerchief" in the author's *Death Ride at Euclid Beach*) or the 1887 slaying of Detective William Hulligan by "Blinky" Morgan. These two homicides featured colorful killers, prolonged manhunts, suspenseful trials, and the satisfying finality of the hangman's noose or the electric chair. But the mundane reality is that for every such exciting drama, the annals of Cleveland's police murders also provide counternarratives of shabby, sordid, and just plain stupid killings, generally perpetrated by pathetic nonentities and lacking conclusive denouements. The tale of Patrolman Louis Weik's murder is one such story, and it might well serve as a template for the banal horror that characterizes so many police murders.

By all accounts, Louis D. Weik was a nice young man. Just 24 years old in December 1903, Louis had only been a member of the Cleveland police force for nine months. A Spanish-American

War veteran, he had worked as a clerk in the McIntosh-Huntington hardware firm before taking Badge #330 and a patrolman's round in downtown Cleveland. And it was just that second week of December when he was assigned to the Eagle Street-Sheriff Street (East 4th) beat around the old Central Market, situated where Broadway and Woodland Avenues converged with Ontario Street. Here it was that death found him in the early hours of Wednesday, December 9, only minutes away from the end of his nocturnal shift.

PATROLMAN LOUIS D. WEICK.

Cleveland Police Patrolman Louis D. Weik.

Boisterously drunken men stumbling through the streets were no novelty in turn-of-the-century Cleveland. The municipal policy toward drunks was a tolerant one under the regime of Mayor Tom Johnson and his police chief, Fred Kohler, both disciples of the "Golden Rule" policy first pioneered by Toledo, Ohio, lawmen. The idea was to move public inebriates along if possible, or lock them up for the night if necessary—but not to penalize them with a criminal record unless they proved unusually belligerent or recidivist. Unfortunately for Louis Weik, Gaetano Pisciotta was something much worse than your run-of-the-mill feisty drunk.

It all began about 2:30 that Wednesday morning. Patrolman Weik was walking his customary beat near the Central Market, checking store doors, when he heard the familiar and unmistakable sounds of drunken carouse. Tracing the commotion to the corner of Eagle and Sheriff Streets, he encountered a group of men arguing in front of 231 Sheriff Street. Their names were John Polito, Thomas Gaetano Pisciotta, Angelo Vasi, and John Valotta. They were all Sicilian immigrants, they had just left a dance held by the Societe Trinacra Fratellanza Siciliana at Germania Hall on Erie Street (East

9th Street), and three of them were trying to shepherd the severely inebriated Pisciotta toward a streetcar that would take him to his Superior Street home. Pisciotta, in the invariable manner of drunks, was unwilling to go, and it was his drunken shouting and profanity that drew Weik to the scene.

Recollections of the encounter would differ, but it is undisputed that Patrolman Weik ordered the group to keep quiet and keep moving along. All complied, except Pisciotta, who muttered that he "didn't give a damn about policemen!" and then proved it by cursing a blue streak at Weik. Then, as now, Cleveland police officers did not tolerate lip meekly, and Weik soon grabbed Pisciotta by his shoulders and prepared to haul him off to jail.

The twosome didn't get far. Pushing Weik away, Pisciotta spun around, whipped out a .38-caliber revolver, and fired three times at point-blank range. The first bullet somehow missed Weik. But the second and third slugs plowed into his abdomen and drilled his stomach and intestines. Amazingly, although he staggered backwards, Weik did not immediately fall. Warning Pisciotta's stunned companions to step aside, he shouted, "Stop or I'll fire!" When Pisciotta didn't

EXTRA

MAY RESULT IN MURDER

PATROLMAN WEIK IS PERHAPS FATALLY SHOT BY MAN ON EAGLE STREET.

THREE BULLETS TAKE EFFECT

OFFICER OF THE LAW SUSTAINS WOUND IN THE STOMACH THAT MAY PROVE FATAL.

HAD NO CHANCE TO DEFEND HIMSELF

Cause of Shooting Not Clear—Tony Bishallo Arrested on the Charge of Shooting to Kill.

Cleveland Leader, December 9, 1903

halt, Weik pulled his service revolver from a pocket and fired at him three times. All three bullets missed, as did another fired by Pisciotta as Weik, bleeding heavily, slumped to the ground.

Drawn by the sound of gunfire, two policemen on Eagle Street, Patrolman John Becker and Watchman John O'Shea, arrived at the scene just as Weik fell in the street. They pursued the fleeing Pisciotta to Ontario Street, where they grabbed him in front of the Central Market. Denying any wrongdoing, he surrendered without resistance and was relieved of his revolver. It was still warm and had four empty chambers. Meanwhile, plainclothes patrolmen Carl

DeHeck and Charles Whelan rushed to aid the wounded Weik. As they approached him, he muttered, "Boys, I am done for! Catch him!" and lapsed into unconsciousness. The officers were about to call for an ambulance when a passing Woodland streetcar motorman saw the group and offered to take Weik to Cleveland General (now MetroHealth) Hospital. Carefully placing the wounded patrolman on the car seats and pillowing his head with their jackets, they brought him to the hospital's operating theater within minutes.

Weik's pessimism about his wounds proved prescient. Although hospital surgeons were able to extract one bullet from his abdomen, the other was lodged in his spine and could not be removed. Moreover, his condition continued to worsen from massive abdominal bleeding. It was clear he could not survive, although he regained consciousness long enough to identify Pisciotta as his killer when the suspect was hauled to his bedside. When Police Captain John Schmunk asked him if he was the shooter, Weik distinctly replied, "That is the man." "Are you absolutely sure of it?" asked Schmunk. "Yes, I swear by the eternal God that he is that man," replied Weik. His wife, brother, and mother were with him when he died the next morning at 8:50. He also left behind Wilbur, an infant son.

Meanwhile, the badly hung over Pisciotta was enmeshed in the predictable routines of Cleveland justice. During the preliminary phase of a severe interrogation, personally conducted by Chief Fred Kohler, the 27-year-old immigrant claimed he did not remember or know anything about the shooting. Indeed, he had even forgotten his name, which he insisted was "Thomas Bishotta." But by late afternoon of December 9, his memory had improved remarkably, perhaps encouraged by questioning that left him bruised and bloody by the time his attorneys, Conway W. Noble, Hy David, and Sidney Vesey were permitted to see him. Kohler and his men, naturally, insisted that Pisciotta's injuries had been unavoidably incurred during his struggle with Weik and afterwards, when he had allegedly "resisted" arrest. Kohler furthermore offered his opinion that Pisciotta was feigning insanity. Whatever the truth, Pisciotta soon changed his demeanor. During his police court hearing on the morning of the murder, Pisciotta simply repeated a litany of denial in broken English: "Everybody say I shoot. I no shoot. I know nothings." (Pisciotta had only been in the United States for four years and claimed to know only a few words of English.) But that same afternoon, he admitted shooting Weik, confessing through his interpreter: "I did it; the drink was responsible." At the same time, however, he insisted that he had shot Patrolman Weik in self-defense after the patrolman had attacked him without provocation.

Louis Weik's funeral was a well attended and touching affair. The Reverend August Kimmell, the pastor of Trinity Evangelical Church, conducted the services at the home of the deceased on Holmden Avenue. The floral tributes were impressive, one a column of flowers supporting a dove of peace. A squad of 14 men from Company K of the 5th Regiment of Ohio Volunteer Infantry, Weik's unit in the Spanish-American War, fired three rifle volleys over his Riverside Cemetery grave before buglers Walter K. Patterson and Harry Gibbons played "Taps." Then the coffin, covered by an American flag, was lowered into the family burial vault. Besides his Holmden Avenue

MURDER

Profile Study of the Italian Accused of Murdering Policeman Weik.

Accused cop killer Piscoiotta.

house, Weik left his widow the sum of $500, paid from the police pension fund. In addition, she received $1,500 from the Police Protective Association, raised by the customary levy of $5 on each association member. She and Louis had only been married for 11 months.

If the murder of Louis Weik was a shabby tragedy, the fate of his killer proved something of a farce. Following a speedy indictment on a first-degree murder charge by a Cuyahoga County grand jury on December 14, Pisciotta's trial before Common Pleas Court judge George L. Phillips commenced on April 29, 1904. Represented by crack defense attorney William H. Boyd (paid with funds provided by the Societe Trinacra Fratellanza Siciliana and Pisciotta's brother John), Pisciotta pleaded a combination of alcohol-impaired judg-

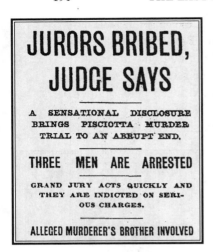

JURORS BRIBED, JUDGE SAYS

A SENSATIONAL DISCLOSURE BRINGS PISCIOTTA MURDER TRIAL TO AN ABRUPT END.

THREE MEN ARE ARRESTED

GRAND JURY ACTS QUICKLY AND THEY ARE INDICTED ON SERIOUS CHARGES.

ALLEGED MURDERER'S BROTHER INVOLVED

Cleveland Leader, May 10, 1904.

ment (the result of imbibing copious quantities of some potent Sicilian beverage known as "Hundred Herbs") and self-defense. Asserting that Weik had choked Pisciotta and beaten him with his nightstick, Boyd told the jury that his client had been "unlawfully assaulted" and was guilty of nothing more heinous than manslaughter. Pisciotta's self-defense plea was initially supported by the testimony of John Polito, who swore that Weik had treated Pisciotta with unprovoked brutality. The import of Polito's testimony, however, was severely diminished when Cuyahoga County prosecutor Harvey Keeler noted that Polito had testified to Weik's blamelessness at Pisciotta's police court hearing on the morning of the murder. Pisciotta's plea of self-defense was further undermined on May 4, when eyewitness Andrew Drushel testified for the state. Drushel, a carpenter who lived in a flat just above the shooting scene, swore that he had seen Pisciotta shoot Weik as soon as the officer tried to arrest him, and that Weik had fired only after Pisciotta shot him.

Cognizant that the momentum of the testimony was against his client, Boyd put Pisciotta on the stand on the afternoon of Friday, May 6. Acting out his own version of the killing with court interpreter Angelo D'Anna playing the role of Weik, Pisciotta forced D'Anna to the floor and handled him so roughly that the jurymen laughed and D'Anna refused to participate in a second reenactment. Nor did Pisciotta help himself during his evasive sparring with Prosecutor Keeler:

> Keeler: What was in your mind as you were standing there shooting at the officer?
> Pisciotta: Who can tell?
> Keeler: And so you were peaceable, talking lowly, making no disturbance?

Sketches of principals in jury tampering.

Pisciotta: Yes.
Keeler: Then why did the officer attack you?
Pisciotta: I don't know.

All of the trial testimony became irrelevant on Monday morning, May 9. As soon as court convened, a solemn Judge Phillips read a statement informing the jury that there had been attempts to bribe some of the jurors. William E. Driffield and Walter Gates had been approached in early May by fellow juror Marcus Greenspan and offered $25 apiece for their aid in either acquitting Pisciotta or insuring no verdict worse than a manslaughter conviction. Phillips declared a mistrial and dismissed the jury, and Greenspan was arrested as he left the box.

The facts of the bribery attempts were conclusively proven at subsequent trials. Acting in concert with Frank Mercurio, a janitor at the Central Market, and John Pisciotta, Greenspan had approached Driffield and Gates on separate occasions. Both jurors had immediately reported his offers to Prosecutor Keeler, who had told them to pretend to cooperate with Greenspan. A meeting at the latter's house on Perry Street (East 22nd Street) soon followed, after which Driffield and Gates took the bribe cash. Suitably marked, it was turned over to Keeler, who brought the matter to Judge Phillips's outraged attention. Only a month later both Greenspan and Mercurio began serving three-year terms for jury fixing, the more prudent John Pisciotta having fled to Italy. Greenspan's sentencing on June 13 featured a distinct tinge of anti-Semitism, as Judge William A. Babcock raked the Russian Jewish refugee over his judicial coals:

> It would seem that one in your place, as you have said on the witness stand, "without a country and an exile from Russia"—would have looked upon these beautiful children of yours and said, "These are the product of the free air and institutions of America". . . . There would have been no favored land for your asylum if others had not built up what you were willing, for a few pieces of silver, to tear down.

Pisciotta's second trial, several months later, was no more satisfactory than his first. Although uncontaminated by any "fixing," his jurors could not agree, some voting for first-degree murder, some for second-degree, and some for manslaughter. The third trial, held before Judge Duane Tilden in December 1904, proved the charm. It consumed only six days, both sides in the contest being wearily familiar with the evidence and testimony, and Pisciotta was convicted of second-degree murder after 24 hours of deliberation. He betrayed no emotion as the verdict was read, nor did he protest when sentenced, on January 20, 1905, to life imprisonment in the Ohio Penitentiary.

It was just as well that he remained mute. Then—as now—"life imprisonment" wasn't what it should be. Just 10 years later, on December 28, 1914, Ohio governor James Cox commuted Pisciotta's sentence to 15 years. It wasn't even that, as Pisciotta was released from prison that very same day.

Louis D. Weik's name is inscribed on the National Law Enforcement Officers' Memorial Wall, Judiciary Square, Washington, D.C. (Panel 25, West Wall, Line 15).

Chapter 13

THIRD-RATE ROMANCE, PROSPECT AVENUE

The Murder of ?

Just tell them that you saw me,
She said, they'll know the rest,
Just tell them I was looking well you know,
Just whisper if you get a chance to mother dear, and say,—
I love her as I did long, long ago.

—"Just Tell Them That You Saw Me"
(1895 song by Paul Dresser)

Big isn't necessarily better when it comes to murder. Which is to say that sometimes the obscure slayings of humble persons shed more light on the inner workings of society than the deafening cultural reverberations of a Nicole Brown Simpson or Sunny von Bülow slaying. Or—to put it in an utterly Cleveland context—we can learn a lot more about the historical texture of the Forest City social fabric from the murder of a forgotten prostitute than the killing of a Marilyn Sheppard. Consider if you will the case of Dolores Evans.

Oddly or ironically enough, the first thing you should know is that her name was not Evans or probably even Dolores. Nor, probably, any of the other dubious monikers she assumed during her short and shabby career as a discount prostitute plying her trade in the grill rooms, all-night restaurants, and "stag hotels" of 1916 downtown Cleveland. Her multiple aliases included Dolores Evans (which is what we will call her hence to avoid confusion) or Evens (Cleveland newspaper editors could decide whether she spelled it "Evans" or "Evens"), Elizabeth Myers, Bertha Smith, and Emma Smith. Not that her real name mattered much in the end—for not even her mother or father came forward to claim kinship when she lay battered and dead on a slab at the Cuyahoga County Morgue.

The telephone call came in to Cleveland's Central Police Station on Champlain Street at 1:45 p.m., January 12, 1916. The male caller, refusing to identify himself, told police that someone was dead at the Hotel Perry, 2111 Prospect Avenue, and hung up. Minutes later, Patrolmen David Sifling and Stephen Majores arrived at the hotel and were led up to the third floor by proprietress Jennie Smith. Entering Room 19 in the northwest corner, the officers found the 20-by-20-foot room in considerable disorder, with the dark red carpet and some of the furniture obviously displaced. There were some wire hangers, a couple of metal hairpins, a cheap imitation ruby ring, and a paper cigar band lying on the floor. On the dresser was a pair of gloves and a lavaliere, set with a cheap fake ruby stone. Inside the fingers of one of the gloves were two nickels, the only money found in the room. At the foot of the bed lay a heap of women's clothing. On the wash basin was a small bowl containing some suspiciously red liquid. (Chemical analysis by Cleveland city chemist Wilbur White eventually disproved the popular theory that it was blood washed off a killer's hands.) And on the bed, weltering in pools of her own blood, lay the body of a young woman. Clad only in her stockings, she had obviously been dead for some hours. Although a hotel towel was wrapped and knotted very tightly around her head and nose, it did not conceal that her face had been brutally beaten before death came. There was also considerable bruising on her torso, breasts, and thighs, and on her broken neck what very much looked like the impressions of the thumb and finger of a left hand. Neither the corpse nor the contents of the room offered a single clue as to the dead woman's identity.

Sifling and Majores were soon joined by Police Detective Captain Alfred Walker and other sleuths, who proceeded to grill the staff of the Hotel Perry. It didn't take these savvy policemen long to surmise that owner Jennie Smith, maid Ada Coffman, and night clerk Sidney Blumenthal were not only lying but had carefully "cooked" their story together before the cops arrived. That story, such as it was, went like this: At 11:45 the previous night, a young man and woman had entered the Perry and requested a room. Coffman was on the desk, and she led them up to Room 19 before returning to fetch a pitcher of ice water the man had requested. When Coffman brought it up, the young woman was already disrobing and seemed calm, comfortable, and unworried. A minute later, the man came down to the desk, tossed Coffman a $10 bill, and signed in as "Lou White and wife." Apologizing for not having a smaller bill, he waited for Coffman get him his change and then returned to Room 19. Nearly two hours passed without incident, and then at about 1:30 a.m., the man, fully dressed, came to the desk, casually tossed the Room 19 key to Coffman, and said, "Be back in five minutes." Walking out the door, he stood for a moment on Prospect before turning and striding west into the darkness. Coffman never saw him again that night.

Here, Hotel Perry owner Smith took up the tale. While making what she said were her customary rounds at 8:30 the next morning, she had found the door to Room 19 open and went in. It was winter and one of the shades was down, so it was pretty dark. But Smith could see what she thought was the form of a sleeping man under the bedsheet. So she locked the door behind her and thought no more about it until early afternoon, when she realized no one had yet emerged from Room 19. In short order, Coffman was sent up to investigate, the corpse was discovered, and the police were notified.

It didn't take Walker's men long to demolish this fabricated version of events. They knew the telephone call hadn't come from the Perry, and they found it suggestive that *all* of the Hotel Perry's residents had vanished by the time they arrived. It was painfully obvious what had really occurred: hours, perhaps, before the police had shown up, the hotel staff had discovered the corpse and immediately alerted their guests—most, if not all, of whom were abed with persons not their legally wedded spouses—to vamoose before the police arrived. What upset Walker most about their mass exodus was his reasonable guess that someone—surely the guests in adjoining rooms 18 and 20—had heard the sounds of the mortal struggle that must have taken place in Room 19. And now they were all gone.

But not quite. Walker's investigation was less than an hour old when it got a huge break from the arrival of Clara Dille and George Pierce. Dille, 17, was no stranger to the Cleveland police, having already appeared in juvenile court as a runaway, receiver of stolen property, and a consorter and cohabiter with older men. She told Walker that she had come to the Hotel Perry because she was concerned about the welfare of her chum, Dolores Evans. Evans, Dille explained, had checked into the Hotel Perry with a stranger the previous night, after agreeing to meet Dille later at an all-night restaurant at 2 a.m. When she hadn't shown up, Dille had gone looking for her. When told that there was a dead girl in Room 19, she burst into tears, sobbing "Oh, I just know it's Dolores!" More helpfully, Dille had brought a photograph of the dead girl with her, which she gave to the police. They quickly identified its subject as "Elizabeth Myers," a 19-year-old small-time prostitute they had arrested on suspicion of soliciting on November 4, 1915.

Dille's story didn't hold together much longer than the fictions of the Hotel Perry staff. Police soon learned that she and Pierce, a 31-year-old film operator at a St. Clair Avenue movie house, had previously shacked up together at the Hotel Perry, and more importantly, had signed in that very morning at 5 a.m. as "man and wife." More intriguing still, Dille and Pierce had taken Room 5, almost directly beneath Room 19, the scene of the murder. Told of this juxtaposition, Dille sobbed, "I might have been there when the murder was committed and slept in entire ignorance of the fact my chum probably lay dead almost directly over my head!" Arresting both Dille and Pierce, police also scooped up night clerk Blumenthal and hauled them all off to jail for a good sweating.

Pierce, who prosecuted a second career as a small-time pimp, was a hard nut to crack, but Dille started singing as soon as she was removed from his presence. She told police that the previous night she had been at the Chinese Republic Restaurant, a chop suey joint on the west side of East 9th Street, just across from where Chestnut

Street began running east. Although she remained generally un-
forthcoming about her career as a prostitute, Dille admitted she had
been sitting at a table with her friend Dolores Evans, while Pierce,
in an anteroom, attempted to procure clients for the two girls. Pointing to two men at a table, he asked the girls in sign language if they
would mind going out with them. Mouthing vehement "No!"s they
resumed conversation, and Pierce returned to his pandering. His

patience was rewarded only a few
minutes later, when a well-dressed
man entered the restaurant. He was a
25-year-old Italian named Louis Bianchetti, and walking into the Chinese Republic turned out to be the
worst decision of his life.

Pierce would later insist that he
had met Bianchetti on a number of
previous occasions, stretching back
to a first encounter in an all-night
restaurant in November, 1915. It is
immaterial whether he knew him or
not, as Pierce's intention that January night, stranger or no, was to vic-
timize him. Engaging in small talk,
he drank the beer Bianchetti bought
him and noted with discreet satisfaction the huge wad of bills the Italian
pulled out of his pocketbook to pay

*New Photo of Murdered Girl,
Midwife Thinks She Knows Her*

Photos of "Elizabeth Myers" aka
"Dolores Evans" and midwife.

for them. A moment later, Pierce moved on his mark. As Clara Dille
sauntered by their table, he said to Bianchetti, "That's an awful nice
girl. Would you like to meet her?" "No," said Bianchetti, probably
thinking the girl looked a little young. "Well, how about the other
one?" purred Pierce, indicating Dolores Evans. Perhaps because he
had been drinking all evening, Bianchetti merely grunted, "I don't
care," which Pierce correctly interpreted as a "yes." Minutes later,
Bianchetti paid the tab, and the two men and two girls filed out of
the second-floor restaurant and down the stairs. As they descended,
Bianchetti urged the girl to come to his room, an apartment on

East 18th Street near Payne Avenue. Evans refused, insisting that she would only accompany him to the Hotel Perry. Moreover, she continued, they must take a taxi there, as she feared the scrutiny of the vice squad if she was seen with a man on Cleveland streets. Taking charge, Pierce whistled a taxi from a stand on East 9th, and cabbie Thomas Sweeney wheeled his cab over. Two minutes later he stopped in front of the Hotel Perry. Running to the lobby, he asked Ada Coffman if she had a room available for a couple. She said yes, and a minute later Louis Bianchetti and Dolores Evans walked through the door.

What exactly transpired after that would eventually become the focus of a sensational seven-and-a-half-day murder trial and a judicial marathon that put half a dozen people in jail. Almost everyone who appeared as a witness for the state was either an accused or convicted criminal and had something to lose by telling the truth. So what follows is the most probable sequence of events.

In the aftermath of the murder, Cleveland mayor Davis and public officials pretended to be shocked to learn that downtown Cleveland was honeycombed with "stag hotels" and "hot pillow" joints of the Hotel Perry variety. Such resorts, and the grill rooms and all-night restaurants where commercial sex was arranged, were well known to Cleveland policemen, newspaper editors, and taxi drivers, and it was quite understood, if not necessarily approved, that anyone wishing to illicitly cohabit for a night, even with someone not of legal age, could be accommodated at places like the Hotel Perry.

There's no reason to doubt Ada Coffman's story up to the point where she left the couple together with a pitcher of ice water. What she couldn't know was what occurred after Bianchetti returned to Room 19. It may not have even been the most likely event. Dr. Philip A. Jacobs, who helped Coroner Byrne perform the autopsy on Evans's body, would testify that the couple did not have sex, or at least sex that left physical evidence. Indeed, County Prosecutor Cyrus Locher would suggest at Bianchetti's murder trial that Bianchetti had assaulted Evans because she sexually spurned or mocked him, a vindictive scenario that might explain why her thighs were so badly bruised. But whether or not they had sexual relations, Bianchetti and Evans decided to go to sleep. Before coming to bed, however, she complained of the heat and opened one of the windows. Some minutes later, while Bianchetti was unable to sleep—or pretending to be asleep because he mistrusted Evans—she arose and went to the dresser, where she had placed her jewelry. Muttering that she wished to put the bracelet and necklace in his coat for safety, she placed them in the right-hand pocket. At the same time, her back to Bianchetti in the bed, her left hand reached around and stealthily filched his cash-filled pocketbook from the inside pocket of his chinchilla coat.

Although Bianchetti had no criminal record, he was not naive enough to misconstrue what was happening. Shouting, he grabbed for Evans, clad only in stockings, even as she scurried to the open window. He was a second too late. Even as he began dragging her back to the bed, Evans managed to toss the pocketbook through the open window. Then she turned to resist Bianchetti. It was an unequal struggle at best. Powerfully built and athletic, Bianchetti had worked at manual labor since he was a child and was known for his strength. He was also known for his fiery temper when aroused, and he turned both loose on Evans in Room 19. He later claimed that he only hit her once, twice, or maybe three times, but the autopsy evidence suggested otherwise. Bianchetti suffered only a few scratches on his hands and face, but Evans wound up with a broken nose, blackened eyes, severe bruises on much of her body, and the unmistakable evidence of a strangler's grip on her throat, a grip that broke her windpipe and took her life. Sometime during the flurry of blows, Bianchetti managed to grab a towel, which he tied around her mouth to stifle whatever noise she was still capable of making. No one knows whether her death or the subsidence of his temper came first, but after she stopped moving, he pulled the sheet and bedspread over her and sat down to contemplate his next move. He would always insist that he did not know that she was dead when he left the room.

Bianchetti testified at his trial that he just "threw" his clothes on and stumbled downstairs. But Coffman saw nothing amiss in his attire or demeanor when he sauntered out at 1:30 a.m. His hair was combed, his tie was straight, and his brown suit was clean and

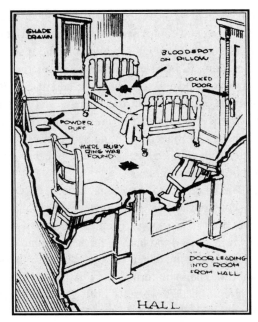

Diagram of the murder room 19, Hotel
Perry.

brushed, as was his sporty chinchilla coat. If he later told the truth,
his first act after going outside was to search the alley just west
of the hotel, where he believed Evans's confederate had waited to
retrieve the wallet thrown from the window. Bianchetti testified at
his trial that he found no pocketbook but did discern some footsteps
in the winter snow. He followed them to East 19th before the trail
petered out in the still-falling snow.

Bianchetti's conduct after he left the Hotel Perry was hardly the
behavior of a man with a bloody murder on his conscience. Returning to his flat on East 18th, he slept until 7:30, arising to go to his
job as a roast chef at the Cleveland Athletic Club on Euclid Avenue.
Reproached for his tardiness, he made up for it by cooking up 300
chickens for the lunch crowd. He explained away the scratches on
his hands and face to his coworkers, saying simply that he had gotten into a fight with a girl who had tried to roll him for his money.

Bianchetti showed up again for work on Thursday, January 13, at 7 a.m. If he hadn't known the Evans girl was dead, he knew it now, because there was the front-page headline of every Cleveland newspaper, and his fellow employees were chattering excitedly about it. By 10 a.m. he was in a state of panic. Speaking to Desire Weyer, head chef at the Cleveland Athletic Club, he told him he was quitting and demanded his back wages at once. Bianchetti was a prized employee, and the puzzled and unhappy Weyer asked him why he was leaving. All Bianchetti would say was "I got into some trouble—just a little trouble. I must leave the city immediately." Taking his $32 in wages, Bianchetti left the Club and began preparing to leave Cleveland.

An hour after he left the Athletic Club, Bianchetti appeared at Charlie Shields's garage on East 18th and hired Shields to drive him to East 71st and Broadway for $1. An hour later, Shields showed up at 1738 East 18th, where he helped Bianchetti haul his heavy steamer trunk into his automobile. Bianchetti's flight almost ended several minutes later. Telling Shields he had a bad cold and was probably contagious, he huddled, almost hidden, as Shields motored out Broadway. As they approached the intersection at East 71st Street, however, Shields cut off a streetcar and almost ran down a policeman. Inexplicably, the policeman didn't seem to notice, and a nervous Bianchetti ordered Shields to continue on to the Willow Inn on Schaaf Road. There, porter James Connors helped lift his trunk from Shields's auto, and Bianchetti settled down to kill time before catching the 5:30 train to Akron at the nearby Baltimore & Ohio Railroad station.

If Louis Bianchetti feared pursuit by the law, he certainly didn't show it that Thursday afternoon. For five hours that afternoon he drank, smoked, and played pool with other men at the Willow Inn, taking a brief interval out to grab a shave at Lou Gabb's barber shop down the road. Jo Margienean, 24, a Willow Inn habitué, remembered the handsome stranger well. He laughed easily, even when he lost at pool, ate a lot of sandwiches, and said he was going to Akron to get a job as a cook.

Bianchetti made an equally positive impression on the B & O run to Akron. Dressed in his brown suit and a dark brown overcoat, and wearing a dark fedora hat, he chatted with baggage master John

Ranft in four languages and offered him a drink of whiskey. Arriving in Akron at 7:19, he detrained at the Howard Street Station and arranged to have his trunk transferred to the Erie depot, where he planned to catch a train to New York.

Meanwhile, back in Cleveland the manhunt for Bianchetti was just getting started. It took police some time to identify him, let alone mobilize an effective search. First identifying him, confusingly, as "Lou Whits" or "Louis Koehler," police wasted valuable hours in fruitless questioning before some anonymous soul furnished them with a photograph of the suspected killer. But the photograph didn't turn up until midnight, January 13, almost 30 hours after police had learned of the murder. And it would not be until Friday afternoon—72 hours after the murder—that the first police circulars bearing Bianchetti's photograph and description began going out to police stations all across the country. Its particulars included:

Age: 28 or 30
Weight: Between 150 and 170 pounds
Height: 5 foot, 7 inches
Complexion: Dark, almost swarthy
Hair: Dark brown, parted on side
Eyes: Dark, shifty
Face: Smooth-shaven
Overcoat: Blue, chinchilla
Hat: Black, soft felt, creased into crown
Suit: Dark
Muffler: Black and white silk, with fringe
Collar: Plain, white turnover
Tie: Dark

Eventually, as Thursday passed, a flood of information about the Cleveland Athletic chef began pouring into police headquarters, much of it volunteered by his coworkers, former employers, and friends, who were almost unanimous in their praise for his character and disbelief that he could have perpetrated such a bloody deed. The only dissenters were brother and sister Arthur and Rita Rondino, who talked to police late Wednesday night and were the probable source of both the fugitive's photograph and current address. Arthur told police Bianchetti had roomed at his house until July of 1915, but had been ejected after he attempted to force his attentions on Rita. She took issue with the carefree, happy-go-lucky portrait of Bianchetti painted by his friends, telling police, "I was afraid he would kill me if we were alone together, he acted so strangely."

If you had read the Cleveland newspapers during the week after Delores Evans was murdered, you would have gotten the impression that the presumed killer was a mastermind who had cunningly masked his tracks. The weekend papers made much of the fact that after Bianchetti was traced to Akron, his baggage, invariably described as a "yellow trunk," had been routed to the West Coast on an Erie train. This disclosure prompted a telegram to police in Dodge City, Kansas, where armed squads prepared to stop both Bianchetti and his "yellow" trunk. They found the trunk when the train reached Dodge City, but there was no sign of Bianchetti—nor of his actual trunk, for it seems that police or railroad officials or *someone* had simply misidentified the "yellow trunk" as his.

Bianchetti's capture was due to far more prosaic and fortuitous police work. Although press accounts stated that Bianchetti had effaced all traces of himself and his identity from his East 18th Street room, he had, in fact, left an envelope behind, which was all the more conspicuous in the nearly bare flat. On the envelope was the address of one of his sisters, Mrs. Olympia Cairola, dwelling at 315 West 35th Street in New York. With that mundane clue in hand, the rest was child's play for cooperative New York City police. After receiving a telegram from Cleveland police chief Rowe, detectives Anthony Guinta and Charles A. Picco and two other New York City policemen staked out the Cairola home on the evening of Saturday, January 16. They hadn't waited long when they saw a man fitting Bianchetti's description—five feet, five inches in height, 175 pounds, well dressed and groomed—walk out the door. Tailing him carefully, they watched as he entered first a tavern, then a grocery. They grabbed him from behind as he came out of the grocery. "Your name Bianchetti?" snarled Guinta. Pulling his watch out, which had the initials "L. B." clearly engraved on the back, Picco said, "Yes, you're the man. We want you for murder."

Bianchetti seemed to take his arrest well. In a calm voice he said, "Yes, I am Bianchetti, the man you want. I killed the girl, and I'll tell you everything you want to know." But his mien deteriorated rapidly as they walked him back to his sister's home to search for evidence. Her hysteria after learning of his arrest quickly pushed him over the edge. In his bedroom, the detectives opened his suitcase to find the necklace and bracelet that Evans had been wearing the night of January 11. Suddenly, as the two detectives examined the trunk, Bianchetti lunged for the bed, where all 14 of his razor-sharp chef's knives were spread out. Screaming, "I'll kill myself—I won't go back to that!" he was overpowered by the detectives before he could harm himself. Taken to the Jefferson Market police station, he agreed to sign a complete confession. It is probably true, as Guinta and Picco swore later in court, that Bianchetti's confession was uncoerced, although the two detectives may have slyly implied that a full confession would "help" Bianchetti with Cleveland authorities. But the "confession" ultimately would lose much of its persuasiveness when Guinta freely admitted in court that he had dictated a good deal of the text that was written in Bianchetti's hand.

Meanwhile, Bianchetti stayed in jail, under a 24-hour suicide watch, pending his extradition to Cleveland. Increasingly nervous and despondent, he became extremely aggressive whenever a photographer hove into view. Fearful that his other siblings or his aged parents in Italy might see his picture in a newspaper, he went almost berserk when anyone tried to take his picture, struggling like a maniac and attempting to hide his face from the camera. Finally, on Thursday, January 20, nearly a week after his arrest, Cuyahoga County sheriff Ed Hanratty and county detective James Doran came to bring him back to Cleveland for trial.

Bianchetti's return to Cleveland was the most tumultuous—and disgraceful—event of its kind since cop killer "Blinky" Morgan had been brought back to Cleveland for trial in October 1887. An estimated 10,000 Clevelanders were waiting at Union Station on West 9th Street when Hanratty and his handcuffed prisoner stepped off the train at 5:30 that Friday evening. Hustled with difficulty into a waiting automobile, Bianchetti was whisked to the Cuyahoga County Jail on West 3rd Street (attached to the old County Courthouse by the "Bridge of Sighs"), followed all the way by a jeering, angry mob that repeatedly shouted, "Murderer!" and "Kill him!" As a Cuyahoga County grand jury had already indicted him the previous Monday, Bianchetti settled in to await his scheduled trial date on February 23. By the end of his first full day in jail he had recovered his usual aplomb, and had already commenced what became a daily routine of chatting with his many visitors, playing casino with the sheriff's deputies, attending to his continual grooming duties, smoking an endless number of cigars, and watching the jailhouse kittens, "Mike" and "Jennie," perform tricks taught to them by a former prisoner. He also spent much time reading and rereading his considerable fan mail, most of it from addled but adoring young women. His most awkward moment came just after his arrival at jail, when he was confronted with Clara Dille. "Is that the man?" asked Detective Doran. "Yes, that's the man!" replied Dille, Then she burst into tears and stretched out her hand to Bianchetti, saying, "I'm sorry, Louis—sorry I peached on you. They made me tell. Won't you shake hands?" "No! Never!" barked Bianchetti as he was led away to his cell.

Strangely enough, the mob- and newspaper-fueled sensationalism of Bianchetti's return to Cleveland was almost overshadowed by two related phenomena. The first was a firestorm of criticism of the Cleveland police that was ignited by the Evans murder. There had been lots of prostitutes in Cleveland, and they had been there for a long time. And some of them, going back to Christina Sigsby's appalling death in 1853 or the more recent butchery of Maggie Snedegar at her Lake Street home in 1903, had been murdered with wanton ferocity. But there was some special poignancy about the death of Dolores Evans that tugged hard at the heartstrings of Clevelanders—especially the heartstrings of its articulate clergymen and newspaper editors. Cleveland's ministers began attacking police laxity about downtown prostitution the day Evans's body was found. The Reverend E. R. Wright, executive secretary of the Federated Churches, weighed in that day with a demand that police work to prevent "improper meetings" in downtown hotels. The Rev. M. J. Keyes of the People's Methodist Church on Bridge Avenue followed up Wright's call for more strenuous moral policing but also suggested direct involvement by the church militant:

> Let ministers visit grill rooms in pairs. Let them watch at hotels that have careless night clerks who let in persons when they know, or ought to know, they come for immoral purposes. . . . It should be our duty to hold out a warning to the girl on the street when she takes her first step leading to prostitution, and which leads to such an event as the one which has so recently shocked our whole city and land. The church cannot escape her responsibility.

Inevitably, the rest of Cleveland's religious heavyweights began to chime in, and Mayor Harry Davis, hitherto indifferent to downtown vice, decided it would be better to be in front of such a crusade than behind it. Sternly vowing that downtown "stag hotels" and grill rooms would be cleaned up, Davis cleverly diverted attention from his previous laxity in enforcing public morals by attacking . . . Cleveland's police force. Insisting on Thursday that Evans's killer should already have been caught, Davis threatened to sack the entire Cleveland detective force and reorganize it under a new system more closely directed by him. Captain of Detectives Alfred Walker took the hint and resigned his position on Friday—the moralistic baying of unappeased Protestant ministers continued apace. Particularly eloquent was the Reverend George Birney, pastor of the Euclid Avenue Methodist Church, whose Sunday, January 16 sermon thundered:

> Cleveland's social jungle, which caught the unfortunate girl, lies at the doorstep of every Clevelander home. None are safe from the beasts that inhabit it. This swamp could be drained if all good people would get together to do so.

Unimpressed by Mayor Davis's soothing rhetoric and his sacrifice of Walker, Birney revved up his crusade the following Sunday, describing Cleveland's "underworld" as an "actual jungle where beasts snare their prey in rank entanglements and kill for the lust of

Cleveland News, January 13, 1916.

killing." Noting the pending licensing of "female cabaret shows," he lamented, "Just now it would seem the jungle is to be extended in its special liberties." He then warned of even worse moral plagues to come and assigned the true moral responsibility:

> I have not the time to speak of the opening of the Sunday theaters, the official permission to allow public gambling, the line of waiting madams paying rent on Hamilton Avenue N. E., all ready for the official signal to open the jungle's path to their doors as of yore. The murder of Elizabeth Myers opened the eyes of even those desiring to be blind. And this is the prevailing order of the jungle district. Those who have known conditions [there] are not surprised. The police know, but do not act. Has the public a right to ask the reason why? Just so long as the beasts do not slit each other's throats, nothing is done. When this happens, a great blare of trumpets is heard and the man hunt is on. A uniformed policeman is actually stationed at the mouth of the den. When the slayer is brought back the public becomes morbidly curious and that is as far as the interest goes. But the jungle remains. Not a single assignation house has been closed; not a grill room has lost its license; nothing is done to change the conditions that will make other murders inevitable, and the jungle is a permanent city institution.

Not content with such scorching jeremiads, the Reverend Birney, alas, also descended into verse. A paralyzing 14 stanzas in length, his "Dolores Evans" painted a doleful, indeed Dantesque, picture of the Forest City:

> Dolores Evans. So she called herself.
> As she plied her trade for her sinful pelf.
> And prowled through the midnight restaurants
> Like a she-beast prowls through its jungle haunts.
>
> Dolores Evans. A sweet, sad name
> To be bandied about in toasts of shame.
> While men—no Beasts—with slavering mouths
> Give tongue thereto in their wild carouse.

Brevity, alas, forbids inclusion of all 12 other stanzas, but readers will be grateful to learn that Birney's pessimistic vision of Cleveland ended with at least the hope that a benevolent Providence might speed the day when Vice no longer strutted scarlet and unopposed through the streets of Cleveland:

> Dolores Evans. Dear God bring the day,
> When the Jungle of Cleveland shall pass away.
> And the reign of the tooth and the claw be o'er,
> And the prowling night beasts be no more!

As is so often the case, this public clamor for a moral renaissance in Cleveland did not last long. Two weeks after the murder Davis had recovered sufficient political aplomb to state, presumably with the straight face: "Cleveland is the cleanest city in the United States and will remain so."

Cuyahoga Juvenile Court judge George S. Addams was not the only one unimpressed by the fustian rhetoric of Davis and the clergyman and dismayed by their scapegoating of the police. But he was the only public official willing to say so in print. The hysteria triggered by the Evans murder had just begun to subside when he talked to a Cleveland *Plain Dealer* reporter on February 2: "I think it is a shame the way some people are jumping into print and criticizing the police just because they think they will advance their own personal causes a little." Asked if he meant Mayor Davis, Addams retreated a step, saying, "It is not necessary for me to name specifically whom I mean. The people know who has caused all this vice agitation and who has helped it along by criticizing the police." Addams, who was no softy on crime, went on to put the vice hysteria in perspective:

> If it had not been for the murder of Elizabeth Myers there would have been no vice crusade and no attack on the police. When the newspapers and the public became generally interested in that story, these politicians saw opportunities to get into the limelight, and they immediately assailed the police department.

In their reaction to the Evans murder Cleveland newspaper editors were less pious than Mayor Davis or local clergymen, their editors skeptical, no doubt, that Cleveland would ever submit to the degree of moral reformation demanded by its clergy and some public servants. But they were not squeamish about taking advantage of the Evans murder to do what they did best in that era of "Yes, Virginia, there is a Santa Claus" and O. Henry–style journalism. I like to think that the following *Cleveland Press* editorial was written by a young Louis Seltzer, but it could have been authored by any seasoned Scripps Howard hack of the day:

> They found her murdered one morning. She was but a child, yet she had a profession. It is not named in polite society. Nice persons, when they have need to refer to it, call it "the easiest way." It did not take the police long to inventory her belongings. She had but one dress. Hundreds of girls will read the sordid tragedy—and not have the slightest idea of the circumstances which led up to it, although they will remember that "She had but one dress."
>
> There's a more important lesson for girls in this story. The murdered girl was innocent once. Perhaps her mother had guarded her—had protected her well—from the knowledge that there is a special evil always waiting, lurking for girls.

It is not for newspapers to dwell on this angle of the tale. But someone should do so. And who but mothers should point the warning in the truth about the girl who had but one dress? Who but mothers dare dwell on the horrid lie in the words, "the easiest way."

Compared with the public response to the mystery of Dolores Evans's identity, the official, clerical, and journalistic reactions to the Evans murder were models of restraint. Evans was killed on a Wednesday, and, following her autopsy, her body was sent to the county morgue on Lakeside Avenue. The next day it was exposed to public view from 5 a.m. until 9 at night, and before it was removed the following Tuesday, as many as 100,000 Clevelanders filed into the morgue and past the gray casket to gawk at the murdered "Dolores Evans." There were many families in the passing parade, many of them with young children and even babes in arms. Coroner Byrne's announced purpose in permitting this public spectacle was his hope of identifying the victim, but not a single person successfully identified the corpse. Not that there weren't many anxious claimants; before the body was removed to the Woodland Cemetery chapel, 30 persons would claim, many of them with copious tears, that the girl in the casket was their long-lost and beloved daughter, wife, granddaughter, or niece. Typical of such aspiring relations was A. M. Rossow, a farmer from Garrettsville in Medina County. He didn't get to Cleveland in time for the morgue corpse circus because he only learned about the murder while reading his German-language newspaper on Monday night, January 17. Arriving at the Woodland Cemetery chapel on Tuesday morning, he demanded to see the dead girl. Looking at her face, he cried tearfully, "That's my daughter! There can be no doubt of it!" and began making arrangements to take the body back to Garrettsville. That same evening, at 7 p.m., a young woman walked into the morgue and announced to morgue keeper Richard Dufflin, "I am Minnie Rossow." And she was—although Minnie had assumed the name Kennedy and was now living on Kinsman Road. The backstory to her father's misidentification was a template for virtually all of the other sincere but mistaken identifications of the body by anxious relatives saddened by the disappearance of a loved one. Tired of farm life, Minnie had run away from her father's home three years before and vanished into the anonymity of big-city Cleveland. His desperate need to find her had climaxed with his pilgrimage to the Woodland Cemetery vault for closure.

All other attempts to identify the dead girl proved similarly fruitless. A man and woman appeared at the morgue on Friday, January 14, saying the corpse was that of Elizabeth Myers, a girl from Braddock, Pennsylvania, who had run away with a carny show and never come back. Harry March of Massillon stated that the dead girl resembled someone he'd known there. The father, mother, and stepchildren of Anna Statch of 13603 Crennell Avenue, Cleveland, unanimously identified the body as her, only to have Anna turn up the next day. Anna De Wolfe of Pittsburgh opined that the girl was her brother George's missing wife. Rose Russell of 2091 West 61st Street thought it might be a girl she'd known seven years before in Beck's Run, near Pittsburgh. Russell's hunch gained credibility after

Louis Bianchetti.

the Reverend August Shoppol, retired rector of St. Joseph's Church in Beck's Run, heard about the dead girl. Shown her photograph, he said he thought it was a picture of a girl he'd baptized some years before who had attended his parochial school. Her name was Elizabeth Myers, and she had come back to him in the summer of 1914 to obtain a copy of her baptismal certificate so she could get married. And on and on, hour by hour, day by day, the misidentifications continued to explode as often as they blossomed. Most observers of the phenomenon eventually concluded that if the mother and father of the dead girl had recognized her or were aware of her fate, they weren't eager to come forward into the spotlight of public sensationalism. The general ghoulish tone of the public spectacle was captured in an exchange between morgue keeper Dufflin and a father who had dragged his young toddler to gape at the corpse. "That child is too young to be here!" Dufflin reproached him. "Oh," replied the father, "don't worry, she's too short to see up there anyway." Most of the adult viewers behaved as if looking at a dead stranger's corpse was no more solemn a pastime than attending a sporting event or bargain sale. Most of the men did not remove their hats, and many continued smoking as they passed by the casket.

There were some Clevelanders, of course, who neither desired nor needed facts to support their suppositions about the dead girl or her killer. One such was Alva H. Hooper, secretary of the National Psychic Science Association. Interviewed by a *Cleveland Press* reporter the day after the murder was discovered, Hooper pronounced as his own profound insight what any reasonably alert newspaper reader already knew:

> The slayer was a man of exceptional strength and this strength was used in a fit of unexpected anger. The killing was not premeditated, but after the crime the murderer did not regret the deed. Material facts show it. He washed his hands deliberately, then walked out, cool and calm. It will be a long time before the murderer is caught, if at all.

More perceptive still was Stella Western, a "gypsy queen," who was found with her family at their Bedford encampment. The killer was still in the city, she told a reporter on Friday, January 14, but he was going to leave that night. More interesting was her claim that she had known about the murder the moment it occurred and could prove it, as she had awakened her husband to tell him about it even before the cops were called. Then there was Ernest George, a palmist and self-proclaimed "student of fatality." Peering at the dead girl's hand as he walked past the casket at the county morgue, he generously shared his prompt analysis with yet another *Press* reporter:

> Her sudden death in youth is shown by a branch of the heart line falling to the head line under the mount of Saturn. Her

ambition is indicated by the conical sensitive fingers and the stiff thumb of determination, which shows that she would always go to the extreme to get what she wished. Her finger tips are conical but spatulate enough to give her great action in life. She would never sit and dream. She had a scrutinizing mind. Great impulsiveness is shown plainly. Her heart, head and life lines come together with a spray or tassel, which shows its sudden and mysterious ending. The mount of Jupiter at the base of the index finger, shows her to have been a leader of her crowd. She was generous to a fault. She had courage of a sort, too. Had it not been for this determined brain, she would have escaped her tragic death.

Last to join the newspaper nonsense chorus was "character analyst" William Judson Kibby, who informed the ever-obliging *Press:*

She put up a game fight. Perhaps her resistance was what led the assailant to kill her. She was a very determined girl, rather a masculine than a feminine type. That short chin shows fight. The high bridge of the nose means she was aggressive. Look at her picture. See the high spirited look. She was kindly and generous and she wanted to have people admire and like her, as her full lips show. But notice that cynical, critical look in her eyes. I imagine for all her kindliness, in a fit of temper she would have said some very ugly, cutting things. The girl, I think, was a very close observer—the partly-opened eye shows that. And she had pretty good self esteem. You can see it in the curve of her lips. There's a dash about her that indicates cleverness, and that same dash, the cynical look, the curled ringlets, shows she was coquettish and fickle.

The only relatively dignified interval in the obsequies for Dolores Evans came at her funeral, held at the Woodland Cemetery chapel. In attendance that chilly morning were 250 persons, most of them women and children. The Reverend H. C. Hinds of the Calvary Presbyterian Church officiated in a simple ceremony. In his brief remarks, the Reverend Hinds recited Tennyson's "Crossing the

Bar," made allusive mention of the Prodigal Son, and asked forgiveness for those "who, in a moment of strong passion, do things which they would not otherwise have done." A minor stir was created by a well-dressed woman who alighted from an expensive-looking automobile and sat through the service with tears pouring down her face. Her disinclination to identify herself inevitably sparked a rumor that she was the dead girl's mother.

The wheels of justice had begun to turn even before Bianchetti fled Cleveland. Coroner Byrne's inquest into the death commenced on Thursday, January 13, and was a model of dispatch. All of the relevant Hotel Perry employees gave testimony, as did Patrolmen Sifling and Majores, Clara Dille, and George Pierce. That set the stage for the grand jury, which began hearing the same witnesses on Monday, January 17. As soon as Dille and Pierce finished testifying, they were rearrested and jailed. The following Monday they were both tried and found guilty in Judge George S. Addams's Cuyahoga County Juvenile Court. Pierce, who had been unable to make his $1,000 bail, was sentenced to a year in the workhouse for contributing to the delinquency of a minor. That minor, Clara Dille, who had been on juvenile court probation at the time of her friend's murder, was sentenced to the Girls' Industrial School in Delaware, Ohio. Also sentenced was Hotel Perry night clerk Sidney Blumenthal, who received 90 days in the workhouse and a $500 fine, his reward for signing Clara and George into the Hotel Perry as "husband and wife" in the wee hours of January 12. The trial proceedings disclosed that it was also Blumenthal's hand that had added "and wife" to Bianchetti's signature in the hotel register.

If the murder of Dolores Evans was a sharp, short tragedy, its culmination, the trial of Louis Bianchetti, was a prolonged farce. Opening in the common pleas criminal court of Judge Thomas M. Kennedy on February 23, it featured Cyrus Locher in the county prosecutor's chair and attorneys John J. Sullivan and Joseph V. Zottarelli for the defense. And it was Locher who was responsible for both the length and unintended comedy of proceedings. For unknown and possibly inexplicable reasons, he chose to pursue a first-degree murder indictment against Bianchetti, even before the accused was returned to Cleveland and most of the facts were known. It is true that Locher's early decision accurately reflected public opinion, which had already been much inflamed by the statements of public officials, especially Coroner Patrick J. Byrne. His comments, offered the day after he completed his autopsy on the victim, were echoed by Cleveland lawmen and prosecutor Locher:

> This crime was one of the most brutal in Cleveland's history. The man who killed this girl must have had fingers of steel. He crushed her throat till the trachea, or windpipe, collapsed. The eyes, the cheeks and the chin show that the murderer battered the girl with powerful blows of his fist. The towel which he knotted about her throat and head was pulled tight by a marvelous strength. I believe Miss Myers' murderer must either have been a degenerate, or a man so mad with anger that he was insane. . . .The slayer was a man of powerful physique, and was prompted apparently by a degree of passion rarely found in any but the lower animals.

Such comments were amplified in Cleveland's newspapers, which repeatedly referred to Evans's unknown killer as a "superstrong maniac" and "demon." The problem for the prosecution was that by the time the trial opened, six weeks after the murder, wiser heads had begun wondering how Locher was going to demonstrate malice aforethought and premeditation in a killing that had all the earmarks of a spur-of-the-moment crime of passion. Rather than backing down, however, Locher stuck to his capital charge, opining, just a week after Bianchetti's capture, that he need only prove "momentary premeditation" to put the accused in the electric chair. Or as he explained somewhat disingenuously to reporters, "Premeditation may be of only a moment's duration. It may be of months or a year." To which defense attorney Zottarelli rightly riposted: "Premeditation is not measured by time."

Locher's difficulties in securing a first-degree murder conviction were apparent from the moment Judge Kennedy gaveled the trial into motion on the morning of February 23. Manacled to burly deputy sheriff Dwight Nutting, Bianchetti was brought into the courtroom at 9:30, nattily attired in a brown suit (his garb on the murder night), tan shoes, white hose, pink and white shirt, and blue-and-white-striped tie, and sported a fresh haircut and shave. No one summoned on the first venire of 37 talesmen seemed anxious to serve on the Bianchetti jury. Indeed, it soon developed that nearly all of them had previously formed an unalterable opinion about the guilt or innocence of the accused. Over the next four days, nearly 100 prospective jurors were methodically examined, almost all of whom insisted they were already hopelessly prejudiced. Threats by Locher and Judge Kennedy failed to stem this weary trend, even after Kennedy ordered that talesmen be segregated so that they couldn't exchange tips on how to avoid jury duty. Jury selection dragged on from Tuesday morning until almost noon Saturday and became increasingly acrid as an irritated Locher grilled reluctant talesmen. Typical of the exchanges in the hot, airless courtroom was his dialogue with carpenter Harry Luther:

> Locher: You are not anxious to serve on this jury, are you?
> Luther: No.
> Locher: Isn't that why you are answering as you do?
> Luther: No.
> Kennedy: Do you realize that you are testifying now under oath and that you can be sent to the penitentiary if it is found you are testifying falsely?
> Luther: I do and I stick to my testimony.

More testy still was Locher's dialogue with talesman Clark L. Clinker, who told Locher and Judge Kennedy his mind couldn't be changed by testimony:

> Locher: Suppose that you were told it was raining outside. Then you would look out and see it was not raining, you would change your opinion, would you not?
> Clinker: I would know it was not raining.
> Locher: You change your opinion when you find you are wrong, don't you?
> Clinker: No.
> Locher: You're like the old maid who was open to conviction, but was sure there was no man living who could convince her.

Kennedy: You have a firm opinion you are going back to
work, don't you?
Clinker: Well, I think so.
Kennedy: Don't let anything change it, keep right on, we
don't want you.

The nadir of the jury selection marathon came on Thursday,
February 24. Bedford night watchman John Baughman had been
the first talesman to actually make it into the jury box. But just a day
later, Judge Kennedy looked over to find him fast asleep there. He
excused him gently, explaining that he wanted "wide awake" men
deciding Bianchetti's fate.

In addition to problems with jury selection, the proceedings
were troubled by death threats and charges of jury tampering. On
the first day prospective juror James C. McIntosh informed Judge
Kennedy that he had been approached at his home by someone
claiming to be a deputy sheriff. McIntosh had refused to discuss the
case with the "deputy," but Prosecutor Locher demanded an immediate investigation. McIntosh's story was subsequently probed by
Cuyahoga County detective James Doran to no effect, and, in any
case, talesman McIntosh never made it into the jury box.

As jury selection entered its third day on Friday, Locher en-
livened the monotony by announcing that he had received a death
threat, warning him to go easy on Bianchetti. Dramatically characterizing it as a "Black Hand" warning, Locher released its clumsy
text to the press:

County Locher. Inclosing you few lines to give you a fair
warning if you are any cause of of Louis Bianchetti Death
i will kill you if it takes me life time to do it. So don't insist upon his Death so much. Because if he dies you will
to. Don't think it's a bluff. If they get him to the chair in
Columbus then they are ready for you in hell for I will send
you there.

It was subsequently revealed that Assistant County Prosecutor
Samuel Doerfler had found the note on his desk a couple of days

prior to Locher's disclosure. Cleveland newspapermen might have given it more play, had not Doerfler twice denied the note's existence to them before Locher chose to brandish it in court.

As the prosecution and defense bickered over jurors, death threats, and tampering allegations, some comic relief, or at least distraction, was generated by the appearance of an elderly, distinguished-looking gray-haired woman who sat in court every day, intently watching the proceedings. According to Judge Kennedy, she identified herself only as "Mrs. Smith," flashed him a badge that said "Secret Detective Agency," and claimed merely a professional interest in the trial. Locher, who probably knew better, let it be known to reporters that he thought the dignified woman was the dead girl's unknown mother—after all, Evans had also used "Smith" as an alias—and the newspapers had sport with that speculation as one talesman after another struggled mightily to avoid jury duty.

Finally, at 11:55 a.m. Saturday, jury selection was over, and Judge Kennedy asked the 12 jurors to rise and take their oath. Except that it *wasn't* over. Even as the jurors began to raise their right hands, juror Frank Leska blurted out, "I refuse to be sworn in a case involving the life of a fellow man!" After a hurried conference with the three attorneys, Judge Kennedy patiently explained to the jurors that the law couldn't force a juror to act against his own conscience:

> Under the law it is entirely optional with the juryman whether he shall believe in capital punishment, unless the attorneys on one side or the other raise the question. A man can be an eligible juryman and not believe in it if the state does not object to him on this ground. He can enter the box with the foreknowledge and determination that he will not, under any circumstances, impose the death penalty.

Kennedy's ruling was simply an exposition of current Ohio law, but it was a precedent for Cuyahoga County, establishing for the first time that a man could be an eligible juror in a capital case without believing in capital punishment, if the state did not object.

Sketch of scene as Bianchetti arrives at the Union Depot, *Cleveland Press*, January 22, 1916.

Locher—who, oddly enough, did not himself believe in capital punishment—chimed in, insisting that he would only ask the jurors for an "honest" verdict. But that wasn't enough for juror Morris B. Spero, who stood up and shouted, "I am absolutely opposed to the death penalty. I refuse to be sworn in!" Judge Kennedy promptly excused Spero from the jury and replaced him with Jacob Amster, only to be confronted by a third dissenter, John Stofko, who demanded to know why his views on capital punishment *had* been solicited during his examination. Kennedy retorted, "I have no explanation to make to you. Sit down!" Then it was juror Rick Hallin's turn. "I want off the jury! My wife is ill!" "You'll not be excused," replied Kennedy firmly, and he again asked the jurors to rise for their oath. At which point the newest juror, Jacob Amster, whined, "My mother is 85 years old and I should be with her!" Kennedy had had enough. "Hold up your right hand," he commanded. "I'll commit you to jail or you'll be sworn." Muttering to himself, Amster took the oath, as did juror Francis Stewart, who registered a protest by remaining seated, chewing an unlit cigar. "I'm sitting here with an opinion," he archly volunteered to Judge Kennedy. "You also want to attend some stockholders' meeting this afternoon," replied the unimpressed justice.

With juror Leska still on the jury, it was clear that there would be no death verdict, but Locher manfully pushed on. Speaking for only five minutes in his opening statement, he explained that he would let the state's witnesses paint "word pictures" of the murder victim and the events surrounding her death. But Locher didn't just leave his case to simple words. He made sure the jury saw all of the mute evidence collected from Room 19 and elsewhere: the clothing Evans shed before she got into bed with the accused (a black mosquito bar skirt, a corduroy coat, and a little round hat), her cheap jewelry, and the gloves containing her last two nickels.

Locher's state witnesses—the Hotel Perry staff, George Pierce, Clara Dille—gave persuasive evidence on the stand, and the prosecutor's use of the physical evidence was blunt but effective. But, leaving aside the nebulous reference to "momentary premeditation" in his opening statement, Locher failed to explain to the jurors just what motivation Bianchetti could have had for beating an apparent stranger to death in a semipublic place. If Bianchetti was reacting to an attempt to steal his money—and Locher insisted that such was not the case—then the only explanation for his violent actions was that he was, as Coroner Byrne put it, a "degenerate" maniac and, ergo, not responsible for his actions, much less subject to a first-degree murder prosecution.

Who were these two strangers who, on the night of January 11, found themselves in a death struggle in a shabby Prospect hotel room? What little information is known about Dolores Evans came mostly from her peers—girls of easy virtue like Clara Dille and other habitués of Cleveland's seamy nightlife, a garish and mean-streeted realm of grill rooms, all-night restaurants, and inexpensive and incurious hotels. It is easy to suppose that their lives were much like hers: a desperate, hand-to-mouth struggle fought in shabby rented rooms, disreputable restaurants, and bars, and controlled by hard-hearted pimps and petty criminals. It seems Dolores turned up in Cleveland sometime in late 1915, at least late enough to be rousted for suspected soliciting on November 4. Clevelander

Raymond Schenkelberger told police he met her on October 1 of that year, and that he gave her the suitcase that contained most of the few possessions found after her death, mostly cheap clothing, shoes, and postcards from various gentlemen callers.

Perhaps because of her dubious occupation, Dolores moved around a lot during her few months in Cleveland, living at a series of low-rent dwellings, including the Hotel De Luxe on Prospect and the Weddell House on West 6th Street. She showed up at the Hotel Rexford, 1038 Chestnut Avenue, on January 3 and lived there until her death, although she was about to be expelled by landlady Jennie Leisure for what she charitably termed "irregular hours" when death found her.

The biography Evans gave Clara Dille and others implied much but offered few facts. The impression derived from her oblique and infrequent disclosures was that she had left home at 13 to seek adventure and independence with a traveling carny show, working as a singer and dancer. Somewhere along the way, the show had either disintegrated or abandoned her, and she had ended up in Pittsburgh. If she had relatives there, she didn't see them, for as she told her landlady Jennie Leisure, she "never dared return home." Sometime in 1915, for unknown reasons, she had gravitated to Cleveland.

Elizabeth Lanning, a waitress at an all-night restaurant on East 9th Street, was able to add some darker tints to the sketchy portrait of Dolores Evans. Lanning met her there around Christmas 1915, when the hungry Evans begged 50 cents from her to pay for her dinner. They had a few chats during the following month, and Lanning would recall that Evans usually seemed morose, sometimes weeping uncontrollably. She told Lanning that she came from Pittsburgh but never mentioned her parents, except to say she had been orphaned at a young age. She claimed she had been a member of the Ziegfeld Follies chorus and some unnamed traveling shows. She also confided to Lanning that she lived in terror of a man named "Joe"—her pimp?—and that Joe had forced her to take drugs. Significantly, perhaps, one of the few items found in her threadbare lodgings was a postcard containing the lyrics of a maudlin contemporary song, a line of which the unhappy Dolores Evans had underlined: "I write these lines to tell you that I'm sorry I left home."

Much more is known of Evans's accused killer, although some of it seems at odds with the clean-cut, cheerful young man that most of his Cleveland acquaintances and friends knew. Born to the parents of a large, impoverished family in the small village of Messarno, Italy, on May 4, 1891, Bianchetti had been apprenticed to a carpenter at the age of 11. Coming to America in 1906, he lived with a brother in Wilmington, Delaware, and worked at a tannery before striking out on his own to New York. There he started at the Hotel Imperial for $18 a month as a potato peeler but soon exhibited culinary skills that kept him in demand wherever he went. After cooking stints in various New York hotels, he worked at a Maine coastal resort and several Philadelphia hotels before coming to Cleveland in March 1915. After working for six weeks at Dominic Portinaro's Roma Restaurant, 1052 Prospect Avenue, Bianchetti secured a job in the kitchen of the Cleveland Athletic Club. Quickly working his way up to roast chef, he was making $80 to $90 a month when his night in Room 19 wrecked his life. Practically everyone who knew him at work or play liked him, although some remarked that he was capable of frightening displays of temper, especially if he thought someone was trying to take advantage of him. It is significant that many of his coworkers at the Athletic Club were willing to appear as supportive character witnesses at his murder trial and that they and his other friends contributed generously to the defense fund that paid attorneys Zottarelli and Sullivan.

One fatuously diverting naysayer to the chorus of Bianchetti admirers was inimitable character analyst Judson Kibby. One look at Bianchetti's newspaper photograph instantly disclosed to the astute Kibby the presence of a "destructive brain":

The destructive brain is shown by the thickness of the head where the ears are attached. It is so developed that the ear fairly bulges out. A destructive brain indicates a tendency to tear down. When controlled by a strong moral brain, the destructive brain becomes useful. A butcher, for example, must have a destructive brain, but without control or moral restraint a destructive brain leads to wanton destruction. The face is that of a strong masculine type of man, cunning, ob-

servant, with well developed self-esteem, exceedingly sensitive in personal matters, intense, affectionate, impulsive and
aggressive. Combativeness, self-esteem, sensitiveness, impulsiveness and other characteristics show clearly that, when
aroused, he would give way to anger and might be unable to
control himself. Power to observe is show by the keenness
of the eyes and the bulge in the forehead above the eyeballs.
The small eyes indicate cunning. The general expression of
the face indicates self-esteem. So do the jaunty tie, the but-
tonhole bouquet, and silk handkerchief in the watch pocket
and the manner of combing the hair. The set look of the face
indicates intenseness; the thick lips and the dimple in the
chin show the strong affectionate nature. His self-esteem
and shrewdness and desire to have people approve of him
must combine to make him sensitive in personal matters.
The short chin indicates the impulsiveness and the high ridge
of the nose shows him aggressive. He has a very combative
nature, being a man who would strike back quickly. He has
the appearance of great physical strength and is a man of
rugged stock.

On Tuesday, February 29, Locher scored a significant point
when he put Dr. Philip A. Jacobs on the stand to testify about his
autopsy. Bianchetti claimed that Evans had been alive when he left
Room 19, but Jacobs said his analysis of the chop suey in her stomach indicated that her digestion—and her life—had stopped only an
hour after she finished her meal at 11:30 p.m. The prosecutor was
also victorious in getting Bianchetti's New York City confession
read into the record, over vigorous objections from both defense attorneys. But the confession was actually pretty vague on the details
of Bianchetti's physical struggle with Evans—which he described
as just "three or four punches"—and its impact was mitigated by
Guinta's admission that he had written most of it in Italian for Bianchetti to sign.
    Early afternoon, Locher made one final attempt to demolish the
defense contention that a cash-flush Bianchetti had been the victim
of a simple "badger game," lured by the promise of sex to a room

where he could be robbed. Locher made much of the fact that witness Parrodi Amico, Bianchetti's coworker at the Athletic Club, had lent $5 to Bianchetti on the murder night. If Bianchetti really had a roll of $250 in his pocketbook, Locher wondered aloud, why was he borrowing $5 from a friend?

The prosecutor's ploy fell flat, however, as numerous persons had testified to Bianchetti's impressive wad of cash on the murder night and his inflexible insistence on picking up the tab. The testimony of Clara Dille and George Pierce further undermined Locher's contention that Bianchetti had not been the target of a premeditated robbery. It was, no doubt, crystal clear to the jurors after hearing Clara Dille and George Pierce's sordid testimonies, that the presence of these two persons on the murder night was more than coincidental to what happened in Room 19. Then at 2:10 p.m. the state rested and the defense went to work.

From the moment Sullivan began his opening statement, it was clear that his strategy would be mainly a character defense, heavily dependent on the circumstances of the defendant's biography and his impression on the jury. So Sullivan (like most of the best defense attorneys something of a ham actor and later a most persuasive seller of War Bonds after the United States entered World War I) set the stage by painting a highly sentimental portrait of a hardworking, innocent Italian boy who left his aged parents to follow the American dream. He found that dream in Cleveland, only to have it destroyed by a chance encounter with designing criminals. Every action taken by Bianchetti on the murder night, Sullivan asserted, could be justified in terms of self-defense and the preservation of his property.

Bolstering Sullivan's hagiography of Bianchetti, Joseph Zottarelli introduced the jury to his client's friends and coworkers, all of whom said lovely things about the industrious roast chef, all of them emphasizing his generally cheerful disposition and unfailing generosity. Then came Dr. M. G. Platt, who impeached the autopsy findings of Dr. Jacobs, charging that his claim about the rate of digestion in Evans's stomach was mere guesswork, and could be off by as much as 24 to 36 hours.

Then it was time for the main event, Bianchetti's appearance on the stand. Bianchetti was at his best that morning—well groomed, well dressed, and possessed of an amiable, polite manner. At his best Bianchetti was an attractive person and he must have made a good impression that long morning and afternoon, as first Sullivan and then Locher led him through his narrative of the murder night. Bianchetti didn't offer any significantly new details, but his testimony was consistent with the few indisputable facts. He insisted that Evans was still alive when he left the room; hence, he explained, his tying a towel around her face to prevent her from crying out. And his version of the climatic moments was remarkable for its concision:

> I jumped from the bed and grabbed her. She said, "You leave me alone!" and she cursed me. She pushed me away and threw the pocketbook out of the window. I hit her in the nose two or three times.

Remarkably, neither Sullivan nor Locher pressed Bianchetti on the matter of how much he had to drink that fateful evening. Leaving the Athletic Club at 6:30 p.m. after a hard day's work, Bianchetti had visited his friend Parrodi Amico from 9 to 11 p.m. imbibing "five or six" drinks of red wine. Then it was on to the Roma Restaurant, where he downed "five or six" Benedictines. He further acknowledged having at least two beers at the Chinese Republic Restaurant, so it is odd that neither of the contending attorneys probed the possibility of alcohol-impaired judgment. Indeed, in his New York confession, Bianchetti had acknowledged that he was "nearly drunk" on the night of January 11.

The state produced one rebuttal witness, who contradicted Bianchetti's account of his search in the snowy alleyway for his pocketbook by stating that there was only a four-hundredths-of-an-inch snowfall that wintry night. Then it was on to the closing statements. Samuel Doerfler spoke first for the state, charging that Bianchetti had known Evans was dead when he left Room 19 and had baldly lied to the jury. He scored his best point with his portrayal of the physical disparity between the hulking Bianchetti and his five foot two, 120-pound adversary:

Bianchetti is a big, strong, young man, weighing, he says, about 175 pounds. The dead girl was a frail little girl who weighed about 120. And yet he has the audacity to tell you that this frail little girl was able to push him out of the way and, despite him, throw his pocketbook out the window.

Zottarelli followed Doerfler, sketching for the jury one last time the crude robbery scheme that had so fatally miscarried for Dolores Evans and her sleazy accomplices. Sticking mainly to the facts, he saved the corny melodrama for his closing peroration:

If the Great Nazarene could come down now and call forth Dolores Evans from her grave, she would come forth saying, "Gentlemen, it is the truth Bianchetti has been telling. I obeyed orders and I took that money from his pocket. That is why he struck and beat me. [Turning to Bianchetti] Bianchetti, there are the masters of your fate. I see no Judas Iscariot among them. Look, Bianchetti, there they are, twelve good apostles. I leave you with them, and Bianchetti, I am not afraid of the result.

The only surprise in Zottarelli's passionate defense was his unexpected and perhaps injudicious praise of Bianchetti, who, he piously stated, did not carry a stiletto, dagger, or pistol, "as most young Italians of his age have."

Sullivan's closing statement for the defense was a masterpiece of emotional appeal, if not logic. Asking dramatically that the doors of the courtroom be locked, he addressed the packed courtroom, most of the rapt spectators being female. Picking up where he'd left off in his opening statement's portrait of Saint Louis Bianchetti, he emphasized the harsh contrast between his splendid and sterling client and his client's foul accusers:

Gentlemen, the greatest recommendation for a man is an affirmative answer to the question, "Does he work?" Bianchetti has scarcely had an idle day since he was eleven years of age. He is a moral boy. An idle brain is the devil's workshop. In this case, some witnesses put on by the state are either in

Sketch of scene at Bianchetti trial, *Cleveland Press*, February 23, 1916.

the jail, the workhouse or under sentence.

Next, calling Zottarelli to him, he had the aged attorney act the part of the victim, as the two attorneys reenacted their version of the events in Room 19 for the jury. Aware that the jurors might retain some compassion for Dolores Evans, Sullivan was careful with his words about her, painting her as a helpless pawn manipulated by more feral beings:

> Pierce was her master. She obeyed him like a slave. Ah, Mr. Prosecutor, you talk all you like of pity for Dolores now that she is dead. But who pitied her when she was alive? We are not condemning her. We pity her. But she had gotten so deeply into the clutches of this Pierce that even her mother was ashamed to come forward and identify her when she was dead.

Aware that the trial of a young Italian immigrant had raised ethnic tensions and triggered accusations of anti-Italian bias on the part of Cleveland authorities, Sullivan cited the frequent references to Bianchetti as a "degenerate," and angrily challenged Locher to prove it, shouting, "I defy the prosecution to cite me one example of an Italian who is a degenerate! Oh, God! Oh! thou state of Ohio, prince of the commonwealth of the Union, can't you give this jury something better to take to the jury room in deliberation on this boy's case—something better than a theory?"

Moving on to Bianchetti's claim that he left Evans alive, Sullivan surprised everyone by offering a new and startling explanation for his client's assertion:

> You heard him say, "I didn't kill her." Bianchetti cannot believe, even now, that Dolores Evans is dead, unless . . . [dramatic pause] unless somebody came creeping up to the room after he had left. And who would have come? One of the State's star witnesses [George Pierce], who the testimony will show, was interested in money, money—he tried to conceal from you on the witness stand where he was between the time Louis Bianchetti left the Evans girl untying the towel from about her face and 4:30, when he again appears on the scene—following right on the tracks of his "operative" to the very place where Dolores Evans had taken this boy. Where was he for those two hours? And was he so interested in fixing up an alibi, which was exploded by Clara Dille, another one of the state's own witnesses, because both of them were in jail and he couldn't get to her to fix up her story. Money was the motive back of all this. When Bianchetti and the girl got into the cab they were followed! . . . All of them, including one of the clerks at the Perry Hotel, were in a plot which caught this young man like a rat in a trap.

An enraged Locher jumped up, demanding, "Is there any evidence of that?" But it was too late; the notion had been planted, Judge Kennedy had not objected, and Sullivan returned to his opening theme, elaborating on Bianchetti's fine qualities and what devastation his conviction would bring upon his aged, infirm parents back in Italy. He ended his plea on a note that exceeded in theatrical shamelessness any excesses he and Zottarelli had previously committed. Standing directly in front of the jury, he warbled anew his pastoral vision of Bianchetti's beatific childhood home and the saintly parents who had always believed in him and his successful life in the New World. His last words to the jury were a soulful rendition of Rudyard Kipling's 1891 poem "Mother O' Mine":

> If I were hanged on the highest hill,
> Mother o' mine, O mother o' mine!
> I know whose love would follow me still,
> Mother o' mine, O mother o' mine!
>
> If I were drowned in the deepest sea,
> Mother o' mine, O mother o' mine!
> I know whose tears would come down to me,
> Mother o' mine, O mother o' mine!
>
> If I were damned of body and soul,
> I know whose prayers would make me whole,
> Mother o' mine, O mother o' mine!

By the time Sullivan finished reciting the poem, three of the jurors had broken down in tears, one of them, Robert Fawcett, sobbing helplessly.

Allowed the last word, Locher tried to destroy the emotional impact of Sullivan's sentimental appeal. Deriding Sullivan's portrait of "sunny Italy" and dismissing the defense's arguments as simply a "string of lies," Locher tried to divert some of the compassion so acutely aroused by Sullivan for his client to the dead girl. Brandishing her photograph repeatedly in front of the jury, he thundered:

> This case started the day the poor little girl was born. Not as Sullivan told you, the day Bianchetti was born. There came a time when she had nothing to sell but her body—she sold that.

Zottarelli had angered the prosecutor with his innuendos suggesting anti-Italian bias, and it was now Locher's turn to play the ethnic card. He was "shocked," he told the jury, at Zottarelli's stereotyping of young Italian males as invariable pistol packers and stiletto wielders:

> I resent such a statement because it is not true about most young Italians. I tell you that Louis Bianchetti is not entitled to a single thing more than anyone else, and none of those self-respecting Italians in this court room or anywhere else ask anything more. . . . I hurl those charges back into your face with scorn, Mr. Zottarelli!

Summarizing the evidence against Bianchetti one last time, Locher ended his plea, after speaking for almost two hours:

> There were only two things necessary for the state to prove in this case: First, that Elizabeth Myers is dead; second, that she died at the hands of Louis Bianchetti. These two points have been proved beyond a reasonable doubt, and they complete the state's case.

Bianchetti's jury soon demonstrated that Locher was both right and wrong in his final assertion. He had proved that Evans was dead and that Bianchetti had killed her. But the charge was first-degree murder, and he hadn't come close to proving that the killing was premeditated. He had presented no evidence to support malice aforethought, and it is significant that Locher never mentioned his novel legal doctrine of "momentary premeditation" after his initial opening statement. So surely he was not surprised when the jury returned after eight hours' deliberation with a unanimous verdict of manslaughter. As foreman William J. Martin read the verdict, Zottarelli turned to Bianchetti and exclaimed, "Oh well, we won!" The jury had only taken two ballots, and the tally of the first was nine for manslaughter and three for second-degree murder. Locher's odd legal strategy becomes even more puzzling when one considers that the defense lawyers had offered to plead their client guilty to manslaughter, rather than first- or second-degree murder, a full month before the trial began. And virtually every lawyer and journalist with an opinion on the outcome had predicted a manslaughter conviction from start to finish. Even Bianchetti agreed, remarking as he was led back to his county jail cell, "I got what I thought I would. It suits me fine." Seven and a half arduous days had been consumed in a struggle for an outcome that had been suggested on January 22, 10 days after Evans's body was found.

Judge Kennedy deliberated for some time before deciding Bianchetti's sentence. His options were to send him to the Ohio Penitentiary in Columbus for an indeterminate sentence of 1 to 20 years, which would make him eligible for parole application after a year. The alternative was to send him for an even more indeterminate stay in the Mansfield Reformatory, his release dependant on the estimate made of his progress toward "reform." Ultimately, Kennedy opted for the former, and Bianchetti entered the penitentiary on March 8, 1916, less than two months after the death of Dolores Evans. Proving himself a model prisoner from his first day in prison, Bianchetti soon won a transfer to the model prison honor farm at London, where he likewise won praise for his good conduct and his excellent cooking. During World War I, he demonstrated his patriotism by making blankets for the Red Cross. He failed to win release at his first parole hearing in April 1917; the members of the Board of Clemency were well inclined toward him, but they deferred to public opinion that the "community hurt" inflicted by his crime had been too great to permit his early release. But Forest City passions cooled soon enough, perhaps eclipsed by war fervor, and Bianchetti's diligence and good behavior were rewarded on October 7, 1919, when the Ohio Board of Clemency voted him a parole. On November 1, he walked out of the Columbus prison and disappeared into the obscurity whence he had come. Clara Dille also disappeared after entering the Girls' Industrial School at Lancaster on March 4, 1916. Her name briefly surfaced later that year, when her mother was killed in a tragic trolley accident on the West 3rd Street bridge. Cuyahoga County closed the Evans case for good on July 19, 1916, when they donated the last clothes worn by Dolores Evans to the Salvation Army. No one ever came forward to identify or claim the body of Dolores Evans or Elizabeth Myers. Her identity remains unknown.

Chapter 14

CLEVELAND'S GREATEST HISTORIAN

S. J. Kelly's
Forgotten Treasures

It could be said that Cleveland has not been well served by its modern narrative historians—but it would be more accurate to say that it has hardly been served at all. Cleveland's first century and a half notoriously produced nothing but celebratory and triumphal paeans to the evolution of the Forest City, with scarcely any general narrative Cleveland history written during the last century. No one can belittle the massive achievement of David D. Van Tassel and John J. Grabowski's *The Encyclopedia of Cleveland History*, which after two decades remains an invaluable research arsenal of Forest City subjects in both its print and online versions. The same can be said, too, of its bicentennial spin-off, Carol Poh Miller and Robert Wheeler's briskly written *Cleveland: A Concise History, 1796-1996*—but it's way too damn short. Four other books still deserving of space on the Cleveland history lover's slim shelf of essential works are William Ganson Rose's *Cleveland: The Making of a City*, George Condon's *Cleveland: The Best-Kept Secret,* Jan Cigliano's *Showplace of America,* and Eric Johannesen's *Cleveland Architecture, 1876-1976*. The first, although little more than a dense chronology, is still an indispensable source of names, dates, and facts; the second, a lively celebration of some of Cleveland's more colorful personalities and phenomena, remains the best-written and most fun of any book ever written about Cleveland; the third is a history of Euclid Avenue's "Millionaires' Row" that makes you really wish you'd lived there; and Johannesen's book is a loving and graphically lavish tribute to a time when Cleveland still built beautiful public buildings and dwellings. In addition to the far too many books on its professional sports franchises, there have also been several dozen estimable books published on narrow facets of Cleveland history, which have chronicled some of its educational, religious, and cultural institutions. The fact remains, though, that if it's a good, general, up-to-date narrative history of Cleveland you want, you're out of luck—as I first discovered 20 years ago when, under my secret identity as a mild-mannered librarian, I compiled a comprehensive bibliography of every book on Cleveland. Who knows when someone will produce the Great Cleveland History Book—but while you're waiting, let me introduce you to the greatest Cleveland historian of them all: S. J. Kelly.

S. J. Kelly? I hear you muttering. *Who he?* I've always prided myself on my knowledge of Cleveland's past, but I nearly asked the same question the first time I heard his name spoken back in the early 1990s. As was his custom when researching his Cleveland books, historian/journalist George Condon had dropped by the Fairview Park library to ask me some questions in my capacity as the library's history specialist. George found me in the back stacks and smiling impishly, as was his wont, uttered the words that changed my life: *"Have you ever heard of S. J. Kelly?"* "Y-e-s," I hesitantly replied, "wasn't he some old geezer who used to write some kind of editorial column for the *Plain Dealer* way back in, I don't know, the twenties or thirties? I know I've seen his name a zillion times, but I've never stopped to read him, because I'm sure he doesn't have anything to say about murder." Demonstrating his unfailing tolerance for my flippant ignorance, George merely handed me a sheaf of smudgy-looking photocopies. "You should look at these," he said. "You know, Kelly may have been the best Cleveland historian ever! I mean, Kelly knew *everybody*, saw *everything*—and he never forgot anything or anybody. You know, an anthology of his columns would make a helluva Cleveland history book!"

Reader, I took a look at those sloppy photocopies the moment George left, for the simple reason that I thought *he* was the greatest Cleveland historian ever—so his opinion of Kelly's work carried all the more weight with me. Little did I know what I was getting into. Before a week had elapsed, I found myself completely besotted by

Kelly's work, indeed so much so that I had already embarked on the daunting challenge of photocopying his entire run of columns, some 1,336 pieces of the most fascinating Cleveland history I'd ever read. Within a month, I, like George, had become a monomaniacal Kelly fanatic, who, when not reading my favorite Kelly "bits" aloud to irritated auditors in the staff lunchroom, was given to accosting complete strangers and tormenting them at length with my fervor for the great journalist's oeuvre. More than fifteen years on, my great appreciation for Kelly's achievement remains undiminished, and it only remains for me to explain why S. J. Kelly is the best Cleveland historian you've never read.

A word about the background and format of Kelly's *Plain Dealer* columns is in order before offering an assessment of his work. Kelly was 69 years old when he began his history column in 1935 and had already spent nearly half a century as a working journalist at virtually every newspaper in the city: the *Plain Dealer,* as well as the *Herald, Press, Leader, World, Voice,* and who knows how many more extinct sheets. Early that year he persuaded *Plain Dealer* editor-in-chief Paul Bellamy (the author's grandfather) to let him write columns featuring personalized historical reminiscences of Cleveland, 500 to 700 words in length, which would appear three to five times a week on the editorial page. The first column, an affectionate remembrance of Judge Rufus P. Ranney, appeared February 13, 1935; the last, a captivating visual description of downtown Cleveland on a moonlit night in 1850, was published on August 4, 1948. Sometimes the columns expanded to a length of 1,000 words, especially during the early years; later, World War II newsprint shortages curtailed space to only 200 or 300 words. Often, particularly when telling a complex narrative, such as Moses Cleaveland's first journey to the Western Reserve or events in Cleveland during the War of 1812, Kelly would relate his story over a series of columns, sometimes lasting for several weeks. He was not a great stylist, and his work was often carelessly edited. (Indeed, the slapdash editing of his columns lends sad credence to the gibe that newspaper proofreaders of Kelly's era were invariably superannuated widows or knackered rummies.) But—like most journalists—S. J. Kelly was not writing for stylists. He was writing for curious Clevelanders like himself, and far more importantly, he was a born and inveterate storyteller, who over the course of 14 years and 1,336 columns brought a vanished Cleveland to vibrant life for his readers.

Samuel Jewett Kelly came from an unusually comfortable background for a journalist of his or any era. His grandfather, lawyer Moses Kelly, attended Harvard and then came to Cleveland in 1836 and, in tandem with his law partner, Thomas Bolton, built one of the most successful and prestigious legal practices in Cleveland. Moses was also active and prominent in the burgeoning city's political affairs, as was his son, Frank Kelly, who served as a Cleveland councilman in the 1870s and later as a municipal judge. Thanks to this elite background, Frank's son, Samuel Jewett, born in 1866, enjoyed lifelong entrée to the homes, clubs, schools, and recreational resorts of Cleveland's ruling circles. It was an unusual social background for a journalist, and it would pay large dividends in the 1930s when S. J. Kelly began publicly reminiscing about his decades spent mixing with the movers and shakers of Cleveland. When he took you on an exhaustive walking tour of Cleveland's "Millionaires' Row" you knew he'd been into every one of those fabled homes and talked to the people who lived in them.

But a life of easy entrée to Cleveland's Social Register was not Kelly's only resource when he sat down in the dark years of the Great Depression to re-create bygone Cleveland in the pages of the *Plain Dealer*. For a journalist of his time—or for that matter, any era—Kelly had an extremely broad range of interests and enthusiasms, all of which he drew upon successfully in his work. He liked the theater, and could recall seeing theatrical luminaries like Edwin Booth, Maude Adams, Lawrence Barrett, John Ellsler, Edwin Forrest, and James O'Neill at the ornate Euclid Avenue Opera House and the old Empire Theater on Huron Road. He also enjoyed the opera, sometimes recalling the great Cleveland performances of Enrico Caruso and Nellie Melba. But Kelly was no snob in his pleasures. His columns often celebrated the more raffish amusements of his—and Cleveland's—younger days. These diversions included seeing P. T. Barnum's midget, "Tom Thumb," at the old Athenaeum Theater on Superior Street, gaping at Mervine Thompson, "The Strongest Man in the World," and staring at Chang Woo Gow, "The Chinese Giant," who displayed his entire nine feet at Stone's Levee on August 10, 1881.

It was in Kelly's columns on the popular amusements and everyday sights of olden Cleveland that his most attractive personal trait was displayed, a truly democratic ethos. Notwithstanding his privileged background, Kelly was genuinely interested in all sorts of people, and he discovered many of the most memorable characters he wrote about in saloons and at prizefights, bicycle races, and torchlight political rallies, or even downtown street corners, where he encountered colorful figures like perennial sidewalk orator Howard Dennis, "Newspaper Annie" (the first female to hawk newspapers in Cleveland), and "the Old Apple Woman," who peddled fruit for years on Superior near Bank Street. Sixty years had passed since Kelly had seen Annie, but he made his readers see her again:

> Wrinkled and old she was, but with a strange ruddy complexion like her apples, witching sharp eyes, an old lady's cap with its white trimming, a winning smile and brogue and jargon with which she wheedled children and grown folks. Sometimes she faded from the picture. Then she would be found crouched at the foot bridge into the Union Depot. She was the same person. She knew you but she would start all over again, with all her talk and coaxing, as if she had never seen you before. Thousands of Cleveland people must have bought apples from her. She would rise or fall to the mental status of her customer, glibly and at once. She had queer powers of speech. Something that made you think of broomsticks, midnight and tall, pointed caps. It was well that she lived not in old Salem.

One of the most remarkable, if inexplicable, things about S. J. Kelly was the serendipitous fatality with which he happened to be around when big news broke. It wasn't just that his profession led him to hot news, it was more like, in some uncanny way, that hot news sought him out. Kelly just *happened* to be in Mentor on June 21, 1905, when someone left a railroad track switch open and the 20th Century Lake Shore Limited crashed, killing 19 and injuring scores, some of whom Kelly interviewed as they lay bleeding and stunned that terrible night. Similarly, Kelly just *happened* to be sitting down to dinner with his family one night when, across the street, L. M. Hubby's new brick mansion suddenly blew to pieces in a spectacular natural gas explosion. Five years later, he was in Alexander Taylor's Euclid Avenue home and watched its walls shudder and sway from the impact caused by a titanic explosion at the Austin Powder works, 10 miles away. Kelly was also on hand when the first Case Institute building went up in flames, and he had inexhaustible eyewitness memories of what he'd seen while covering the epic blizzard of November 1913, a catastrophe that paralyzed the city for days, killed 300 persons and sank many ships throughout the Great Lakes region. Kelly long cherished a moment of macabre comedy occasioned by the blaze that burned the Academy of Music on Bank Street on September 8, 1892. A *Cleveland Herald* reporter at the time, Kelly by chance saw the first flames burst through the roof and sprinted to the nearby *Herald* office, hollering, "The Academy of Music's on fire!" The editor on duty gazed "stupidly" at Kelly for a moment and said, "The *what* is on fire?" Glaring reprovingly at the young reporter, he added, "Young man, we have a *fire* reporter!"

Kelly didn't get his boundless curiosity and relish for the telling detail from strangers. His grandmother, Jane Howe Kelly, was the sister of Henry Howe, the first genuine historian of the Buckeye State, and all three generations of the Kelly family seem to have been open to all the sights, sounds, and diversions their bustling city on the make had to offer. One of Kelly's most vivid word portraits was a childhood memory of a day spent at the North Union Shaker settlement, where the entire Kelly family made a bumpy journey to the Middle Settlement one Sunday morning in a horse-drawn wagon. The building where community religious services were held was located in an area that is now part of the Beaumont School for Girls campus, just east of Lee Road. Kelly never forgot the scene that followed the prayers and preaching:

> Then came the dance. The old and young Shaker men with their hats on formed a long row, facing them, the women and girls in another row, still in their sun bonnets. The dance began with a queer shuffling movement. They held their hands before them puppy fashion. The men and women kept a dignified space between them, all of them chanting their

querulous Shaker religious song. As the dance grew stronger, they were apparently seized with violent shakings and tremblings, caused by strong religious emotions. It was not exactly a "shimmy," but some of those girls could dance better than others—and they knew it.

When it came to describing spectacles, Kelly didn't play favorites. He delivered the same effective application of vivid detail to the maneuvers of a barroom brawl as he did to a droll afternoon spent in the company of John D. Rockefeller or a nocturnal meeting of the Garfield-Perry Stamp Club. And though he frequently capitalized on his memories of Cleveland's biggest big shots, he more often than not showed them in their less staid and stuffy moments. His memory of John Farley had nothing to do with the wily politician who dominated Cleveland politics before Tom Johnson; he recalled Farley merely as a kindly old man who carved boats for child visitors. He remembered Myron T. Herrick, another canny Cleveland politico, a banker, and a personal friend of President McKinley, simply as the generous childhood neighbor who brought him two baby alligators from Florida. His recollection of Worchester Warner, cofounder of Warner & Swasey, was not of the imposing industrial mogul, but the enthusiastic amateur astronomer who invited his friends over to his house in 1881, where they took turns lying on a mattress gazing spellbound at the moon through Warner's new telescope. Several of Kelly's most ingratiating installments concerned James H. Clark, one of John D. Rockefeller's original partners in his Standard Oil empire. Kelly often played billiards in the Clark home and listened carefully while Clark reminisced about his early buccaneering days with John D., played sentimental solos and marches on his silver cornet, and planned the spectacular July 4 fireworks displays that annually delighted his Cedar Avenue neighbors. One day he told Kelly a story that would have burned the ears of John D. and his more hagiographic biographers. It seems that Rockefeller had sent Clark to collect $5,000 from a creditor:

This had taken several days and he did not report until he had the money. Rockefeller had become suspicious, and when he entered the office he acted uneasy. Finally he approached

Clark in a determined manner and demanded what he had collected, and in a choking voice upbraided him. This was a signal for fight with "Jim" Clark. He grasped Rockefeller, swung him from his feet and threw him to the floor. All his bulldog nature aroused, Clark seized Rockefeller's necktie and half choked him. Maurice and Richard Clark were present and dragged "Jim" from the prostrate Rockefeller. The future oil magnate arose, adjusted his clothes and went on with his accounts as if nothing had happened.

Kelly struck a similarly irreverent note with an anecdote about Edward Hessenmueller, an early Cleveland police court judge and one of the great legal lions of late-19th-century Cleveland. Whatever his public demeanor, the judge, it seems, took no guff from his private clients:

Judge Hessenmueller is busy. Here comes a client—a duplicate of Judge Hessenmueller—white bearded—carries a cane. They are in conference now. They are bending over the judge's desk. The conversation grows warmer. You can see the bearded client bring his fist down on the judge's desk. He shouts: "Judge, you are a liar!" Out shoots Judge Hessenmueller's fist. The bearded client hits the floor! The judge, like "Pickwick," who has struck his cellmate in the debtor's prison, stands there. The client picks himself up, and says: "Oh, judge, how could you do that?"

During its 14-year run, Kelly's column was the place to go if you wanted to know what Cleveland had looked like, smelled like, felt like, and sounded like between the 1860s and the early 1900s. One day he took you into Burwell's Bakery on Euclid Avenue in the 1870s. Even in his eighties, Kelly could savor the remembered taste of Burwell's hard caramels and white paraffin gum. The next day Kelly favored you with a guided tour of Edward Decker's old photography studio on Superior Street, where everyone who was anyone in Cleveland sat stiffly for their formal portraits.

("Look at this point. There, that's all right. Wait until I count nine.") All of the fondly remembered places of his boyhood and early manhood had their day in Kelly's columns, and they furnished a voluminous register of how Clevelanders lived, shopped, worked, and amused and expressed themselves 150 to 100 years ago: Frank Douttiel's barbershop, Tom Powers's gun store on Superior Street hill, Lane's Drugstore, Seaman & Smith's boot and shoe store, Alfred England's smoke shop, the Ontario Bird Store, Jake Steinfeld's clothing emporium at 242-244 Superior Street ("We can meet the requirements of any style of man!"),Van Tassel's hardware store on Detroit Street, Kimball's Newspaper Depot (where the young Kelly furtively devoured the pink sheets of the *Police Gazette*), Jones's Restaurant in the old Payne block, the first Burrows bookstore on Euclid Avenue, and dozens of others. Kelly also lovingly re-created the innocent pastimes of his youth: the Civil War Cyclorama at Euclid and East 9th Street, Frank Drew's Dime Museum on Superior (featuring "Human Freaks," "Living Skeletons," "Animal Monsters" and other delights), Clinton French's museum of outré curios on Bond Street, the Casino roller-skating rink on Forest Street, and the White Elephant auditorium on East 4th Street, where the young Kelly attended legendary wrestling matches. Some of his most engaging columns were devoted to the blood sport of prizefighting, then a respectable hobby of even well-born men, amateur foot-race contests, and competitive bicycle races, hair-raising spectacles that invariably ended in shattering collisions and blood on the course.

Although Kelly excelled at limning such popular topics, his columns also celebrated what had made the city of Cleveland great in his lifetime: the accomplishments of the pioneers, industrialists, merchants, politicians, and civic, institutional, and religious leaders who had transformed Cleveland from a struggling, malarial hamlet in 1800 into an economic colossus and sixth-largest American city by 1930. The following is but a brief sample of the individuals whose lives and deeds found a place in the columns of S. J. Kelly: Alfred Kelley, Jared Kirtland, Alexander Winton, Cassie Chadwick, Liberty E. Holden, Henry B. Payne, Leonard Case Sr., John P. Green, Jeptha Wade, Harvey Rice, Mark Hanna, Lorenzo Carter, Moses Cleaveland, Amadeus Rappe, Samuel Livingstone Mather, Ambrose Swasey, Henry Chisholm, Charles Schweinfurth, William J. Gordon, Charles Brush, Linda Eastman, and hundreds more. Most of his stories about these figures included colorful personal anecdotes, and Kelly's columns also provided three-minute histories of practically every historic street (Public Square, Coleman Court, Short Vincent, old Bond Street, Rockwell Street, old "First Street," which led to Cleveland's first cemetery) and structure (the old Union Depot, the original Hower & Higbee store, the Sheriff Street Market, the huge "Emma" furnace in the old Newburgh steel mills, Doan's Armory at East 105th Street, the Society for Savings bank on Public Square, St. John's Cathedral, the Old Stone Church, the Hollenden Hotel, the Old Arcade of downtown Cleveland). But Kelly never forgot the human side of the Cleveland story, and some of his most ingratiating columns were tender memories of his first toy locomotive, reading and rereading Horatio Alger's *Ragged Dick,* a beloved dog also named "Dick," and a comically rueful reminiscence of running from the police after a childish escapade.

Ironically enough for a curious journalist, S. J. Kelly himself was a highly secretive person with a passion for anonymity, a human sphinx who did not tell even his wife his exact age until the night before he died in 1948. George Condon, whose first half decade on the *Plain Dealer* overlapped with Kelly's final years, noted his ghostlike character with his usual humor in a 1995 essay on Kelly. He himself never saw Kelly, and remembered him only as:

> a shadowy, unreal person who moved through our journalistic workaday world like a wraith. His editorial page copy seemed to emerge effortlessly out of the mists that usually are so effective in screening the present from the past. Nobody on the City Room staff knew Kelly in person, or could remember ever seeing him in the flesh.

Frustrated by Kelly's personal reticence, *Plain Dealer* city editor James Collins made a heroic effort to penetrate his shield of silence in 1947, assigning crack investigative reporter Joseph Wadovick to write a profile on Kelly. Wadovick struggled for a fortnight to pry biographical information out of Kelly, but his sole trophy from the ordeal was Kelly's grudging confession that he had begun working at the *Cleveland Herald* in 1885. Any more personal queries were answered with the dismissive reply "That's not important." Wadovick recalled his frustrating interview after Kelly's death, stating:

> [The] interview itself was a two-week affair, a ruse to coax telltale data out of Kelly. It ended in a labyrinth of fuzzy dates and the tracings of a leer on the Kelly countenance.

Some hints of Kelly's life did emerge occasionally in his columns, most often in sentimental recollections of his youthful school days. Like most boys of his social class he first attended Linda Thayer Guildford's Academy on Huron Road. Moving on to the Brooks Elementary School in 1874 and later graduating from the Bolton School, he briefly attended the Kenyon military academy in Gambier, Ohio. His desire was to go to Yale, but that dream died when his family suffered financial reverses. Showing some talent as a painter he attended the Western Reserve University School of Design, the precursor of the Cleveland Institute of Art. But he was a restless young man, and when adventure beckoned, he sought it in the wilds of Florida. Mrs. Julia Tuttle, a well-to-do woman of his acquaintance, owned some undeveloped property on the coast there, and she offered Kelly and two like-minded friends 10 acres of it for free, on the condition that they homestead there and take her cow with them. They talked Mrs. Tuttle out of the cow mandate but subsequently almost lost their lives when their sailboat foundered off the Florida coast. The shipwreck was followed by a harrowing three-week battle for survival in the uncharted jungle of the Everglades. The trio eventually made their way back to Cleveland, and Kelly finally settled down to a more prosaic life as a sports reporter. Mrs. Tuttle's property, of course, ultimately became the nucleus of the future city of Miami.

Academic purists might look at Kelly's voluminous work—as some have—and say, "Well, it's a superior order of nostalgia, perhaps, but hardly the deep and profound matter of History Proper." I don't think so, and I don't think most Clevelanders who got a chance to read Kelly would think so, either. Kelly had actually *lived* through the times of most of the persons, incidents, and phenomena he described, and what he didn't know firsthand, he more often than not learned from people who did. He conversed with people who still remembered when there were savage wolves, impromptu horse races, and annual cattle fairs on lower Euclid Avenue, who had heard the sound of Commodore Perry's guns at Put-in-Bay in 1812 and could still recall the boisterous days when Cleveland's volunteer firemen happily battled each other in the streets, sometimes more frequently than they fought fires. Yes, S. J. Kelly came from the topmost social class, he knew John D., Samuel Mather, and all their ilk, and he was always comfortable, at ease, and welcome in the homes of Cleveland's upper crust. But he also knew and liked a lot of beat cops, bartenders, pugilists, ward heelers, manufacturers, and storekeepers, and they liked him right back. Reading his many pages, it's manifest on every one of them that he was comfortable with as broad a range of humanity as might be found in the novels of Emile Zola or the engravings of William Hogarth. Call it journalism, call it nostalgia, or call it history, with or without a capital *H*: S. J. Kelly's addictive prose is the closest you will ever come to walking down a Cleveland street of the 1870s, '80s, '90s, or the decades that followed. S. J. Kelly didn't just make and write Cleveland history—he lived and embodied it, and any Clevelander who hasn't been exposed to his columns has been cheated.

Somewhere in the subterranean bowels of my Vermont cellar sits a scrupulously edited but unpublished anthology of the best of S. J. Kelly's Cleveland history columns. Quarried from the intimidating and unwieldy 800,000-word bulk of his total work by this humble author, it represents about 40% of his columns. Prefixed to it is an entertaining and informative introduction to the world of S. J. Kelly composed by George Condon and once intended for what we desperately but vainly dreamed would become a Cleveland Bicentennial rediscovery and republication of his work. It sits there yet, awaiting resurrection and admittance to the woefully underpopulated realm of enduring books on Cleveland history.

Chapter 15

MY FIRST DISASTER

How I Got to Be "The Cleveland Historian Your Mother Warned You About"

During my two decades as a purveyor of Cleveland woe I have frequently been asked why I have spent so much of my life immersed in the details of murder and catastrophe. I have given several different answers to that question, and all of them are true. A strong family background of colorful journalists, a lifelong curiosity about the wellsprings for motives of heroes and evildoers, and a general passion for Cleveland history have all contributed to my obsession with stories about Cleveland's most violently memorable moments. But there are other, more personal reasons for my peculiar preoccupations, most of them stemming from a number of childhood and adolescent episodes, episodes which I am mostly saving for my interminable autobiography in progress, *Wasted on the Young*. In the meantime, what follows here may at least explain my interest in loud explosions and death-defying acts . . .

Looking back from the vantage point of almost half a century, it's clear to me that it was all Steve McQueen's fault. *Steve McQueen?* I hear you thinking. Steve McQueen, the badass cop of *Bullitt*, who single-handedly made cardiac car chases de rigueur in action films forever and ever, amen? *That* Steve McQueen? No—the Steve McQueen I'm thinking of played Virgil Hilts, the insouciant American prisoner of war, five years earlier in the best World War II film ever made, *The Great Escape*. Long before he became iconic by laying serious rubber in a snazzy 1968 Ford GT Mustang, McQueen looked incredibly cool astride a big-ass motorcycle as he fled from hordes of evil Nazis. Now, it's true that when *The Great Escape* was released in the summer of 1963, my brothers and I were too young to torque around Cleveland Heights on snarling motorcycles. But we weren't too young to do the other thing we saw during multiple viewings of *The Great Escape*, which was to dig our own escape tunnel in our own backyard.

I know what you're thinking: how could we possibly confuse the half acre of my parents' house lot in suburban Cleveland Heights for the menacing prison camp of Stalag Luft III, deep in the malignant heart of the Third Reich? How could we possibly have deluded ourselves into the fantasy that we could dig a functional tunnel the length of our yard, some 200 feet? Well, I suppose you could put it down to the power of adolescent imagination, but there was more to it than that. After all, it wasn't as though we lacked the know-how for the job. For some years we had tirelessly explored the vast underground storm-sewer system of Cleveland Heights, and only come close to drowning once or twice. And at least four or five times that summer we had watched our heroes, supermen like Charles Bronson and David McCallum, burrow their way past barbed-wire fences and Nazi goons to freedom, again and again and again at Loew's State Theater on Euclid Avenue. Indeed, we considered ourselves practically postdoc tunnel escape scholars, having also seen other tunnel films like *Escape from East Berlin* and *The Password Is Courage*. Given this wealth of expertise and the smarts to profit from the mistakes of our movie heroes, it was obvious that our Kenilworth Road tunnel was going to be a piece of cake.

Nor was it hard to keep the project a secret from my parents. Although the remotest corner of their large lot was nominally my father's compost pile, he never actually visited it from one summer to the next. And I don't believe my mother even knew its location, as it was partially screened from her ruthless scrutiny by a large garage. So we knew from the outset that we had a free hand and soon made the most of it. One sunny morning, after enlisting the participation of our chum Butchie Green, we swore each other to secrecy in solemn blood oaths, assembled our tools (shovels, ropes,

John, Christopher, and Stephen Bellamy, c. 1963, co-conspirators at the Cleveland Heights annex of Stalag Luft III.

buckets, and a supply of wooden slats), and set to work on our own Great Escape.

It didn't take many minutes in that hot August sun for us to discover that the creative minds behind *The Great Escape* had made tunneling look deceptively easy. Perhaps, too, we had failed to adequately note that the *Great Escape* tunnelers numbered some hundreds, whereas we comprised a mere quartet of pathetic suburban striplings. Then there was the soil itself, which we immediately discovered was not anything like the loose sand underneath Stalag Luft III but solid, unyielding midwestern clay. But we stoutly persevered, impelled ever onward by the hormone-driven power of adolescent fantasy. After all, we figured, if we were willing to risk digging our tunnel *under the very noses of our fiendish Nazi captors,* we certainly weren't going to let a little marbleized clay compromise our powerful blow against the Axis powers.

So the secret work went on as, day after day, stripped to the waist under the pitiless sun, we bored deeper and deeper into the earth. Six feet down in a three-by-three-foot shaft after a week, we switched to the horizontal phase, pushing a tunnel westward toward freedom, or at least in the probable direction of the Cedar Road-Fairmount Boulevard intersection. And say what you will of our childish lunacy, that tunnel wasn't just a hole in the ground. Thanks to the technical expertise of my elder brother Stephen, it boasted nearly all of the fancy refinements of tunnels we'd seen in the movies: functional ventilation pipes, sturdy wooden slats to support the tunnel roof (daringly filched from the back stoop of a local furniture store), and a reinforced wooden cover that cunningly camouflaged the opening to the vertical shaft from any potential airborne surveillance. My memory is that brother Stephen was actually preparing to install electric lights in the tunnel when the great catastrophe struck . . . but I get ahead of myself.

In retrospect, it is clear that if we had been paying closer attention to our movie tunnel models, we might have also noticed the obvious fact that *all* the movie tunnels had begun in sheltered, dry, indoor sites. Situated as it was in a reeking compost heap, our tunnel decidedly did not—which meant that it was, notwithstanding its wooden cover, pretty much open to the elements. Those elements duly arrived during the third week of our labors, in the form of torrential rains, which promptly flooded the entire tunnel and stopped all digging. More mortifying to our self-esteem, the rain also brought home to us the realization that the flooding issue might have been avoided, or at least mitigated, had we not carelessly demolished virtually all the backyard drain tile in the careless enthusiasm of our initial excavations.

Well, the rain finally stopped after five days, and it was precisely at this juncture that our already demented enterprise graduated to the supreme level of total, self-destructive insanity. Time was of the essence, for we were but two weeks away from the beginning of school, and an exhausting marathon of bailing had left us with a stubborn foot of water still on the tunnel floor. What to do . . . what to do . . .

I'd like to be able to say that it wasn't *my* idea—but, mercifully, I don't really remember who first thought of the deranged plan. But I *do* remember that I heartily agreed to the concept, which was simplicity itself. Indeed, why hadn't it occurred to us sooner? Since we couldn't bail the water out, we decided we'd *burn* it off instead.

View from the scene of the crime: Branches in lower right helped mask the tunnel entrance.

Anyone who has ever watched the sun burn a puddle of water away knows that heat causes evaporation. So a few minutes later, Butchie and I were at Gene's Sohio station, where we pumped five gallons of leaded, 33-cent gasoline into a can. Lugging it home, we trucked it out to the compost pile, removed the shaft lid, poured the gasoline down . . . threw a lit match after it, slammed the lid down, and ran like hell.

Two minutes passed. Nothing. Another minute elapsed. A lot more nothing. Butchie looked at me—I looked at Butchie. It was time to step up and be a Man, and I'm sure we were thinking the same thing: *What would Steve McQueen do?* Exactly, no doubt, what we now did. Gingerly creeping back to the lid . . . we carefully opened it. Nothing. There was only one thing left to do—and we did it—which was to trot back up to Gene's Sohio, pump another five gallons of gasoline, and go through the whole harebrained sequence again.

Our second try was more successful, and, I must confess, far more exciting. Again pouring the gasoline down the shaft, we lit a match, slammed the lid down, and ran for cover. A minute went by.

Nothing. Shrugging our shoulders, we walked back toward the lid . . . and got there just about the instant the ground underneath us erupted with a mighty roar, hurling us into the air, along with smithereened fragments of the tunnel cover, wooden slats, several hundred pounds of Cleveland Heights clay, and about a ton of muddy water. Perhaps the only one more surprised by the explosion than Butchie and me was my mother, who just happened to look out her kitchen window in time to see the two of us actually flying through the air. We were still on the ground, stupefied, singed, wet, and scared, when she arrived on the crime scene, demanding to know what in holy hell was going on. I don't remember what we told her, except that it sure wasn't the truth, which—aside from the potential consequences—was simply too embarrassing to admit. She made us fill in the ruined tunnel that very afternoon—but she never did learn the true facts behind the Mysterious Compost Pile Catastrophe of 1963. Fortunately, that deranged episode proved to be the end of our tunneling escapades—but our memorable summer mishap was to yield unforeseen fruit in my later and enduring love

Lawrence "Butchie" Green at work at Gene's Sohio, mid-1960s.

affair with lethal explosions, catastrophic events, and the heroes and heroines who rise to their occasions. Tragically and ironically, Butchie Green, my brother Steve's best friend and a young man beloved by all, was killed in an inexplicable industrial accident at Nela Park in February 1967. Then again, that very day, just hours after his death, his U.S. Army draft notice arrived in the mail . . .

PHOTO CREDITS

Anyone wishing to contact John Stark Bellamy II regarding the contents of this or his other Cleveland woe titles may do so at this e-mail address: jstarkbi@tops-tele.com. Those wishing to do so may rest assured that the author welcomes criticism, as Winston Churchill once said, "even when, for the sake of emphasis, it for a time parts company with reality."